Approaches
to Welfare

Edited by
Philip Bean
and
Stewart MacPherson

Approaches to Welfare

Routledge & Kegan Paul
London, Boston, Melbourne and Henley

First published in 1983
by Routledge & Kegan Paul plc
39 Store Street, London WC1E 7DD,
9 Park Street, Boston, Mass. 02108, USA,
296 Beaconsfield Parade, Middle Park,
Melbourne, 3206, Australia, and
Broadway House, Newtown Road,
Henley-on-Thames, Oxon RG9 1EN

Photoset in Ehrhardt by
Kelly Typesetting Ltd, Bradford-on-Avon, Wiltshire
and printed in Great Britain by
The Thetford Press Ltd, Thetford, Norfolk

Library of Congress Cataloging in Publication Data

Main entry under title:
Approaches to welfare.
Includes index.
1. Public welfare – Great Britain – Addresses, essays, lectures.
2. Welfare state – Addresses, essays, lectures.
I. Bean, Philip. II. MacPherson, Stewart.
HV245.A76 1983 361'.941 82–21402

ISBN 0–7100–9423–X
ISBN 0–7100–9424–8 (pbk.)

For Professor David C. Marsh

Professor of Applied Social Science,
University of Nottingham 1954–1981

Contents

Notes on contributors

Philip Bean

Philip Bean is a Lecturer in the Department of Social Administration and Social Work, University of Nottingham. Prior to that he was a Research Officer for the Medical Research Council, and before that a Probation Officer in the Inner London Probation and After-Care Service. In 1979 he was Visiting Professor at the University of Manitoba, Canada, this award being granted by the Canadian Federal Government on an open competitive basis. Philip Bean's main interests are in the fields of Criminology, Mental Health and Social Philosophy where he has published widely. Among his publications are *The Social Control of Drugs*, Martin Robertson, 1974; *Rehabilitation and Deviance*, Routledge & Kegan Paul, 1976; *Compulsory Admissions to Mental Hospitals*, John Wiley, 1980; *Punishment: a philosophical and criminological inquiry*, Martin Robertson, 1981, and he has recently edited a book entitled *Mental Illness: changes and trends* published by John Wiley, 1983, which is a contributed volume from international authorities in mental illness.

Roger Cox

Roger Cox is a Lecturer in Social Administration at the University of Nottingham. He has previously been a teacher and has taught in a College of Education. His main research interest is in the construction and political development of images of childhood. He has written previously on education and on the educational expectation of social work students.

Nicholas Deakin

Nicholas Deakin read history at Oxford and then entered the Home Civil Service, which he left in 1963 to join the Institute of Race Relations where he worked on the Nuffield Survey of Race Relations in Britain. Subsequently he spent three years at the University of Sussex before joining the GLC in 1972 as Head of Social Studies, becoming head of the Council's Central Policy Unit in 1979. In 1980 he was appointed Professor of Social Policy and Administration at Birmingham University. He has published books and articles on race relations, inner city policy and new towns.

Victor George

Vic George, Professor of Social Policy and Administration and Social Work, University of Kent at Canterbury, worked for a number of years as a social worker before joining the LSE and the University of Nottingham where he spent a number of years as a lecturer in Social Administration before taking up his present post at the University of Kent in 1973. His writings have been in the field of social welfare, both on a national and comparative level. His books include: *Foster Care: Theory and Practice, Social Security and Society*, 1973, *Ideology and Social Welfare* (with Paul Wilding), 1976, *Poverty and Inequality in the Common Market Countries* (with Roger Lawson), 1979, *Socialism, Social Welfare and the Soviet Union* (with Nick Manning), 1980, all published by Routledge & Kegan Paul.

John Greve

John Greve has been Professor of Social Administration at the University of Leeds since 1974. He is a graduate (BScEcon) of the London School of Economics where he subsequently lectured on social administration. Afterwards he held a senior post at a housing research institute in Oslo, Norway, where, as later, he divided his time between pursuing and promoting housing research and developing comparative studies across the broader field of social policy.

Professor Greve, who is Norwegian speaking, has been a frequent visitor to the Scandinavian countries as researcher, lecturer, visiting professor, and consultant both on research and policy matters. He has lectured in Denmark, Norway, Finland and Sweden, and participated in several official Scandinavian conferences and seminars.

Besides his academic work in Britain, Professor Greve was a member of the South-East Economic Planning Council from 1969 to 1972, was on secondment to the Home Office from 1969 to 1973, and a member of the Royal Commission on the Distribution of Income and Wealth from 1974 to 1979. He visited Sweden on behalf of the Commission which later published his report on low incomes in Sweden.

Professor Greve has published extensively on housing and social policy both in this country and Scandinavia and his major publications include *Housing, planning and change in Norway*, Norwegian Building Research Institute, Oslo, 1969, *Voluntary housing in Scandinavia*, University of Birmingham, 1971, *Comparative Social Administration* (with B. Rodgers and J. Morgan), Allen & Unwin, 1971 and *Homelessness in London* (with D. Page and S. Greve), Scottish Academic Press, 1971. He is joint author of a book on sheltered housing for the elderly published by Allen & Unwin, 1983.

Robert Holman

Robert Holman went to London University and gained a BA Hons and PhD in Social Administration. He was a Child Care Officer with the Hertfordshire Children's Department, then entered academic life having held positions at Stevenage College of Further Education, Birmingham University, Glasgow University and finished up with the Chair of Social Administration at Bath University. Since 1976 he has worked as a Community Social Worker for the Church of England Children's Society on a council estate.

His publications include: *Poverty: Explanations of Social Deprivation*, Martin Robertson, 1978; and *Kids at the Door* (with D. Wiles and S. Lewis), Basil Blackwell, 1981.

Kathleen Jones

Kathleen Jones is Professor of Social Administration and Head of the Department of Social Administration and Social Work, University of York, and is the author of *The Teaching of Social Studies in British Universities*, Bell, 1964, *The Compassionate Society*, Routledge & Kegan

Paul, 1965, *A History of the Mental Health Services*, Routledge & Kegan Paul, 1972, *Opening the Door: a study of new policies for the mentally handicapped* (with J. Brown), Routledge & Kegan Paul, 1974, *Issues in Social Policy* (with J. Brown and J. R. Bradshaw), Routledge & Kegan Paul, 1978. She is general editor of the *International Library of Social Policy*, and chairman of the Social Administration Association, and is now working, with A. J. Fowles, on a study of prisons and mental hospitals.

Peter Leonard

Peter Leonard graduated in politics at the London School of Economics and subsequently took a research degree in social administration, qualifying as a psychiatric social worker. He practised in social work for ten years in the fields of community work, child care, intensive family casework and child guidance before entering social work education. After teaching casework at Liverpool University and being Director of Social Work Education at the National Institute for Social Work, he established the Department of Applied Social Studies at Warwick University in 1973. He was a member of the Seebohm Committee (1966–8). His publications include *Sociology and Social Work*, Routledge & Kegan Paul, 1966; *The Sociology of Community Action* (ed.), University of Keele, 1975; *Social Work Practice under Capitalism* (with Paul Corrigan), Macmillan, 1978, and *Marital Violence: Social Construction and Social Service Response* (with Eileen McLeod), University of Warwick, 1980. He is currently a scientific adviser to the Mental Illness Research Liaison Group of the DHSS.

Stewart MacPherson

Stewart MacPherson was born in 1945. He left school at sixteen and worked in a number of jobs, including the Civil Service and Ford. After a year at Technical College he went to the University of Keele (joint Honours Sociology/Politics, 1970); postgraduate work at the University of York (MPhil Social Administration, 1972). In 1972–3 taught social administration at Makerere University, Uganda. Took up present post as Lecturer in Social Administration at Nottingham in 1973; visiting Lecturer, University of Dar es Salaam, Tanzania, 1974; from 1977 to 1979, and in 1982, Lecturer in Social Policy and Community Development, University of Papua New Guinea. Awarded PhD in 1980 for study of basic health services in Papua New Guinea. Recent publications include *Social Policy in the Third World*, Harvester, 1982.

Terence Morris

Terence Morris, Professor of Social Institutions in the University of London, has taught at the LSE for almost thirty years. After studying Social Anthropology he became a research student in Criminology under Hermann Mannheim. Over the years he has travelled widely, and has advised Colonial governments in the English-speaking Caribbean areas and the Western Pacific. He has also travelled extensively in the United States and was Visiting Professor in the University of California, School of Criminology at Berkeley, 1963–4. Appointed a Justice of the Peace in 1967, he has sat as a magistrate in a busy South London court. He has been associated with the starting of a number of groups including the British Society of Criminology and the Institute for the Study of Drugs Dependence. He has been a supporter of the Howard League since 1948 and is currently a member of its council. His best-known researches have led to the publication of *The Criminal Area*, Routledge & Kegan Paul, 1957; *Pentonville: The Sociology of an English Prison*, Humanities Press, 1963; *A Calendar of Murder* (with Louis Blom-Cooper), Fernhill, 1964. His *Deviance and Control: the Secular Heresy*, Hutchinson, 1976, has been translated into Portuguese.

R. A. Parker

Roy Parker has been Professor of Social Administration at the University of Bristol since 1969, having previously worked for ten years at the London School of Economics. He has recently transferred to a research chair. Before joining the LSE he worked in the Berkshire Children's Department. His major research interests have centred upon child care policy (especially foster care); housing and rent policies; administrative issues in the social services, and the politics of social reform. His publications include: *Decisions in Child Care*, Allen & Unwin, 1966; *The Rents of Council Houses*, Bell, 1967; *Planning for Deprived Children*, National Children's Home, 1971; *Change, Choice and Conflict in Social Policy* (with P. Hall, H. Land and A. L. Webb), Heinemann, 1975 and, as editor, *Caring for Separated Children*, Macmillan, 1980.

Gillian Pascall

Gillian Pascall is lecturer in Social Administration at the University of Nottingham. She has a Diploma in Social Administration from the London School of Economics and a PhD from Nottingham. Her main interests are in health and women's studies, and she has recently been on an Inter-Universities Council visit to Papua New Guinea.

Robert Pinker

Robert Pinker is Professor of Social Work Studies at the London School of Economics and Political Science, University of London. He was previously Professor of Social Administration at Goldsmiths' College (1972–4) and Professor of Social Work Studies at Chelsea College (1974–8). He has served on the committees of various statutory and voluntary bodies including the CNAA, the SSRC and the Centre for Policies on Ageing. He is a former editor of the *Journal of Social Policy*, and currently edits a series on Studies in Social Policy and Welfare for Heinemann Educational Books.

He is a member of the Central Council for Education and Training in Social Work, and has recently served as a member of the Barclay Working Party on the Roles and Tasks of Social Work, to which he submitted a minority report.

His main research interests include the content and aims of social work education; alternative patterns of care for the elderly; the uses of discretion in income maintenance; and the comparative study of social welfare. His publications include *Social Theory and Social Policy*, Heinemann, 1971, *The Idea of Welfare*, Heinemann, 1979, and various monographs and articles.

Richard Silburn

Richard Silburn graduated from the University of Nottingham in 1961; he was appointed Assistant Lecturer a year later. He has worked in the Department of Social Administration ever since, where he is now a Senior Lecturer. His principal research interests have been in the field of poverty studies. He is the joint author of *Poverty: the Forgotten*

Englishmen, Penguin, 1970, and a number of other monographs on social conditions in the East Midlands. More recently his work has focused upon welfare rights and social security policy.

Adrian Webb

Adrian Webb is Professor of Social Administration and Head of the Department of Social Sciences at Loughborough University. Previously he was research secretary to the Personal Social Services Council between 1974 and 1976. He began his academic career as a Lecturer in Social Administration at the London School of Economics (1966–74). He is co-author of *Income Distribution and the Welfare State*, Bell, 1971, *Change, Choice and Conflict in Social Policy*, Heinemann, 1975, *Across the Generations: Old People and Young Volunteers*, Allen & Unwin, 1975, *Teamwork in the Personal Social Services and Health Care*, Croom Helm, 1980, *Whither State Welfare?* (with G. Wistow), RIPA, 1982. He has written widely about management, research and policy in the personal social services in both the statutory and non-statutory sectors. He is also Chairman of the Volunteer Centre.

John Westergaard

John Westergaard is of Danish origin. Born in 1927, he was educated at a secondary school in Denmark and at the London School of Economics (1948–51). After work as an assistant on research into social aspects of town planning at University College London (1951–4) and a year as a research fellow at Nottingham University, he returned to the LSE, where he was successively assistant lecturer, lecturer, senior lecturer and reader in sociology. He moved to his present post as Professor of Sociological Studies (and head of the department of that name) at Sheffield University in 1975. His research and publications have been mainly in the fields of class structure, including relevant aspects of public policy, and urban sociology. He was part-time Deputy Director of the Centre for Urban Studies, University College London, till 1975; and serves or has served on committees or boards, *inter alia*, of the Council for National Academic Awards, the Social Science Research Council, the International Sociological Association and the Council for Academic Freedom and Democracy.

Paul Wilding

After postgraduate work at the University of Manchester, Paul Wilding was lecturer and then senior lecturer at the University of Nottingham between 1967 and 1975. From 1975 until 1981 he was senior lecturer in Social Administration at University College, Cardiff. In 1981 he returned to Manchester as Professor of Social Administration. His publications include *Motherless Families*, 1972 and *Ideology and Social Welfare*, 1976 (both with Vic George) and *Professional Power and Social Welfare*, 1982 (all published by Routledge & Kegan Paul).

Barbara Wootton

Barbara Wootton was born in 1897, the youngest of the three children of two Cambridge dons, and was educated at the Perse High School Cambridge and Girton College, where she took a first-class degree in economics with a mark of special distinction. In the course of her subsequent career, spread over more than sixty years, she has held the posts of Director of Studies in Economics at Girton College, Research Officer in the Joint Research Department of the TUC and Labour Party, Principal of Morley College London, Director of Studies for the University of London's (Adult) Tutorial Classes, Professor of Social Studies in the University of London, and Nuffield Research Fellow at Bedford College London. In 1958 she was among the first creation of Life Peers and has been Deputy Speaker of the House of Lords for the past fourteen years.

Barbara Wootton has also served on four Royal Commissions and a dozen Government Committees investigating social or economic problems. Besides being a London magistrate for forty-four years and a BBC Governor for six, she has written one volume of short stories, one novel and ten books on social or economic subjects, and is an honorary doctor of Columbia University, New York, and eleven UK universities. In 1977 she was made a Companion of Honour.

Barbara Wootton has been twice married – in 1917 to Jack Wootton who was killed in the First World War, and in 1935 to George Wright who died in 1964, after many years as a member, and subsequently an Alderman, of the LCC.

Introduction

It is now forty years since the publication of the Beveridge Report. For a large part of that forty years the report, the legislation emanating from it and associated with it, and the approach to welfare that it represented have dominated the study of welfare in Britain. Behind this collection of essays lay the notion of providing an opportunity for a number of authors to contemplate 'approaches to welfare' across that span of time. The train of thought which produced this collection was set in motion by the retirement of Professor D. C. Marsh, whose career in teaching and writing about social administration began in the 1940s and continued until his retirement in 1982. His best-known books, on 'The Welfare State', served to focus the attention of the subject for many years. As a number of contributors to this collection show, both the study of welfare and its practice have changed significantly over the forty years since 1942.

In bringing together this group of essays there was never any serious intention, indeed any hope, of ensuring a comprehensive and systematic treatment of all the major issues. Rather, and here we do claim purpose, not serendipity, it was hoped that the collection as a whole would be in some way representative of the diverse range of work embraced by that elusive term 'social administration'. In that hope we believe we were justified. Thus we have a wide range of specific topics, a variety of styles and a number of different approaches to the subject-matter: as all editors know to their cost, the degree of editorial control is unpredictable at best – in this case we were fortunate that our contributors needed little or no advice or assistance from us. We are also fortunate to have essays which deal in general terms with the complex pattern of intellectual forces which have shaped, and are shaping, the contemporary study of welfare. In so doing, some authors discuss the history of welfare provision or emerging approaches to analysis of welfare in society. Others deal with more specific topics in rather different ways, for example by tracing the emerging patterns of service provision. Whatever the form adopted all the essays illuminate issues in the contemporary debates within and about the study of welfare. It is clear that we are now facing years in which the older notions and certainties of the 'welfare state' will be even more seriously questioned. That questioning will come, as it already has, from many, very different, directions. There have always been, as several essays show, those opposed to organised welfare because they believe it to be redistributive, pauperising, or a threat to morals. From the beginning there have also been systematic attempts to analyse welfare institutions in terms of efficiency and effectiveness – with the goals as given. But since the 1940s, and indeed long before, there was also a current of analysis which saw welfare as part of the total distribution of resources of all kinds and thus analysed its role against both the needs of the mass of people and a perception of the social divisions in society.

Recent work in this country has more clearly broken with the almost totally dominant Fabian tradition of the 1950s and 1960s. That this has taken so long must surely be seen as only partly a function of our declining economic position; it is surely also a result of looking inward upon a set of institutions the fundamental goodness of which went unquestioned. Several contributors indicate the insularity of British approaches to welfare which may be seen as a result of that long period of intense self-regard.

We hope that this collection will give, to those new to this area of study and the issues it tries to deal with, a rather different introduction to approaches to welfare than is generally available in one place. To those more familiar with material in this field, we offer the collection as containing a number of readable and stimulating essays; not the least advantage of such a collection is that of exposure to diversity. There can be little doubt that the study of welfare is not marked by unanimity of approach.

We thank all the contributors most sincerely for their work, their patience and forbearance and their promptness in completing the essays, and we are very grateful for the secretarial assistance without which we could not have coped.

Philip Bean
Stewart MacPherson
Nottingham

Chapter 1
The evolution of social administration
Paul Wilding

My concern is to explore the changes which have taken place in social administration as a subject of academic study in the last thirty years – roughly the years spanned by the careers of the first generation of professors of social administration. The essay falls into three parts. First, I shall try to outline the essential characteristics of what I have called the traditional social administration approach – described by many as the Titmuss tradition. Then I shall look at the factors which weakened the dominance of that approach and led to new conceptions of the subject. Finally, I shall examine the nature of what I describe – rather unimaginatively perhaps – as the new social administration, its emphases, insights and preoccupations.

The traditional social administration

When the Department of Social Science was established at the London School of Economics in 1912 its purpose was clear and limited. 'It is intended', the Calendar stated, 'for those who wish to prepare themselves to engage in the many forms of social and charitable effort' (Titmuss, 1963, p. 15). Until the Second World War this remained the essential purpose of what subsequently became known as the Department of Social Administration. Marsh writes:

> The study was essentially descriptive and designed to answer the question how do the social services operate, when did they come into being and when, and by whom, can they be used? All too often 'the social services' were studied as a 'useful' subject which one had to

know in order to be a social worker, and few attempts were made to analyse the economic and sociological relationships and implications of the social services as social institutions, or to question their aims, purposes and methods of administration (1965, p. 10).

The development of state welfare services after 1945 raised many new issues of academic study for a subject which saw itself as essentially concerned with the study of the social services. In the years between 1950 and the early 1970s what I have called the traditional social administration developed, flourished and began to be the object of criticism.

Throughout these years there was, of course, a process of continuing evolution. There was what might be called the early social administration approach, associated most obviously with Penelope Hall, perhaps, as the writer of the subject's basic textbook in the 1950s and 1960s, and confining itself exclusively to the study of social services and seeing them as the simple product of an expanding humanitarianism (1952). This approach was increasingly challenged by the Titmuss approach which looked at social administration in a broader perspective and saw social policy as the product of a multiplicity of factors and as having a multiplicity of roles and functions in society. Titmuss's own ideas about the nature of the subject also changed quite considerably between his inaugural lecture in 1951 and his last lectures delivered in 1973, and posthumously published in *Social Policy* (1974). Nevertheless, in spite of these two stages in the traditional approach, it is possible to sketch in its essential features.

First, it was characterised by certain shared assumptions about the subject-matter of social administration – the British welfare state and the social services in particular. 'Social administration', Titmuss declared in his inaugural lecture, 'may broadly be defined as the study of the social services' (1963, p. 14).

In 1975 Donnison concluded that the social services were still the main focus of those studying social administration (1975, p. 13). 'What has particularly characterised social administration as a field of study', says Parker, 'has been the attention paid to the description and evaluation of existing social services or policies' (1972, pp. 118–19).

At times Titmuss certainly sought to broaden the scope of the subject. All commentators agree on the seminal nature of his famous paper, 'The Social Division of Welfare' (1963). Sinfield, indeed, describes it as 'probably . . . the most cited paper in the British literature of social policy' (1978, p. 124). Pinker argues that in that essay 'Titmuss broke through the then conventional and narrow definitions of social policy and, by focusing upon aims rather than academic procedures, he brought a new analytical dimension to his subject' (1977, p. vii). Few colleagues or students, however, followed Titmuss in his attempted break-out, and the burden of Sinfield's article is that in the next twenty years few of his colleagues attempted to take up and build on Titmuss's attempt at a reconceptualisation of the subject. Social administration continued to concentrate its attention on government and on its legislation, substantially ignoring the distributional outcomes of decisions made by other important institutions, public and private, and so limiting its analysis of welfare and dis-welfare (Walker, 1981, pp. 226–7).

Second, the traditional social administration was characterised by a shared approach to its subject-matter, an approach which can usefully be summed up as particular, prescriptive and parochial. The approach was particular in the sense that students and scholars tended to focus on particular issues, problems and services rather than to look generally at social policy and social welfare. They took their cue from Titmuss who posed the rhetorical question, to which in his mind, at least, there was only one answer, 'To understand better what it is all about have not we in the end to ask concrete questions about specific policies and services rather than to generalise broadly about "social policy" in the abstract?' (1974, p. 49). Such an approach clearly has value. It can help to delineate the size and nature of specific problems, it can alert administrators and policy makers to shortcomings in services, it 'has value as a watchdog and buttress for the welfare state' (Taylor-Gooby and Dale, 1981, p. 28) but it does limit and narrow the scope and range of the subject.

The traditional approach has been unashamedly prescriptive. It has been committed to the production of knowledge for use by policy makers and governments, rather than knowledge for understanding by scholars and theorists. The concern of the subject, says Mishra, has been

> not in knowledge about social welfare institutions for its own sake but rather in understanding the nature and dimensions of a particular social problem with a view to its solution . . . stated simply, the advancement of welfare rather than the accumulation and refinement of a body of tested knowledge is the central concern (1977, pp. 3–5).

Other commentators make the same point. Social administration,

Joyce Warham argued in 1973, can be distinguished from the other social sciences

> by an overt and primary commitment to the promotion of individual and social welfare *through the process of social reform*. Its pursuit of knowledge is directed not exclusively to understanding how social services function as social institutions, but also to considering how they could be and possibly ought to be modified (1973, p. 193).

This 'commitment to welfare' – and to welfare to be promoted and achieved through the development of certain particular social institutions – limits the subject to those who share such a commitment. This 'heavy load of human longing for a better world' (Pinker, 1977, p. xiv) is clear in the social administration literature of the 1950s and 1960s.

Parochialism is another important element in traditional social administration. All the leading scholars insist that social administration cannot be studied except in combination with the other social sciences and the study of society as a whole. 'Social policies cannot be understood', Donnison wrote, 'if they are treated as a separate sphere to be studied in isolation from the rest of society' (1974, p. 53). Marsh insists on the same point. Social services, he writes, 'cannot be studied in isolation, they must be looked at as one feature of the economic, social and political systems of the society in which they operate' (1965, p. 16).

The sad fact is, however, that in the traditional social administration more often than not social policies and social services *were* studied in a kind of vacuum. Hilary Rose describes herself as brought up

> within an older tradition of social policy [what is described here as the traditional social administration] where – to gently caricature it – the economy was relegated to the background, the social relations of class were to be left to the sociologists, power was to be ignored, and where social policy itself was to be discussed in regal isolation (1981, p. 477).

Students of social administration were expected to know some economics and politics and sociology but social policy was seldom, if ever, firmly located in the context of the kind of society revealed by economic, sociological and political analysis. Social policy *was* regarded in some strange way as susceptible to study in isolation from its environment.

Third, the traditional social administration shared certain values and certain assumptions about society. These assumptions were seldom made explicit but they underpinned – and eventually undermined – its basic approach. There were the assumptions about the continuance and easy inevitability of economic growth which everyone except the congenitally pessimistic held in the 1950s and 1960s. There were the assumptions about agreed social objectives which seemed so evident in the Butskellite years when ideology was clearly dead. There was the belief that gradual reformism on classic Fabian lines was the way to change and improve society and that society could be changed in this way – eventually perhaps fundamentally. There was the faith that the proper mechanism for such change was the state operating through the social services and that all that was needed was rather more of them, rather better directed, staffed and organised. There was the belief that policy making was a rational kind of business and that if needs were proven and 'facts' produced 'society' would respond with policies to tackle the 'problems' which were revealed.

Assumptions about society and shared values fused together. The leading figures of traditional social administration were all implicitly or explicitly Fabians. They were united above all by a shared vision of a more equal, more just society, with 'better' social services financed through redistributive taxation. Scholarship and advocacy coexisted easily in this consensual world. Social administration became identified with a particular political philosophy and a particular approach to social welfare.

This belief in state social services as the road to social welfare is a limiting one. It leads to what Taylor-Gooby has described as the 'perspective of the State that is the hallmark of the social administration tradition' (1981, p. 8). It narrows the subject to a concern with state services and can easily lead to the adoption of the state's criteria for their evaluation.

Any brief description of a subject as broad in its concerns as social administration and one which embraces scholars and students from such diverse backgrounds, must be an oversimplification. In the 1950s, 1960s and early 1970s, however, a recognisable social administration evolved characterised by shared – and limiting – assumptions about subject-matter, by a shared approach which I have categorised as particular, prescriptive and parochial and by certain shared social values and assumptions about society.

The undermining of the traditional approach

For twenty years there was little challenge to the orthodoxies of the traditional social administration. Indeed, its assumptions took on the status of facts and were no longer regarded as contestable. In the early 1970s, however, the dominant view of the subject began to be challenged. Its underpinnings – a consensus model of society, a rational model of policy making, a view of the state as independent arbiter – were all exposed as assumptions which were fundamentally problematic and which could no longer be regarded as necessarily sound.

It is possible to distinguish five main reasons for the challenge to the traditional social administration which led to the broadening and deepening of the subject. First, there was a self-conscious critique which emerged from within the subject. In 1971, for example, Pinker wrote scathingly of 'the current poverty of social administration as a theoretical discipline' (1971, pp. 5 and 12). He concluded:

> The question that faces us is whether or not social policy and administration is becoming little more than a motley collection of skills which are applied, on a largely *ad hoc* basis, to a series of problems in the field of social welfare (1971, p. 13).

In 1974 Parker felt able to write of 'a steady enlargement of the conception of the subject' and asked – rather plaintively – 'was the subject destined to be for ever occupied with description, evaluation and practical prescription?' (1974, p. 567). There was a dissatisfaction within the subject with its implicit ideology, its lack of theory, its failure to establish its claim to be regarded as more than a conglomeration of the *ad hoc*, and with what was felt to be its continuing lack of academic respectability. This contributed to a re-examination of its basis and tools.

Second, the fundamental consensus which had characterised British politics in the 1950s and 1960s came to an end. No longer was there consensus about social ends or how they might be attained. Economics and social policy became political again. There were different views about the proper role of the state in welfare which were the product of different values and ideologies and different economic and social priorities. 'Society' was clearly not agreed about the things which it had seemed to be agreed about. In fact, at times in the years after 1970, 'society' did not seem to be agreed about anything.

Social administration had developed in the consensus atmosphere of the 1950s and 1960s and owed more than most people realised to that particular confluence of circumstances. Students had assumed agreement about means and ends, they had assumed that 'facts' would vanquish mere opinions. The ending of this state of bliss unloosed a barrage of questioning about the nature of social policy, the role of the state in welfare, the costs and benefits of social services – questions which had been unasked in the previous two decades.

A third blow to the traditional social administration was the ending of the assumption of continuing and automatic economic growth which followed the Arab-Israeli war of 1973. The end of growth meant the end of painless welfare expansion. It meant that choices had clearly to be made – and such choices are clearly, at the end of the day, value judgments. The ultimately political nature of welfare policy was emphasised again. Politics re-entered social administration.

So too, more obviously, did economics. The costs of welfare became more apparent and less acceptable. Measurement of benefits became an obvious necessity. Social administration had to seek to adapt to this new harsher world and forge new tools to measure efficiency and effectiveness, and to determine the 'fair' allocation of scarce resources.

A fourth factor in the decline of the traditional social administration was the realisation, which became stronger in the late 1960s and early 1970s, that social welfare services were failing to achieve their objectives. Inequality of opportunity in education had not been abolished. Neither had inequality of access to health care. Poverty still existed. Homelessness had reappeared. Slums still stood. The traditional social administration had never lacked confidence in its chosen instrument – state social services. All that was required was more of much the same. By the early 1970s, more people were questioning whether more resources were the answer or whether there were more deep-seated and fundamental reasons for failure. And if growth had ended and resources in future were going to be more limited, then objectives could never be attained. Prescription became a more complex activity.

In the late 1960s and early 1970s welfare absorbed more central and local government time and energy than it had done since the 1940s. The reorganisation of secondary education began in earnest. The personal social services were reorganised in 1971 and again, following local government reorganisation, in 1974. The National Health Service was reorganised in 1974 after some six years of discussion and negotiation. A series of attempts was made to introduce a new pension scheme which finally came to fruition in 1975. Almost immediately, however, doubts were voiced about these reorganisations – about the size of the new units which had been created, about increased bureaucratisation and about the costs involved. Social services, generally, suffered in public esteem as a result – and social administration suffered another blow to its self-esteem.

But perhaps most important of all in the reaction against the traditional social administration was a group of influences which can usefully be categorised together as new movements of thought. The resurgence of Marxism after 1968 posed all kinds of awkward questions for traditional social administration. Marxists exposed and criticised the implicit assumptions of social reformers – that the state could act as an independent force for social change, that society could work towards agreed social objectives, that state welfare was necessarily benevolent in purpose. Marxism also asserted the primary importance of the system of production in the generation of social relationships whereas Titmuss, for example, was 'entirely uninterested in the Marxist thesis that unequal social relations are located in the relations of production, he was content to leave the economic system to industry, the state and the economist' (Rose, 1981, p. 481).

New developments in sociology also posed difficulties for social administration. For many years sociology had been dominated by functionalism and consensus theory. In the late 1960s conflict theory became the dominant paradigm – the approach which sees society as characterised by conflict about ends and means rather than by a basic agreement. Students of social administration were faced with the task of making sense of social policy in a conflict situation. Whose side were they on?

Sociologists also began to be more interested in social welfare in the 1960s.

> It may be that when the history of social administration as
> an academic discipline during the 1960s comes to be looked back
> upon, one of the most significant developments will be seen to have
> been the growing influence upon it of sociology (Warham, 1973,
> p. 193).

Sociology has provided new approaches to understanding society, new tools of analysis, new perspectives and its own different and at times complementary approach to the study of welfare in society. As Warham points out, traditional social administration was concerned primarily with the aims and purposes of social services whereas the primary focus of sociology was with their *functions*. A focus on the functions of social services – social control, the perpetuation of women's dependency, the maintenance of labour discipline, for example – opened up new and, at times, rather disturbing perspectives for traditional social administration.

Feminism, equally, has helped to expose the dominant values implicit in much social policy. The feminist critique of the welfare state has sought to show how social policy functions to preserve a particular pattern of relations between the sexes, that it reflects, perpetuates and strengthens patterns of dependency. The traditional social administration remained blissfully unaware of the oppression to which it was contributing until feminism's first wave swept through the conference halls and the journals in the early 1970s. It was yet another challenge to the subject's basic assumptions.

Traditional social administration took a great deal for granted – about society, about government, about social services. The fallibility and fallaciousness of some of its central presuppositions were exposed in the early 1970s. Central concepts such as need, which had been assumed to have a certain technical absoluteness, were revealed as relative, contestable and riddled with value judgments and assumptions. From this smokey cauldron rose what might easily, but rather misleadingly, be called the 'new social administration'.

The new social administration

What then is this development which I have called the new social administration? What are its key characteristics? How is it different from the traditional social administration? Measuring the changing characteristics of an academic subject is difficult. Are best-selling or most-used texts the best index of conventional academic wisdom? Should one look at the content of courses offered in universities and polytechnics? Or should the focus be on new ideas which by some kind of academic osmosis come to be widely regarded as important?

What is certain is that the basic content and approach of academic courses changes rather slowly. Well-tried books are not banished when their approach and ideas come to be questioned. Rather they are garnished with more recent productions. Baker's examination of introductory social administration reading lists issued by Departments in 1977 reflects this situation. He found that the recommended reading reflected what he called the 'social conscience thesis' – that social policy is inherently benevolent, that it develops in response to a deepening sense of social obligation, and that it is becoming ever more generous as society gets more aware of the need for social services (Baker, 1979, p. 178). What we don't know, of course, is how far this reflection of the traditional social administration approach is criticised, modified and its assumptions unpacked and exposed, in lectures and tutorials.

The Joint University Council's study of the teaching of social administration suggests a slight cracking of the mould. The material which the JUC gathered suggested that while study of the British social services continued to hold a favoured place in the teaching of social administration, such teaching was tending to be counterbalanced by more generalised and theoretical material. Half the Departments which supplied the Council with detailed information about course content made some reference to the study of the ideologies underlying welfare provision and to theories of welfare (JUC, n.d., pp. 36–7). The Council concluded:

> The main shifts we have been able to identify are towards the presentation of social policy in ways that give greater importance to its philosophical and normative bases as matter for analysis themselves, to the concepts entailed in the promotion, implementation and study of social policy, to the structural context of social policy and the phenomena that it generates or seeks to change, and to the dynamics of change and development in social policy. The relationship between social policy studies and sociology is closer than formerly (JUC, n.d., p. 78).

The Council saw the scope of social administration widening at three levels – the conceptual, the theoretical and the contextual. It is important, however, to bear in mind that, if half the Departments who responded made reference to the study of ideologies and theories, half did not mention such novelties and were presumably continuing in more traditional ways.

While new ideas and approaches will only gradually be absorbed in a subject's literature, be reflected in the kinds of research undertaken or in courses of higher education, there can be no doubt that there are new ideas stirring in social administration.

Social administration is questioning many of its taken-for-granted assumptions – 'that social policy is always in intention and outcome benevolent, that the expansion of social services is necessarily the best way to tackle social problems, that the notion of 'social problem' is objective rather than problematic, that social reform can be achieved through reformist state action, and so on. The traditional social administration, it is now widely recognised, was – or is – itself an ideology and it needs to be dissected and exposed like any other. There is vigorous, critical questioning of ideas, assumptions and approaches – which were taken for granted until the early 1970s.

There is also much more concern with knowledge for understanding rather than knowledge for prescription, with the attempt to understand social welfare policies and institutions as part of a particular kind of society – to look at social policy from outside rather than from inside. The traditional social administration approached the study of welfare from inside, from a policy analysis rather than a social analysis or political economy perspective because of its commitment to description, evaluation and prescription. The new social administration does not reject these roles but argues that they must be complemented by this attempt to understand the roles and functions, the latent and manifest purposes, of social policy, in different kinds of society at different stages of development.

This approach is bound up with a broader view of the subject-matter of social administration. Carrier and Kendall have argued that the subject-matter of social administration is quite simply the welfare activities of societies, the whole complex of social arrangements for meeting needs (1977, p. 27). This seeks to draw the subject away from its concentration on arbitrarily defined social services and from a pre-occupation with public action. Titmuss's attempt in 1952 to broaden the field of social administration to include occupational and fiscal welfare was based on the justification that these were both essentially publicly financed (1963). Carrier and Kendall seek to move beyond this concern with funding to embrace the many and varied ways in which societies seek to influence differential command over resources according to some notion of need – which could embrace such diverse fields as transport policy, regional policy, pay policy, welfare services rendered by families and neighbours to each other, employment policy and tax policy.

Alan Walker has also recently argued for a new, broader approach which would move on from a study of public social services to a concern with 'the *distributional* implications or outcomes of the decisions and activities of a wide range of social institutions and groups' in relation to such social resources as income, assets, property, health, education, environment, status and power. He writes,

It is assumed that the extent to which these resources are distributed equally or unequally relative to need will determine the pattern of welfare in any society. Thus the essence of social policy is the social production and distribution of inequality and welfare (1981, p. 239).

If social administration is the study of social policy, then it must widen its scope 'to include all those institutionalised processes and values which determine the distribution of resources, status and power' (1981, p. 242).

Perhaps the most obvious feature of the new social administration is the move towards a political economy approach – the setting of the study of social policy firmly in the context of the politics and economics of contemporary society. Such an approach sees welfare as essentially and inherently political. It seeks to analyse different approaches to the promotion of social welfare through market systems and through public social services, to explore the assumptions which underlie them, assumptions about society, the state and the role of government, and to examine the values which underpin them.

This approach emphasises the primacy of the economy as the determinant of policy. It sees social policy not as the product of human benevolence, nor as a simple response to revealed need, but rather as an instrument of economic and political policy in a particular kind of society.

The concern essentially is with disentangling the value bases of policy, their source and influence, and with probing the functions of policy, the actual economic, political and social *effects* of policy and the relationship between social, economic and political institutions.

There has been much stress in the new social administration on a need for theory – partly at least because theory is what gives academic subjects respectability and status. At the root of this concern for theory there is also a concern for understanding, for ideas which help to make sense of that strange mix of activities which we call social policy. Economics, politics and sociology have been the source of such ideas.

Without doubt this new drawing on the wells of politics, economics and sociology has enriched our understanding of welfare state policies, and has enriched and extended social administration as a subject of academic study. Hopefully, it will also indirectly have given a blow to the rather pathetic and self-conscious concern within social administration to assert its status as a full-grown independent academic discipline. What the new social administration has made even clearer is that it is an 'area of study', not a 'mode of thinking' – to use Alan Williams's useful distinction (Culyer, 1981, p. 312). What the new social administration has made clear too is that 'none of the more important policy questions can be confined within academic boundaries' (Donnison, 1979, p. 154).

There is a danger, of course, that the heady wine of the new social administration may, as Hilary Rose perceptively points out, lead to a neglect of the strengths of the traditional approach, its detailed, empirical preoccupation with micro studies and the intimate relations of distribution and redistribution. Rose points out the specific relevance of this approach to a feminist analysis (1981, pp. 477–8) and it has a wider relevance too. Assessment of the effects of policies, accounts of the policy making process, suggestions for better directed policies remain as necessary as ever – perhaps even more necessary in conditions dominated by stringency and ideology decked out as economic theory. And such empirical study is the basis of theory building – a point which some of the more excitable theorists seem to forget. But such empirical studies need the context setting – philosophical, political, economic and sociological – which the new social administration has begun to provide.

The two traditions in social administration are complementary. On its own the traditional social administration was limited both in the field of study it cultivated and in the questions it posed. But, at best, the work produced was immensely revealing of the distributional implications of a range of social institutions, public and private. At the same time, such work could be myopic. What is needed is a marrying of the detailed empirical study of the operation of particular social services to a broader notion of the field of study – social policy – and the marrying of this approach to the new theoretical concerns of recent years.

Without proper and careful earthing in detailed empirical studies of the statutory base, operation and effects of a broad range of social policies, the new social administration could degenerate into little more than wild and windy ideological rhetoric. Together, the two approaches can both enrich our understanding of society and social policy and contribute to the design and implementation of 'better' social policies. Alone, either tradition is inadequate.

The traditional social administration has contributed greatly to our understanding of the operation and effects of individual social policies. The new social administration can provide the broader context in which it is possible to start making sense of social policy more generally. Such a focus represents a maturing of the subject. There is no necessary tension between old and new. If we are to build the newer world which was the aim and ideal of the founding fathers of our subject, both approaches are equally vital.

References

Baker, J. (1979), 'Social conscience and social policy', *Journal of Social Policy*, vol. 8, pt 2.

Carrier, J., and Kendall, I. (1977), 'Social administration as social science' in H. Heisler (ed.), *Foundations of Social Administration*, London, Macmillan.

Culyer, A. J. (1981), 'Economics, social policy and social administration: the interplay between topics and disciplines', *Journal of Social Policy*, vol. 10, pt 3.

Donnison, D. (1974), 'Social policy and administration', in B. Chapman and A. Potter (eds),, *WJMM: Political Questions*, Manchester University Press.

Donnison, D. V. (ed.) (1975), *Social Policy and Administration Revisited*, London, Allen & Unwin.

Donnison, D. V. (1979), 'Social policy since Titmuss', *Journal of Social Policy*, vol. 8, pt 2.

Hall, P. (1952), *The Social Services of Modern England*, London, Routledge & Kegan Paul.

Joint University Council for Social and Public Administration (JUC) (n.d., but 1979–80), *Teaching Social Policy and Administration in Britain and Ireland*.

Marsh, D. C. (ed.) (1965), *An Introduction to the Study of Social Administration*, London, Routledge & Kegan Paul.

Mishra, R. (1977), *Society and Social Policy*, London, Macmillan.

Parker, R. A. (1972), 'Social ills and public remedies', in W. A. Robson (ed.), *Man and the Social Sciences*, London, Allen & Unwin.

Parker, R. A. (1974), 'Social administration in search of generality', *New Society*, 6 June 1974.

Pinker, R. A. (1971), *Social Theory and Social Policy*, London, Heinemann.

Pinker, R. A. (1977), 'Introduction', in D. Reissman, *Richard Titmuss: Welfare and Society*, London, Heinemann.

Rose, H. (1981), 'Re-reading Titmuss: the sexual division of welfare', *Journal of Social Policy*, vol. 10, pt 4.

Sinfield, A. (1978), 'Analyses in the social division of welfare', *Journal of Social Policy*, vol. 7, pt 2.

Taylor-Gooby, P. (1981), 'The empiricist tradition in social administration', *Critical Social Policy*, vol. 1, no. 1.

Taylor-Gooby, P., and Dale, J. (1981), *Social Theory and Social Welfare*, London, Edward Arnold.

Titmuss, R. M. (1963), *Essays on the Welfare State*, London, Allen & Unwin.

Titmuss, R. M. (1974), *Social Policy*, London, Allen & Unwin.

Walker, A. (1981), 'Social policy, social administration and the social construction of welfare', *Sociology*, vol. 15, no. 12.
Warham, J. (1973), 'Social administration and sociology', *Journal of Social Policy*, vol. 2, pt 3.

Chapter 2
The aims and consequences of social policy*
Vic George

All advanced capitalist societies are social service societies of a sort: they spend about one-fifth of their gross national product on the five main social services – education, health, housing, social security and the personal social services –, they employ a large number of professionals to administer and provide these services and they apply a complex set of legal regulations either prohibiting or encouraging certain forms of behaviour in the social service field (Larkey *et al.*, 1981). Moreover, in all these societies, there is substantial public support for the idea of social services. Coughlin examined the available empirical evidence from public opinion polls in eight countries – Canada, USA, UK, Sweden, Denmark, West Germany, France and Australia – and concluded as follows:

> The overwhelming mass of survey evidence gathered under diverse circumstances over the past thirty years or so indicates a strongly favorable attitude in all eight nations in our sample toward government efforts to guarantee minimum standards of living for all citizens (Couglin, 1980, p. 18).

This general consensus on the social services does not imply detailed uniformity as well. Social services in advanced capitalist societies vary in their administrative framework, their method of finance, their level of provision and the benefits they confer to different socio-economic groups.

It is obviously important, though extremely difficult, to attempt an

---

*This chapter draws heavily on ideas contained in a forthcoming book by Paul Wilding and myself. I am, of course, alone responsible for any errors contained in this chapter.

appraisal of the consequences of social policy on the structures of such societies. There has been a tendency in social policy literature to confuse aims with consequences and to use these two notions interchangeably. It is, therefore, necessary to distinguish between the two. Aims refer to the intentions or aspirations of social policies; consequences are the actual outcomes of social policy. Clearly intent does not always match outcome; nor do the consequences of social policy always correspond to its aims. There are intended as well as unintended consequences of the aims of social policy.

Any discussion on the aims of social policy encounters two main problems. First, to speak of the aims of a particular piece of legislation is almost tantamount to highlighting the disagreements among the different classes, groups and prominent individuals on what these aims are. There is rarely complete agreement on what a piece of social policy legislation should aim at achieving. Second, even if one adopts as the aims of a particular piece of legislation those given by the government, one is still faced with the problem of identifying them. It is necessary to look for both stated and non-stated aims, for they are both important. There are times when government pronouncements on the aims of social policy reflect reality; there are other occasions, however, where they are mere rhetoric. In such cases the non-stated aims are of greater significance. It is these stated and non-stated government aims that form the basis of discussion in this chapter.

What we are concerned with is not so much the detailed and particular aims of individual services but the broader aims which cut across individual services and which affect the social, economic and political structure of society. An attempt is made to identify these aims and to look briefly at whether such aims are achieved in practice. In addition, an attempt is made to examine briefly the main unanticipated consequences of social policy. In order to give some structure to this discussion, aims and consequences are grouped into social, economic and political – acknowledging, of course, that these both overlap and that they are interrelated.

Social consequences

The first aim of social policy, and perhaps the most basic, is the achievement of certain minimum standards in the areas of life covered by the social services. All political parties and writers on the welfare state of all ideological commitments have expressed their support of this aim. They will agree with Crosland's conclusion that 'The relief of distress and the elimination of squalor is the main object of social expenditure' (1956, p. 113). This general agreement stems from the fact that the achievement of minimum standards poses no threat to the capitalist system. Indeed, it may strengthen it by abolishing or reducing its worst excesses, a claim that we will examine later in this chapter.

This general consensus on minimum standards breaks down when it comes to deciding what constitutes minimum standards for social policy purposes. Thus Churchill, who was one of the first and strongest advocates of minimum standards as a liberal at the beginning of this century, felt concerned enough about the proposals of the Beveridge Report as a prime minister to warn his cabinet colleagues about the 'false hopes and visions of Utopia and Eldorado' (1950, p. 861) that the Report raised.

The concept of minimum standards has three separate but related meanings: Inputs, Outputs and Outcomes. Inputs refers to the standard of service provision, i.e. the number of doctors, teachers, social workers, etc. per 1,000 population; the number of maternity hospital beds, residential places for the elderly, etc. per 1,000 of the specific population; and so on. Outputs refers to the specific results of service, i.e. reductions of general or infant mortality rates, reduction in illiteracy or increase in the number of pupils passing certain examinations, reduction in the number of children in the care of local authorities, reduction in overcrowding, ensuring that no one has an income below the supplementary benefit level, and so on. Outcome refers to the general and non-specific results of a service, i.e. the creation of a healthier, better educated and more humane society. Governments over the years have stressed the desirability of social service outcomes but have been less forthcoming in giving explicit support to the achievement of specific inputs or outputs.

The relationship between inputs on one hand and outputs or outcomes on the other is tenuous. The number of pupils per teacher is no safe guide to such outputs as reading or writing standards or the passing of examinations (Burstall, 1979). The number of doctors and nurses per 1,000 population does not always correlate with such outputs as infant mortality rates. Scotland, for example, has more doctors and nurses per 1,000 population than England but it has a higher infant mortality rate and a lower life expectancy (HMSO, 1979, p. 26). There are two obvious reasons for this lack of strong correlation between inputs and outputs: professionals do not always possess the skills to achieve what they aim at; and the outputs of a service are affected by factors other than its own inputs.

Minimum standards, whether inputs, outputs or outcomes, are relative. They change over time in response to the changing economic conditions, political situations, state of scientific knowledge, pressure-group activity, and so on. This is a well-trodden field in social policy and needs no elaboration here apart from noting the distinction between the minimum standards aimed at by social services and those actually achieved – improvement in the latter is less spectacular than in the former.

Government legislation to achieve minimum standards has been of three types over the years: mandatory legislation which sets explicit standards and provides sanctions to enforce these standards; advisory legislation which sets explicit standards but provides no sanctions against local authorities or other agencies that do not reach such standards; and suggestive legislation which merely expresses the hope that certain desirable but vague goals, such as the welfare of the child, adequate services for all, etc., will be achieved. Most of the legislation has been of the second and third type, particularly at times when governments are anxious to reduce public expenditure.

The unwillingness of governments to commit themselves through mandatory legislation to the achievements of specific standards in inputs, let alone outputs, of services has meant that improvements over the years have been patchy and unreliable. The literature in social policy has documented quite extensively both the successes and the failures in this area and no attempt will be made to even summarise it here (HMSO, 1977; 1978; 1979). All that needs to be said is that though substantial progress has been made over the years, there is still a long way to go before government stated minimum standards are achieved to the full. It is also important to state that this failure is not due to economic reasons. It would not be beyond the economic capability of the country to ensure that no one has an income below the supplementary benefit level; that the pupil–teacher ratio reaches an agreed minimum standard in all areas; that no one need be homeless, and so on. There are, however, problems of how governments can ensure that professionals accept employment in certain areas; that work incentives are not undermined; that the provision of services at minimum standard can cope with the geographical mobility of the population; and so on. These are difficult problems but not insurmountable given sufficient government commitment. What is more difficult is the achievement of minimum standards in outputs for this often depends on such factors as the family, workplace, neighbourhood, etc. which are outside the scope of the social services and to a certain extent beyond the scope of any government activity. Similar considerations apply to an even greater extent to the second aim of social policy – reductions of inequality – to which we now turn.

The use of minimum standards in the social service field in terms of both inputs and outputs has at times been confused with reductions of inequality. It is perfectly possible for standards to rise without necessarily reducing inequalities. Certain types of inequality – geographical, racial and sexual – have been considered as unacceptable by governments and, as a result, policies have been devised with the aim of reducing them. The most crucial type of inequality however – social class inequality – has not featured explicitly in government services, though it is by implication partially covered by policies designed to reduce other types of inequality. It is with social class inequalities that this discussion is concerned and these will be examined along the three related dimensions of access, use and outcome. Before doing this, however, it is important to clarify the meaning of equality in this context. It can be seen in terms of either evenness or fairness. An even distribution does not take into account the needs of the population groups being compared while a fair distribution does. The result is that an 'uneven distribution . . . may be regarded as "fair" if the variation is related to need. Conversely a distribution which is identified as even . . . may be extremely unfair' (Webster and Stewart, 1974). It was equality in terms of fairness that the Plowden Report had in mind when it put forward its policy of positive discrimination in favour of schools in deprived neighbourhoods. 'The first step', the report declared,

> must be to raise the schools with low standards to the national average; the second, quite deliberately to make them better. The justification is that the homes and neighbourhoods from which many of their children come provide little support and stimulus for learning. The schools must supply a compensating environment (HMSO, 1967).

The concept of access, as used here, refers to the geographical distribution of services in terms of the socio-economic character of neighbourhoods. In other words, is the geographical distribution of such services as schools, teachers, doctors and hospitals even between the higher and lower socio-economic neighbourhoods? Or is it fair, i.e. balanced in favour of the lower socio-economic groups which have the greater need for such services? Or is it unfair, i.e. balanced in favour of the higher socio-economic groups which have less need for such services? There is abundant evidence which shows that manual workers suffer from higher rates of illness than non-manual workers and hence have greater need for health services (Le Grand, 1978). Similarly, the academic support which children of manual backgrounds get from their families is less satisfactory than that received by children of non-manual backgrounds and hence their need of the education services is greater (HMSO, 1967; Douglas, 1967).

Using the health services as an example to discuss the concepts of access, the following picture emerges: various studies have shown that working-class areas have fewer doctors per 1,000 population than middle-class areas; that doctors in working-class areas are less well qualified than doctors in middle-class areas; and that doctors' premises in working-class areas are less comfortable than those in middle-class areas. Similarly, the distribution of hospital resources in terms of hospital beds and consultants is balanced in favour of the more affluent regions of the country (Buxton, 1976; Noyce et al., 1974). Moreover, those areas which have more doctors, relatively speaking, have also more hospital resources. Some progress has been made in equalising access to services since the creation of the National Health Service but, on the whole, the general picture has remained unchanged.

Access to services is only important because it facilitates use. It is quite feasible, though improbable, for access to a service to be unfair and for the use of the service to be even and perhaps fair. Most probably, however, unfair access means unfair use and this is what emerges from a discussion of the health services. The available evidence shows that manual groups consult their general practitioners less frequently in relation to their rates of illness than non-manual groups (Hart, 1975). Moreover, as Blaxter (1976) points out, 'middle class consultations have a higher clinical content and working class a higher administrative one'. Equally important, the lower socio-economic groups make less use of the community health services of ante-natal and post-natal clinics than the higher socio-economic groups. The available evidence about changes over the years is not very reliable but it does suggest that only minor changes have taken place since 1948.

The position is quite different in relation to the use of hospitals: all socio-economic groups make equal use of the outpatient services of hospitals but manual groups make greater use than non-manual groups of inpatient services both as regards rates of admission and length of stay in hospital (DHSS, 1980).

The measurement of the outcome resulting from the use of health services is generally accepted as problematic. Nevertheless, it is discouraging to those who saw the creation of the NHS as a means of reducing socio-economic differences in morbidity and mortality rates. Not only has there not been any narrowing of the social gap but, in the case of mortality and infant mortality rates, it has in fact widened (DHSS, 1980). It is a strong indication of the obvious fact that health services are only one of the many factors that affect mortality and morbidity rates. This is not the place to discuss the problems that any egalitarian government will have to face in attempting to reduce inequalities of access, use and outcome apart from noting briefly a few general points. First, it will be easier to tackle inequalities of access than of use; the most difficult inequalities are those of outcome. Second, any such attempts will be expensive and will be resisted by those socio-economic groups who benefit from the existing arrangements. Third, professional groups can veto the plans of any egalitarian government by refusing to work in deprived areas. Fourth, the traditional policies of positive discrimination, though useful, cannot reduce such inequalities – they need to be pursued more aggressively as well as more vigorously and they need to be extended to areas outside the traditional confines of social policy. Fifth, any sustained attempt to reduce inequalities will be far more costly than a policy aimed at achieving minimum standards. In brief, the reduction of inequalities is a much more difficult issue than has hitherto been acknowledged for it strikes at the roots of the capitalist system. It is most unlikely that the existing socio-economic inequalities in social policy will be reduced substantially in the immediate future.

Economic consequences

One of the basic aims of social policy has always been to encourage economic growth. There are numerous statements by politicians and others and in government reports that the various social services are not merely forms of consumption but they are also forms of investment for the individual and for society.

The contribution of social policy to economic growth, irrespective of which group in society benefits most, takes three main forms: it improves the quality of labour, it facilitates the mobility of industry and labour, and it encourages production through increased consumption. These are complex issues and they can only be briefly sketched out here. Moreover, there are the unintended consequences of social policy which, many have claimed, have had the effect of holding back economic growth. These, too, will be looked at very briefly.

Several government reports have referred to the potential effects of social policy – mainly education and health – on the quality of labour, but none so positively as the Robbins Report which declared that 'a community that neglects education is as imprudent as a community that neglects material accumulation', a declaration that the Government of the day accepted wholeheartedly (HMSO, 1963). The Robbins Report reflected the then prevailing optimism of the human capital theory which dominated thinking among experts in advanced capitalist societies. The difficulties involved in disaggregating the effects of education on economic growth from those of capital, labour and natural resources are obviously immense. It was for this reason that the work of Denison in the early 1960s was so important: he calculated that for the period 1950–62, the minimum contribution of education on economic growth was 15 per cent in the USA, 13 per cent in the UK and in Belgium, and for the other Western European countries it was lower, reaching 2 per cent in West Germany (Denison, 1967). Using Denison's methodology, Mushkin (1973) calculated that the effects of health services on economic growth were much lower than those of education, though still important. Similar estimates were later made by various other experts in other countries but all came under increasing criticism so that by the mid 1970s expert opinion was sharply divided on the usefulness of Denison's methodology. The economic recession of the late 1970s in advanced capitalist societies has cast a heavy cloud on the human capital theory because, simply put, education has expanded but economic growth has not. What prevails today is a much more sceptical attitude: education is still considered important to economic growth but there is less certainty about its precise impact, there is greater appreciation of the different effects of different types of education, there is even concern that some forms of education contribute nothing to economic growth, and there is greater appreciation of the importance of international factors on economic development in any one country (Sobel, 1978; Walters, 1981).

Successive governments since the last war have attempted, with varying degrees of emphasis, to influence the geographical distribution of labour and industry through their regional and labour mobility policies. Again, it is very difficult to measure the impact of such policies and not unexpectedly opinion is divided. The work of Moore and Rhodes (1973), and Moore and Tyler (1977) suggests that regional policies from the end of the last war to the late 1970s were successful in encouraging firms to move into the depressed regions of the country, that the economic performance of such firms compared favourably with that of other firms, and that they had an important effect in creating new jobs directly and indirectly. Critics of such policies point to the costs involved and suggest that a better solution would have been to allow market forces to take their natural course. The result, it is argued, would be economic decline in some parts of the country but expansion in others – and a more profitable one at that (Burton, 1977). When one adds to the economic considerations the social and political implications of regional depressions, the pressures on governments to pursue such policies become irresistible. It is partly for this reason that labour mobility programmes which attempt to encourage people to move out of depressed areas have featured far less prominently in government policies. Such programmes have had very little impact, certainly far less significant than that of regional policies. The number of workers who moved as a result of government schemes has not only been small but a significant proportion would have moved anyhow (Beaumont, 1979). There is, however, no reason to believe that such programmes could not be more effective if they were made more generous in the allowances they provide and if they tackled the problem of housing that faces people who move into the more prosperous areas. Both regional and labour mobility policies have lost most of their usefulness in the mass unemployment conditions of the early 1980s. What the country needs first and foremost is the creation of jobs in general; only then can specific policy programmes for particular regions have any chance of success.

The third main way in which social and public expenditure helps to promote economic growth is through the payment of cash benefits to about one-third of the population at any one time. Without this massive injection of income in the economy, consumer expenditure and hence production and employment would suffer. Though there is general acceptance of this, there is a great deal of disagreement about the unanticipated ill effects of such expenditure on economic growth. This is one of various unanticipated adverse effects of public expenditure on economic growth that we shall review briefly here.

The de-industrialisation thesis put forward by Bacon and Eltis

(1976) has been most influential on government policy. Basically the thesis claims that during the 1960s and 1970s public services in general and social services in particular have grown so fast that they have taken up a great deal of labour that would otherwise have found employment in the manufacturing industries. The result has been a growth in the unproductive sectors of the economy and a corresponding reduction in the productive sector. Too few producers have had the responsibility of producing enough to support far too many non-producers. The ensuing scarcity of labour in the manufacturing sector also meant that workers pressed for and received increasingly higher wages with the result that the rate of profit fell substantially. Not surprisingly, industrialists began to invest abroad rather than in Britain, thus adding another dimension to the country's worsening economic position. The solution to the problem, claim Bacon and Eltis, lies in a substantial reduction of public expenditure which will free both labour and capital for the manufacturing sector. Such a policy will cause hardship in the short term but will bring about national prosperity in the long run.

The de-industrialisation thesis has been criticised on both theoretical and empirical grounds. We will not pursue the theoretical criticisms apart from saying that they came from both the Keynesians (Thirwall, 1978) and the Marxists (Gough, 1979). On the empirical side, Thatcher (1979) has shown that the expansion of the social services relied on new sources of labour – women and students – and not on the workers made redundant in the manufacturing sector as Bacon and Eltis claimed. Moreover, the reduction of public expenditure in the late 1970s has not led to a growth of employment in the manufacturing sector – instead rising unemployment in the public sector has been accompanied by rising unemployment in the industrial sector. In spite of these criticisms, however, there is general agreement that beyond a certain level public expenditure has an adverse effect on economic growth in capitalist societies. What is in dispute is the level of such expenditure, the reasons for it, and who benefits from government attempts to curb it.

The second main way in which the growth of public expenditure can undermine economic growth is through its adverse effects on work incentives. This is an old controversy but it has gained weight in recent years because of the two simultaneous processes in British society – rise in public expenditure and economic decline. The debate over work incentives takes several forms but normally it refers to the effects of high taxation and of high social security benefits. Empirical evidence on the effects of both taxation and social security benefits is of two kinds:

evidence based on the opinions expressed by either the public in general or the low-paid in particular concerning such effects; and evidence based on whether different groups of the labour force paying different rates of taxes or receiving certain types of benefits – unemployment and supplementary benefit – make differential work efforts. Both types of studies have their strengths and weaknesses and the conclusions reached so far are inconclusive. On the taxation issue, the general conclusions reached are, first, that the effect of taxes on people's willingness to work can be both positive and negative depending on the individual's financial circumstances; and, second, that whether positive or negative such effects are of minor importance (Meade, 1978; Brown, 1980).

Unemployment benefit and supplementary benefit are said to encourage people to leave their employment too easily and then to prolong their period of unemployment. Research is again inconclusive but the weight of evidence suggests that, first, the vast majority of the unemployed receiving supplementary benefit – 95 per cent – would be better off if they were in full-time employment, particularly in view of the family income supplement (DHSS, 1977, para. 7.24). Second, there is no evidence to support the claim that people give up their jobs lightly in the knowledge that they can qualify for benefits; and third, the earnings-related supplement of unemployment may have had only a minor influence on the duration of unemployment (Maki and Spindler, 1975; Sawyer, 1979). However inconclusive the empirical evidence may be, the present government felt it necessary both to do away with the earnings-related supplement of the unemployment benefit in 1982 and to keep rises in the benefits for the unemployed at a lower level than those for other groups of beneficiaries.

Political consequences

There has been no shortage of views concerning the political consequences of social services in particular and of public policy in general. These views can be divided into those which see social services as helping to maintain or strengthen the capitalist system and those which see them as contributing to its demise. Both sets of views contain writers and politicians of conflicting ideologies.

The first approach has been advanced by both conservatives and marxists. Well-known conservative politicians – Bismarck, Balfour,

Macmillan, Lord Hailsham and others – have seen social reform as an antidote to revolution. In Lord Hailsham's words: 'To yield to legitimate pressure for reform is in reality the surest guarantee against revolution' (Hogg, 1947, p. 26). Marxists, too, have seen social control as one of the aims of social policy. Thus O'Connor (1973, p. 6) speaks for many Marxists when he writes that 'the capitalist state must try to fulfil two basic and often mutually contradictory functions – *accumulation* and *legitimation*'. The social services are particularly vital to the legitimation function of the state.

The second approach, too, has been put forward by writers of ideologically opposite views. The anti-collectivists see the welfare state as undermining political freedom through the excessive power that is being placed in the hands of the government. In the words of Hayek (1944) the welfare state is 'the road to serfdom'. Democratic socialists, too, have seen the social services as undermining the capitalist system and as being one of the many processes that create the appropriate conditions for a socialist society. Titmuss, for example, saw social services as contributing towards a greater sense of altruism and co-operativeness in society. These were also features of a socialist society. 'Socialism', he explained, 'is about community as well as equality. It is about what we contribute without price to the community and how we act and live as socialists' (1968, p. 151).

None of the above writers, however, whether for social control or for social change, provide any evidence to substantiate these claims. They are referring not so much to the actual consequences of social policy but to its aims, aspirations or dangers. Before one can provide any evidence for these claims, one needs to spell out the general ways in which social policy strengthens or undermines the capitalist system. This is the most that can be attempted in this section. The provision of detailed evidence is beyond the scope of the present discussion and may well be impossible anyhow. Clearly, the documentation of the political consequences of social policy is a far more difficult affair than the documentation of its social and economic consequences.

The social control function of social policy is based on two main assumptions: that social reforms have reduced the unacceptable faces of capitalism by abolishing its worst excesses; and that the social services, particularly education, propagate the dominant ideology of the capitalist system. Beginning with the first assumption, evidence from two different areas has been used to substantiate it. First, there is abundant evidence that governments over the years have been anxious to reduce the inherent unacceptable aspects of capitalism for political reasons. In the case of unemployment, for example, Gilbert's (1970) discussion of government policies on unemployment in the 1920s, and Deacon's (1977) examination of the development of insurance benefits for the unemployed during the same period show that fear of revolution or at least serious political unrest was one of the main driving forces behind government policies. Similarly, in the current high unemployment rates among the young and particularly among West Indian youth, government policies were shaped by the potential political unrest among young people. What these and other similar examples show is that governments think that ameliorative social policies can reduce political unrest. Whether they actually have that effect, however, is uncertain.

Second, it has been claimed that the welfare state has come to be accepted by the main political parties (Butler and Stokes, 1969). Any attempt by the Conservative Party to return to laissez-faire capitalism or by the Labour Party to move towards a socialist society are rejected by the electorate. The rise of the Social Democratic Party is seen as evidence of the electorate's rejection of 'extremism' by the right and the left. Butskellism reigns supreme among the public even in the days of a Thatcherite government. The next few years will show how true this claim is.

Let us now look at the ideological function of social policy. There is no doubt that the values underpinning the social services are those generally accepted in society, i.e. they are part of the dominant ideology which supports the existing socio-economic system. It is therefore not surprising to find that work incentives are embedded in the social security system (George 1973); that individualism and competitiveness are inherent in the school system (Bowles and Gintis, 1976); and so on. Marxists and non-marxists are agreed on this. Where they disagree most strongly is on who benefits from this process: Marxists maintain that it is mainly the upper class while non-marxists hold that the whole society benefits. Having said this, it is important to repeat that what social services aim to achieve is different from what they actually achieve. Thus not all pupils or students come to accept the dominant ideology and behave accordingly. Similarly, the effect of work incentive regulations in social security on actual workers' behaviour is unclear, and so on. There is neither monolithic application of dominant values in social services nor necessarily substantial translation of these in people's daily behaviour.

What of the social change function of social policy? The claim that social policy provides stepping-stones towards a socialist society is based on two claims: that social policy makes society more altruistic and that it raises public expectations to a level that capitalism cannot meet. How do social services make society more altruistic? The question has never been answered in any precise or detailed way but the implication has always been that this results from the fact that the allocation of services is based largely on need rather than ability to pay. There is obviously a substantial element of truth in this in relation to health and education but it is less true in the case of social security benefits and it is even less true in relation to housing. Moreover, the available evidence suggests that over the years there has been a trend towards increased private provision in all four social services – a method of provision which reflects ability to pay rather than need. In other words, if social service provision reflects altruism and private provision reflects egoism, the trend since the 1950s has been towards a less altruistic and more egoistic society.

Equally dubious is the claim that social services have raised public expectations to a level that capitalism cannot meet. In the first place, standards in the social services do not simply influence – they are also influenced by standards in other aspects of life. It is not merely a one-way process. In the second place, most studies have suggested that the majority of social service customers are satisfied with the quality of service they receive. Thus a national survey of attitudes to hospital services showed that 'over 80 per cent of patients thought that the service they received was good or very good' (HMSO, 1979, p. 13). Similar findings emerge in relation to general practitioners, primary and secondary schools, and so on. In the third place, even if one accepted the claim that capitalism cannot meet the rising public expectations that are partly brought about by the social services, there is no evidence that the only way out of the crisis is the creation of a socialist society. Indeed, the evidence from several advanced industrial societies in recent years suggests that governments can force or convince the public to reduce their expectations in relation to both public and private goods. In brief, the available evidence suggests – but does not, of course, prove – that social services in themselves have neither undermined capitalism nor strengthened public demands for a socialist society. All that the evidence supports is that the public are loath to give up easily benefits which they have gained over the years.

Conclusion

This chapter has attempted to provide a framework for analysing the broad consequences of social policy on the structure of society. For obvious reasons, Britain was used as the case study but it is hoped that the framework adopted could be applied to other advanced industrial societies. What emerges from this brief discussion is that the study of the consequences of social policy is a very complex affair but also a very important one. It deserves far more serious attention by students of social policy than it has so far received.

References

Bacon, R., and Eltis, W. (1976), *Britain's Economic Problem: too few producers*, London, Macmillan.

Beaumont, P. B. (1979), 'An examination of assisted labour mobility policy', in D. MacLennan, and J. B. Parr (eds), *Regional Policy*, London, Martin Robertson.

Blaxter, M. (1976), 'Social class and health inequalities', in C. O. Carter, and J. Peel (eds), *Equalities and Inequalities in Health*, London, Academic Press.

Bowles, J., and Gintis, H. (1976), *Schooling in Capitalist America*, London, Routledge & Kegan Paul.

Brown, C. V. (1980), *Taxation and the Incentive to Work*, Oxford University Press.

Burstall, C. (1979), 'Time to mend nets: a commentary on the outcomes of class size research', *Trends in Education*, London, HMSO.

Burton, J. (1977), 'Employment subsidies – the cases for and against', *National Westminster Bank Quarterly Review* (February).

Butler, D., and Stokes, D. (1969), *Political Change in Britain*, London, Macmillan.

Buxton, M. (1976), *Health and Inequality*, Milton Keynes, Open University.

Churchill, W. (1950), *The Second World War*, London, Cassell (Appendix F).

Coughlin, R. M. (1980), *Ideology, Public Opinion and Welfare Policy*, Berkeley, University of California Press.

Crosland, C. A. (1956), *The Future of Socialism*, London, Jonathan Cape.

Deacon, A. (1977), 'Concession and coercion: the politics of unemployment insurance in the twenties', in A. Briggs and J. Saville (eds), *Essays in Labour History, 1918–1939*, vol. 3, London, Croom Helm.

Denison, E. (1967), *Why Growth Rates Differ*, Washington, DC, Brookings Institute.

DHSS (1977), Supplementary Benefits Commission Annual Report, Cmnd 7392, HMSO, 1978.

DHSS (1980), Report of a research working group: Inequalities in Health.

Douglas, J. W. B. (1967), *The Home and the School*, London, Panther.

George, V. (1973), *Social Security and Society*, London, Routledge & Kegan Paul.

Gilbert, B. (1970), *British Social Policy, 1914–1939*, London, Batsford.

Gough, I. (1979), *The Political Economy of the Welfare State*, London, Macmillan.

Le Grand, J. (1978), 'The distribution of public expenditure: the case of health care', *Economica*, no. 145 (March).

Hart, J. T. (1975), 'The inverse care law', in C. Cox and A. Mead (eds), *A Sociology of Medical Practice*, New York, Collier Macmillan.

Hayek, F. (1944), *The Road to Serfdom*, London, Routledge & Kegan Paul.

HMSO (1963), *Report of the Committee on Higher Education*, Cmnd 2154, London.

HMSO (1967), *Children and their Primary Schools*, vol. I, London.

HMSO (1977), *Housing Policy: a consultative document*, Cmnd 6851, London.

HMSO (1978), *Royal Commission on the Distribution of Income and Wealth*, Report no. 6, Cmnd 7175, London.

HMSO (1979), *Royal Commission on the National Health Service*, Cmnd 7615, London.

Hogg, Q. (now Lord Hailsham) (1947), *The Case for Conservatism*, Harmondsworth, Penguin.

Larkey, P. D., Stolp, C., and Winer, M. (1981), 'Theorising about the growth of government: a research assessment', *Journal of Public Policy*, vol. I, no. 2 (May).

Maki, D., and Spindler, Z. (1975), 'The effects of unemployment compensation on the rate of unemployment in Great Britain', *Oxford Economic Papers*, no. 27.

Meade, J. E. (1978), *The Structure and Reform of Direct Taxation*, London, Allen & Unwin.

Moore, B., and Rhodes, J. (1973), 'Evaluating the effects of British regional economic policy', *Economic Journal*, vol. 83 (March).

Moore, B., and Tyler, P. (1977), 'The impact of regional policy in the 1970s', *Centre for Environmental Studies Review*, no. 1.

Mushkin, S. J. (1973), 'Health as investment', in M. Cooper and A. Culyer (eds), *Health Economics*, Harmondsworth, Penguin.

Noyce, J., *et al.* (1974), 'Regional variations in the allocation of financial resources to the community health services', *Lancet*, 30 March.

O'Connor, J. (1973), *The Fiscal Crisis of the State*, New York, St Martin's Press.

Sawyer, M. C. (1979), 'The effects of unemployment compensation on the rate of employment in Great Britain: a comment', *Oxford Economic Papers*, no. 31.

Sobel, I. (1978), 'The human capital revolution in economic development: its current history and status', *Comparative Education Review*, vol. 22, no. 2.

Thatcher, A. R. (1979), 'Labour supply and employment trends', in F. Blackaby (ed.), *De-industrialisation*, London, Heinemann.

Thirwall, A. P. (1978), 'The U.K's economic problem: a balance of payments constraint?', *National Westminster Bank Quarterly Review* (February).

Titmuss, R. (1968), *Commitment to Welfare*, London, Allen & Unwin.

Walters, P. B. (1981), 'Educational change and national economic development', *Harvard Educational Review*, vol. 51, no. 1.

Webster, B., and Stewart, J. (1974), 'The area analysis of resources', *Policy and Politics*, vol. 3, no. 1.

Chapter 3
The underdevelopment of social administration
Stewart MacPherson

Development in human society is a many-sided process. At the level of the individual, it implies increased skill and capacity, greater freedom, creativity, self-discipline, responsibility and material well-being. Some of these are virtually moral categories and are difficult to evaluate – depending as they do on the age in which one lives, one's class origins and one's personal code of what is right and what is wrong. However, what is indisputable is that the achievement of any of those aspects of personal development is very much tied in with the state of the society as a whole (Rodney, 1972, p. 9).

In the following chapters the machinery of social administration will be discussed; first, the appraisal of local needs and the spheres of central and local government; second the cohesive and spontaneous efforts of the firm, the trade union, the co-operative and friendly society, and the philanthropic society; third, the problems of vagrancy, feebleness, illiteracy and law-breaking, and how these can be provided for and prevented by building up social services under the Labour, Health and Education departments of government (Gardiner and Judd, 1954, p. 15).

In his foreword to Gardiner and Judd's *The Development of Social Administration*, Richard Titmuss focused his remarks on the deleterious social consequences of rapid economic change in 'the "under-developed" areas'. Arguing the vital necessity of organised social welfare provision to alleviate this misery, he proclaimed that 'This is a challenge which can neither be ignored with a cynical washing of hands in Malthusian waters nor met by imposing, however benevolently, the solutions of the West. "The Welfare State", that unfortunate misleading and illiberal phrase, is no answer' (Titmuss, in Gardiner and Judd, 1954, p. 6). Two crucial themes may be drawn from Titmuss's foreword; the first is that in identifying the nature and role of social welfare as ameliorative and remedial – reactive to rapid economic change – he was clearly representing the dominant views of that time. This was true not just of perceptions of the proper role of social welfare in the colonies of course, but was characteristic of attitudes to welfare and social policy within Britain itself. That the two were so similar was no accident; the pervasive transfer of concepts and practice from the metropolitan countries to the colonies is an essential part of the colonial relationship. Indeed, that transfer has continued long beyond the formal ending of colonial control and forms a crucial part of continuing under-development (Midgley, 1981; MacPherson, 1982a). The notion that social policy was fundamentally concerned with the inevitable conse-quences of the operation of the economic system permeated study of social welfare in the immediate post-war period. It was the acceptance of that inevitability which was so profoundly important. In the colonies, economic exploitation was gathering pace, and on very many occasions direct comparisons were drawn with the social and economic history of Britain in order to justify the horrors which resulted from social and economic changes which were forced on subject peoples (Rodney, 1972).

Second, Titmuss was impressive in his rejection of population-based explanations or solutions. It is tragic that this was of no use; we saw in later years an upsurge of such approaches, in precisely the terms so graphically conveyed by Titmuss in 1954 (Mamdani, 1972). But third, and extremely important, his warnings regarding the imposition of Western solutions were too weak, too late and lacking real understand-ing of the nature of colonial domination. Given the context in which he worked, anything else would have been very surprising. The same cannot however be said so clearly of the authors for whom Titmuss provided the foreword; the fatal flaws in the latter are grotesquely highlighted in the body of the book. Gardiner and Judd present an amalgam of British and African material using problems from the latter and detailed discussion of social welfare provision in the former. Their inclusion of so much irrelevant British material is a clear illustration of the complex phenomenon of cultural imperialism, but, more prosaically, reflects the almost complete lack of substantive literature from within the colonies themselves.

The basic misunderstanding of the nature of colonialism, which so flawed Titmuss's foreword, runs throughout Gardiner and Judd's book. Their concern was to smooth the path of 'economic development' and economic change, to build new patterns of social responsibility and new values consonant with the new economy and society. Above all, they were part of the production of a social administration in the countries of the Third World which was the creature of colonial domination and the attendant to neo-colonial exploitation. In my own experience as a university teacher, I have never seen the printed word provoke a more profound and deeply angry reaction than did that book. In the early 1970s, among students at university in East Africa, the true nature of the book was seen very clearly indeed. Twenty years on, from a different perspective, both the implicit and explicit substance of that earlier view of the world was as clear to those students as it had been hidden from Titmuss.

In that span of twenty years, approaches to the study of social policy and social welfare had changed in the countries of the Third World, though many saw that the changes were slow, and that the influence of metropolitan and 'international' forces could pervert new independent approaches. Elsewhere I have argued that the continuing under-development of the Third World determines both the social problems which bear down upon the poor, and the nature of policy responses which purport to respond to those problems (MacPherson, 1982a; 1982b). I am concerned in this essay to consider the relationship between the study of social welfare in the Third World and such study of the western industrialised countries, and of Britain in particular. I am convinced that there are many ways in which greater awareness of Third World issues, literature and theories would enrich approaches to welfare in the West.[1] Of overwhelming importance however is my conviction that welfare in the West *cannot* be considered in isolation.

From the beginning, the formal study of social welfare in Britain has been parochial, inward-looking and insular. Little if any regard has been paid to theories and practice emanating from the poorest three-quarters of the world; what has become known as the 'Third World'. The use of this term is itself indicative of the dominant perceptions regarding the vast majority of the human population. Although the term has a specific derivation in terms of the major geo-political alignments, its common usage emphasises the distant nature of the societies in question. Here mental distance is far greater than physical distance; areas are perceived as 'remote' when in fact they are relatively close in geographical location or accessibility.

I shall first indicate the profound neglect of events, theories and approaches emerging from the greater part of the world for almost the whole of the period since the Second World War. Second, I shall elaborate the concept of 'underdevelopment' and its relevance to the examination of social welfare, social policy, the distribution of social resources and patterns of social change. Finally, I shall outline the beginnings of a case for the incorporation of such concepts and approaches into the study and analysis of welfare in the West.

Social administration in one country

With very few exceptions, those concerned with writing about welfare have shown little knowledge of, or indeed interest in, the problems of the poorest three-quarters of the world's population. This is quite evident if we take social administration as a focus of such academic activity, though of course by no means encompassing it. To take one rather poor indicator, analysis of the contents of the *Journal of Social Policy* since 1972 shows that of 158 articles only 3 were on topics directly related to issues of development and underdevelopment, and only 2 were concerned with Third World countries.[2] Another indication, and in my view a rather important one, is the extent to which Third World material is included in university and polytechnic social administration courses. This happens in very few places indeed. All these are of course intimately bound up together, the patterns of teaching, research, writing and thinking about the subject being dominated by convention. To the extent that the study of social welfare and social policy manifests this lack of awareness and narrowness of vision, I would argue that the subject has been and is being 'underdeveloped', using that term in the particular and extremely powerful way it is now used in the analysis of poverty in the Third World.[3]

There have been some exceptions to this near-complete neglect of the world. A number of people have drawn on Third World material and, of more relevance to the present discussion, have used that material in analysis of social welfare issues in the West. However, these are extremely scattered and essentially isolated islands in a very large ocean of neglect. One of the most notable exceptions, and one which provides a focus for the present discussion, is Townsend's essay 'Measures and

Explanations of Poverty' (1970). This was the major contribution to a volume based on a conference organised by the International Committee on Poverty Research. Despite the title of the sponsoring body, and their stated objectives, Townsend's was in fact the only essay which drew on material concerned with underdeveloped countries. In the context of that volume, and indeed of the mainstream of writing on social welfare at that time, the essay was notable for that reason alone. Its isolation dramatically underlines the lack of interest. But the essay was notable for other, much more important, reasons. In his treatment of the issues, Townsend began to explore themes and theoretical perspectives which were largely outside the experience of the majority of those engaged on work related to the analysis of social welfare and social policy. Some of the themes and perspectives introduced by Townsend but never developed by him, or others, are among those I wish to examine now, more than a decade later. I believe that the failure of those concerned with approaches to welfare to follow the lead given by Townsend to be a significant loss. Furthermore, I would argue that if we look at the causes of that failure we find important indications of the nature of contemporary work in this area.

Townsend, in his introduction to the collection, argued that in the 1960s 'the dire needs of the poor nations had also come to the forefront of public awareness. . . . Despite the frustrating lack of information an intellectual framework, consistent cross-nationally as well as through time, had to be created' (1970, p. x). Townsend's analysis of the problem of poverty in global terms was notable because of the theoretical perspectives he drew into that analysis. In particular, it was his acknowledgment of the power and relevance of the concept of underdevelopment which so clearly marked that essay out, not just from other writing in what might for convenience be called 'social administration', but from the main body of his own work. Townsend first summarised a number of the deficiencies of conventional approaches to the analysis of development in the Third World. He then identified the first element in the complex web of underdevelopment: 'Many of the societies now acknowledged to be highly developed were capitalised at the expense of those which have remained underdeveloped' (1970, p. 9). Some, including myself, might wish to quarrel with the use of certain terms here, especially 'highly developed', but the basic truth is crucially important, and not at issue. Similarly, in beginning to illuminate the true nature of the relationships between rich and poor countries, Townsend started to place the analysis of poverty on a new footing:

> In many important respects it would be fair to conclude that the structure of underdevelopment has been created by centuries of association with the mercantile and colonialist nations. It would be naïve in the extreme not to recognize that western countries may have much to gain economically and politically even today from the poverty of the so-called developing countries though they may also have a lot to lose by policies of exploitation. Theories of development may unwittingly safeguard western ideology (1970, pp. 9–10).

Here Townsend was drawing on the work of Frank, whose influence on the study of underdevelopment has been enormous (Frank, 1967; 1969; 1972); although the analysis of underdevelopment is not pursued to any depth in the Townsend essay. Given the context, this is hardly surprising: what was impressive was his willingness to use such material at all, and by so doing to move debate on poverty out of the narrow constraints of conventional discourse. Townsend suggested in 1970 that 'The implications of all this for the study of world poverty are far-reaching' (1970, p. 11). They are indeed, and I would repeat my contention that those concerned with the study and analysis of poverty and inequality in the West have largely ignored those implications. We need to study the systems which control the accumulation and distribution of resources, and on a world scale because it is only on that scale that the fundamental patterns of relationship are revealed and the mechanisms of continuing inequality exposed. Again Townsend began to identify this in 1970, and pointed out another aspect of this analysis which is of profound contemporary significance: 'The degeneration or depression of regions, nations and sections of nations into conditions of deprivation' (1970, p. 11). Reports from the community development projects of the 1970s began to follow this direction in their analysis of the underdevelopment of areas of this country (Mayo, 1975), but again it must be said that this aspect of their work was not taken up very vigorously – at least by the mainstream.

I believe that the analysis of underdevelopment must be part of any effort which attempts to move the boundaries of the study of social welfare and social policy outwards and extend the range and depth of its understanding. Without some firm grounding in the realities of contemporary underdevelopment, simple transfers across the present international boundaries, while they may be stimulating, run the very serious risk of being misinterpreted and misunderstood. It is for these reasons that I shall further elaborate the concept of underdevelopment later in this chapter.

But there are other aspects of the neglect of the Third World which I would like to touch on here, and unfortunately I cannot do more than that. Yet again some of these were hinted at in Professor Townsend's 1970 essay. As part of a discussion of the notion of 'development' itself, he began to bring across to consideration of poverty in this country something which is familiar to anyone who has worked in the Third World: the fact that 'Both high and low income countries are a mixture, though to a differing degree, of traditional and modern elements' (1970, p. 31). The importance of seriously understanding both of those elements, in our own society and elsewhere, can hardly be overstated. But there is little evidence that such studies are being seriously pursued. I again agree very strongly with Townsend when he identifies both disciplinary separation and crudeness of terminology as part of the explanation for this: 'Too often extreme analytic polarisations have plagued our attempts to compare different societies – "modern" and "primitive", "developed" and "underdeveloped", "industrial" and "agrarian" ' (1970, p. 31).

Of course, suffusing this kind of categorisation and the related dismissal of such comparisons as irrelevant are the deep-seated ideas of inferiority and superiority which taint a great part of the West. In this, Britain is almost certainly worse than many other countries, and we may look to our colonial past for part of the explanation for this. But rejection of the 'primitive', the 'non-western' or the 'traditional' is not confined to those who have not had the opportunity to consider these matters: 'both the historical and contemporaneous evidence about different societies tends to be insufficiently sought and digested. . . . Every modern society has a traditional one inside it' (Townsend, 1970, p. 32). I cannot explore this theme here but there are very many issues of fundamental significance which are illuminated by consideration of traditional social systems, and perhaps especially when such systems are undergoing rapid change. Similarly, I must defer discussion of the final theme to be drawn from Townsend's essay. The neglect of Third World societies as a source of concepts and theoretical insights is mirrored by the almost total lack of interest in the social policies and programmes which have emerged in those societies. Townsend concluded his essay with one such reference: to the restraints placed on the elites in Tanzania by the Arusha Declaration. The success or failure of that attempt to directly limit power and privilege *by legislation* would, one might have thought, have been of considerable interest within the study of social welfare in Britain.

As I have already contended, the path indicated by Townsend in 1970 has not been followed. In Britain the study of social welfare and social policy has, as yet, developed no 'cross-national intellectual framework', ⟵ despite the considerable advances that studies of poverty and development have made internationally since 1970. What we have rather had is an underlying current of interest, occasionally surfacing, sometimes explicitly, as in the example of overseas staff in the National Health Service (Doyall and Pennell, 1979, pp. 263–6), but more often implicitly or quietly and unobtrusively. Work which has actually picked up and developed the themes outlined above is rare indeed, although recent years have brought some indications of change, but, perhaps predictably, these have tended to come from outside the mainstream (Doyal and Pennell, 1979; Rogers, 1980; Midgley, 1981).

This lack of interest, and lack of awareness, is not confined to Britain. A book which came towards the end of the 1970s dramatically underlines the position I am taking here. In 1977 Michael Harrington's *The Vast Majority* was published. Subtitled 'A journey to the world's poor', it is an intensely personal book with a profoundly serious purpose – to inform Americans of the realities of underdevelopment. The book is important in its own right, but the identity of the author should be, I would argue, of considerable interest. Harrington can be directly compared with Townsend in terms of his contribution to the study of poverty. It was these two above all who exposed the realities of poverty in Britain and America in the 1960s (Abel-Smith and Townsend, 1965; Harrington, 1962; Townsend, 1979). Their separate, and in style and tone quite different, attempts to convey the fundamental importance of underdevelopment should be of significance to the formal study of welfare in the West. What is profoundly evocative in Harrington's book is his identification of what he calls, with a powerful combination of sadness, shame and anger, 'The Cruel Innocence' (1977, pp. 13–33). In that notion I believe that he is as well describing the position of the majority in this country, laymen and 'experts in social policy' alike, as he is his fellow Americans:

> In the nineteen hundred seventies, the government and the people
> of the United States are turning their backs on the wretched of the
> earth. They do so with the best will in the world. Indeed for the
> last eighty years, America has worked against the poor of the planet
> in a spirit of sincere compassion. And one point of this book is,
> precisely, to deprive us of this cruel innocence which prevents us

from even seeing the wrongs we perpetuate (Harrington, 1977, p. 13).

What Harrington saw as true of the United States in the 1970s we must surely see as true of Britain in the 1980s. It is true of governments, and it is true of the majority of people, including those engaged in the study of inequality and welfare. With Harrington, I do not write this arrogantly; I am no better than others, just fortunate to have had the opportunity to work outside the constraints of an underdeveloped discipline. In describing his reactions and responses to India, Harrington conveys several important lessons, not least some indications of an explanation for the continuance of the cruel innocence:

> I had already written seven books of social criticism and observation. But, I came to understand, I am also a very mundane member of the Western middle class, with commonplace emotions . . .
> representative of most of the people who read this book: unheroic, immersed in Western comforts, no Francis of Assisi. I am a contradictory, compromised and somewhat baffled person. If I can transmit the passion for change with which these experiences flooded my middle-class soul, perhaps others will feel them (1977, p. 30).

For the remainder of this essay my objectives are limited; I shall first discuss the concept of underdevelopment at greater length and then conclude by indicating the relevance of that concept to the theory and practice of approaches to welfare.

Underdevelopment

As I have argued elsewhere, recent years have seen a rejection by many in the Third World of Western approaches to the problems of development – which justify continuing exploitation by locating the causes of underdevelopment in the cultures of the Third World itself (MacPherson, 1982a). Above all, underdevelopment has come to be seen as a *process*; it is a powerful active concept, not a static, descriptive one. Thus theories of 'the development of underdevelopment' distinguish between underdevelopment as a state, as in modernisation theories, and as a continuing process. In this conception, underdevelopment does not refer to a society's position on some linear path of progress, indicating a potential for further 'development'. Rather, underdevelopment is a continuing process which profoundly affects both the external relationships of societies and their internal social and economic formations. Both are perverted to ensure progressively more profound integration of Third World societies as exploited elements of the international economy (Frank, 1972; Hoogvelt, 1978; Roxborough, 1979).

Such a concept is in marked contrast to those which dominated discussion of development in the 1950s and 1960s; in that period modernisation theories emphasised the primacy of economic growth and the inevitability of the problems of social change referred to earlier. Underdevelopment theories perceive the relations which exist between poor countries and rich countries as damaging the interests of the former and working to the further advantage of the latter. As Hoogvelt suggests, 'structural-functional theories of modernisation have in fact very usefully served as an ideological mask camouflaging the imperialist nature of Western capitalism' (Hoogvelt, 1978, p. 62). Although largely discredited in terms of both basic assumptions and practical effect, modernisation theories continue to have an enormous influence on the formulation and implementation of policies and programmes in Third World countries, especially where these are mediated through the international agencies. Recently there has been a revival of these theories, particularly in the World Bank, which has begun to reverse policies which had come to reflect an awareness of the realities of underdevelopment (Laar, 1979).

There are of course many different versions of underdevelopment theory (Foster-Carter, 1974). For this essay, two important themes may be identified in what Foster-Carter characterises as the 'neo-Marxist perspective'. First, neither developed nor underdeveloped societies are seen as self-sufficient social systems; emphasis is put on the inter-connections of a global economic and social system. Second, and as a result of examining the patterns of social change in underdeveloped countries, the diffusion of Western systems is seen to create the reverse of development. Rather than bringing greater independence, the nature of social change is such as to bring greater dependence and further entrench exploitative relationships, both within and between countries. It is the mechanisms of unequal exchange which above all operate to ensure the continuing economic subjugation of the periphery (MacPherson, 1982a, p. 26).

Several characteristic features of underdevelopment may be identified, at the price of oversimplification and generalisation. What is common to them all is the notion of *distortion*; this may be seen in both economic and social phenomena. In economic terms, the distortion in underdeveloped societies is that economies may grow, but that growth is primarily geared to the economic interests of the metropolitan powers. Thus, distortions in both patterns of internal economic activity and the nature of external economic relations means a lack of fit between the economy and the achievement of real development. The perverted external orientation of underdeveloped economies will most often mean a lack of internal coherence and dynamic. It is difficult to overemphasise the impact of underdevelopment. The penetration of the cash economy, which now dominates all the societies of the Third World, not only shapes contemporary patterns of social formation, but dramatically restricts the range of future options. In many countries interactions between 'modern' and pre-existing subsistence economies are of major significance. A number of those who have argued for alternative development paths have stressed the values embodied in pre-existing systems. Many have argued that those values can be given expression in development strategies which reject the domination of the international capitalist economy and its attendant social forms (Nyerere, 1968; Waiko, 1977).

In social terms the dominant feature is the emergence of 'a perverse class structure shaped more by external than by internal pressures' (Amarshi *et al.* 1979, p. xv). In post-colonial societies two trends may be seen as characteristic (Gutkind and Waterman, 1977): the emergence of a largely urban, largely public-service-based wage and salary elite and the beginnings of rural class formation. It is the former that I wish to examine very briefly. The urban-based elite is, in crude terms, the most important feature of very many Third World social systems. Where such groups are heirs to colonial administrations they have enormous power, and, with very few exceptions, concomitant privilege (Markovitz, 1977). The extent to which this group, or elements within it, forms a 'bureaucratic bourgeoisie' and the significance of such a formation, will vary. A common factor, however, which is highly relevant to the present discussion, is the dominance of the state (Golbourne, 1979). In any Third World country the relationship between class power and state power is of fundamental importance. 'It should be clear that any analysis of the state in the Third World must examine the mechanisms and institutions through which social classes have access to, and influence on, the making of state policy' (Roxborough, 1979, p. 123).

The class formations of Third World societies are exceedingly complex, and the isolation of one element for cursory examination is obviously unsatisfactory. But for this essay I wish to point to the relevance of underdevelopment as a concept and do not pretend to be doing more. In a more thorough review of material on class formation I concluded that 'the bureaucratic bourgeoisie may be seen to be the dominant exploiting class element within the majority of social formations of the Third World' (MacPherson, 1982a, p. 32). To the extent that this is so, and given the nature of that class, this should be of major concern to those interested in approaches to welfare. In the underdeveloped countries of the world it is the bureaucratic bourgeoisie which has the responsibility for formulating and implementing social policies and programmes.

This very brief discussion has stressed, above all, that underdevelopment must be seen as a powerful and continuing process which produces particular kinds of economic and social formations both within and between countries. Although there may be variation in the specific forms,

> in general terms the perversion of Third World political economies may be seen as directing social change in the interests of external forces. The crucial importance of this perspective is that it enables the economic and social dimensions of what may appear to be vigorous and positive growth and change to be more fully understood (MacPherson, 1982a, p. 33).

The concept of underdevelopment is crucial to any analysis of Third World social welfare; it is also crucial to the proper analysis of welfare in the West. It is not just a moral imperative which should drive us to consider the poor of the world, though surely that is great enough. Neither is it economic self-interest which should persuade us of the relevance of global economic relationships; though the Brandt Report and its reception perhaps demonstrate the strength of support for that. It is rather, as Townsend indicated in 1970, that we must view poverty and inequality in global terms if we are to understand the forces and the mechanisms which perpetuate what are surely basic concerns of any approach to welfare.

Notes

1 This is a vast topic which cannot be pursued in a note. Examples where Third

World material has been used include Freire (1972), Mayo (1975), Dore (1976), Doyal and Pennell (1979), Heatley (1979), Castells (1979), McRobie (1981). In consideration of community development, primary health care, 'relevant' education, mass organisation and participation and very many other themes, there is a mass of extremely rich material which is largely ignored at present (Harrison, 1980; Midgley, 1981; MacPherson, 1982a). One example must serve to indicate another, and major, kind of loss which I believe results from this neglect. The notion of 'the gift', crucial to the concept of altruism, has been discussed by social administration with virtually no reference to traditional exchange systems. A recent article began to do this, but went only a very short distance in its pursuit of the issues (Uttley, 1980).

I must emphasise here that I am not arguing that we can see, in Third World countries, 'ourselves as we were'. As Professor Howard Jones noted in his recent study of crime in Guyana (1981), underdeveloped countries are profoundly different precisely because they have been, and are being, underdeveloped.

2 The January 1982 issue of the *Journal of Social Policy* reported an analysis of the first ten years' content. No reference is made to the lack of Third World material. This is despite the stated editorial policy that 'its scope is international'.

3 Frank (1972) used the concept in this way, to great effect; as did Navarro (1974). In arguing the *underdevelopment* of social administration I am attempting to focus attention on the many elements which serve to distort the subject as an area of study. This distortion has the effect of *preventing* awareness of wider issues and the pursuit of those issues. In very many instances this has happened and continues to happen, despite the *personal* conviction of those engaged in the subject that these issues are both important and relevant. One of the very few fully-developed courses which successfully brought together some of this material is the Open University's 'Patterns of Inequality' (Blowers and Thompson, 1976). It is interesting to note that the Associated Examining Board now have a part of their 'A' level Sociology syllabus devoted to underdevelopment. Most university and polytechnic social science degree courses do not.

References

Abel-Smith, B., and Townsend, P. (1965), *The Poor and the Poorest*, London, Bell.

Amarshi, A., Good, K., and Mortimer, R. (1979), *Development and Dependency: the Political Economy of Papua New Guinea*, Melbourne, Oxford University Press.

Blowers, A., and Thompson, G. (eds) (1976), *Inequalities, Conflict and Change*, Milton Keynes, Open University.

Castells, M. (1979), *City, Class and Power*, London, Macmillan.

Dore, R. (1976), *The Diploma Disease*, London, George Allen & Unwin.

Doyal, L., and Pennell, I. (1979), *The Political Economy of Health*, London, Pluto Press.

Foster-Carter, A. (1974), 'Neo-Marxist approaches to development and underdevelopment', in E. de Kadt and G. Williams (eds), *Sociology and Development*, pp. 67–108, London, Tavistock.

Frank, A. G. (1967), *Capitalism and Underdevelopment in Latin America: Historical Studies of Chile and Brazil*, New York, Monthly Review Press.

Frank, A. G. (1969), *Latin America: Underdevelopment or Revolution*, New York, Monthly Review Press.

Frank, A. G. (1972), *Sociology of Underdevelopment and Underdevelopment of Sociology*, London, Pluto Press.

Freire, P. (1972), *Pedagogy of the Oppressed*, London, Sheed & Ward.

Gardiner, R. K., and Judd, H. O. (1954), *The Development of Social Administration*, London, Oxford University Press.

Golbourne, H. (1979), *Politics and the State in the Third World*, London, Macmillan.

Gutkind, P. C. W., and Waterman, P. (1977), *African Social Studies*, London, Heinemann.

Harrington, M. (1962), *The Other America*, New York, Macmillan.

Harrington, M. (1977), *The Vast Majority*, New York, Simon & Schuster.

Harrison, P. (1980), *The Third World Tommorrow*, Harmondsworth, Penguin.

Heatley, R. (1979), *Poverty and Power*, London, Zed Press.

Hoogvelt, A. M. M. (1978), *The Sociology of Developing Societies* (2nd edn), London, Macmillan.

Jones, H. (1981), *Crime, Race and Culture*, Chichester, John Wiley.

Laar, A. J. M. van de (1979), *The World Bank and the Poor*, The Hague, Institute of Social Studies.

MacPherson, S. (1982a), *Social Policy in the Third World*, Brighton, Harvester.

MacPherson, S. (1982b), 'Mental illness in the Third World', in P. T. Bean (ed.), *Mental Illness: changes and trends*, Chichester, John Wiley.

Mamdani, M. (1972), *The Myth of Population Control*, New York, Monthly Review Press.

Markovitz, I. L. (1977), *Power and Class in Africa: An Introduction to Change and Conflict in African Politics*, Englewood Cliffs, Prentice Hall.

Mayo, M. (1975), 'Community development: a radical alternative?', in R. Bailey and M. Brake (eds), *Radical Social Work*, London, Edward Arnold.

McRobie, G. (1981), *Small is Possible*, London, Jonathan Cape.

Midgley, J. (1981), *Professional Imperialism: Social Work in the Third World*, London, Heinemann.

Navarro, V. (1974), 'The underdevelopment of health or the health of underdevelopment', *International Journal of Health Services*, 4(1), pp. 5–27.

Nyerere, J. (1968), *Freedom and Socialism*, Dar-es-Salaam, Oxford University Press.

Rodney, W. (1972), *How Europe Underdeveloped Africa*, Dar-es-Salaam, Tanzania Publishing House.

Rogers, B. (1980), *The Domestication of Women: Discrimination in Developing Societies*, London, Kogan Page.

Roxborough, I. (1979), *Theories of Underdevelopment*, London, Macmillan.

Townsend, P. (ed.) (1970), *The Concept of Poverty*, London, Heinemann.

Townsend, P. (1979), *Poverty in the United Kingdom*, Harmondsworth, Penguin.

Uttley, S. (1980), 'The welfare exchange reconsidered', *Journal of Social Policy*, 9, 2, pp. 187–205.

Waiko, J. D. (1977), 'The people of Papua New Guinea, their forests and their aspirations', in J. H. Winslow (ed.), *The Melanesian Environment*, Canberra, Australian National University Press.

Chapter 4
Welfare, class and distributive justice
John Westergaard

I

The title may promise a good deal more than a short paper can fulfil. I shall go little beyond annotating two parallel paradoxes associated with the theme (Westergaard, 1978; 1980a; 1980b). They are parallel in the sense that both concern the presence of a moral vacuum where logic seems to require an explicit ethic. The first paradox is familiar, though no less significant for this. It is that, grafted as it has been onto capitalist modes of resource allocation, public provision for welfare in western countries lacks anchorage in any such conception of distributive justice as its ostensible direction to meeting human needs implies. The second paradox concerns critique of welfare policy from the radical left. Such critique has forcefully identified limits set to public provision by its capitalist context; yet the critique has itself been too rarely buttressed by express formulation of a distributive ethic. To that extent it has lacked a distinct moral yardstick for two uses in particular: for clear measure of capitalist shortcomings; and for delineation of policy, so also of social structure, as they might be in an alternative socialist context. My own record is among those open to adverse comment on this score: hence the suggestions which I shall make later in this paper, philosophically unskilled though they are.

II

Neither capitalism as a socio-economic system nor liberalism as its many-headed philosophical companion has had associated with it a principled conception of distributional welfare. Capitalism implies, and liberalism in tune with it proclaims, no general ethic to provide intrinsic justification either for the pattern of unequal rewards as it is at any one time and place, or for this and that attempted modification of the pattern by way of public policy.

Of course capitalist practice and ideology prescribe working rules for distribution; and these indeed give class structure much of its shape. Setting state involvement and its criteria of allocation aside for the moment, there are two such working rules. First, property ownership confers by itself the right to a share in welfare. There are, uniquely, no strings attached to this rule: no questions are asked whether beneficiaries have acquired their claims by service, effort, gift, inheritance or windfall gain. The rule carries heavy weight for class inequality when, as now, substantial ownership – especially of financially productive assets – is concentrated in few hands; and for those whose property is substantial it allows immunity from the obligations tied to rewards under the second working rule. That second rule governs the lives of the majority, though to differentiated outcomes. It allocates shares in welfare as earnings from employment. Rewards here are made and graded, in a sense, according to contribution. Yet contributions are valued, not by reference to some set of moral norms, but by the push and pull of market forces: through pressures in labour markets whose ultimate direction to optimisation of returns to property under the first rule is inhibited only by weight of numbers in union and shopfloor organisation, by professional and craft 'cornering' of particular sub-markets, and arguably by unreflected conventions. The two rules are at odds because the first requires nothing of its beneficiaries, while the second sets a test of a kind – that of market labour service. But they share two features: neither relates rewards to needs; and neither reflects any moral principle which purports to explain the resulting distribution as, in itself, just or fair.

That assessment may be contested on two scores. First, it can be said, capitalism has a code of distributive justice unique to itself: the ethic of equal opportunity, the ideal that 'careers should be open to talent' – and talent only. Whatever the obstacles to its fulfilment, this aspiration provides a yardstick by which to judge equity. But that first counter-argument is flawed, both because the property rule's toleration of gift, inheritance and windfall gain negates the principle of equal opportunity; and because the principle itself has nothing to say about the ultimate equity of unequal rewards. Second, so it may be argued to dispose of just this latter point, market rewards are fair because they represent valuations aggregated from individual choices. But this counter-argument too is flawed. It is circular, because markets aggregate individual choices unequally. The rich have more market-votes than the poor; and market outcomes therefore can be fair only if that inequality of market-votes – of earned and unearned incomes – is in some clear sense fair to begin with. So the argument takes us back to square one, the question of equity in distribution of effective incomes unanswered.

The point is not that capitalist prescriptions for distribution are immoral; it is that they are amoral. The two working rules are just that: operational directives for resource allocation, not norms of distributive justice. The results – substantial, interlocking and broadly persistent inequalities – are not justified in liberal-capitalist *Lebensanschauung* as right in themselves. They are seen instead instrumentally: as necessary by-products of institutions and processes which have other objectives, to which questions of distributive justice are subsidiary or irrelevant. Those other objectives, summarily, are aggregate economic growth, freedom of choice and opportunity.

III

Of course state involvement in distribution – direct and indirect, but in all forms now very extensive – implies and in turn evokes appeal to notions of distributive justice. Yet as embodied either in current practice, or in proposals for reform this way or that which still assume continuation of some kind of 'mixed economy', such notions do not assert an ethic of distributive justice to fill the moral vacuum. With one exception – significant, but also significantly limited – they take account of need only within bounds set by the two working rules for capitalist resource allocation. Those working rules deny equality without simul-taneous proclamation of a principled conception of fairness to provide direct defence of the denial: that is their crucial political weakness. Public welfare policies differ by bringing some notions of equity, even of equality, to bear on distribution; but the contrast is more rhetorical than real.

Equality of opportunity is to the fore among these notions: the ideal of unhampered freedom, and concomitant risk, for individuals to find their own places in the unequal order framed by markets and property, according only to their inherent personal qualities. In some version or other concern with this has been written into a wide range of twentieth-century public policy: into educational provision, legislation against discrimination by skin-colour and gender, measures for mobility and re-training of labour, to take obvious examples. Policy in this mode appeals to considerations both of efficiency and equity; and on both scores its full implementation could help to make continuing inequalities of outcome more palatable – to legitimise a structure of class not otherwise supported by explicit moral principle.

The ideal of equal opportunity is not hostile to the spirit of capitalism. The latter's historical ascendance indeed promoted it; only its twentieth-century translation into diverse measures of public policy is new; and there is no paradox to the fact that aspirations for open opportunity figure prominently in both the public ideology and the social reform programmes of the nation among all most dedicated to the capitalist spirit, the United States. Yet rigorous pursuit of the ideal would contradict capitalist realities. One contradiction concerns principle. To allow inheritance – *de facto*, let alone *de jure* – is of necessity to deny equality of opportunity. Consistent liberals might therefore be expected to favour abolition at least of legal rights to inheritance: to eliminate from capitalism's first working rule for distribution claims to welfare founded only on fortunate accidents of birth. Few liberals have done so. More commonly they have ignored the dissonance between rights of inheritance and opportunity; or evaded the dilemma of principle through measures or proposals for limitation of inheritance falling well short of abolition; or taken on trust conservative assumptions that inheritance is either 'natural', or 'functional' for preservation of basic kinship ties, in a manner rendering it immune from questioning; or, in more pragmatic vein, ascribed to inheritance incentive effects (for those who accumulate property by positive enterprise) which must then be taken to outweigh disincentive effects (for their heirs).

Even apart from legal inheritance, moreover, social inheritance sets high obstacles to equality of opportunity. For all the policy effort invested so far, opportunities by and large have expanded only in the same way as levels of living have improved. The average *niveau* has risen; but relative disparities between classes have remained fairly steady. In respect of formal education, progressively more young people have acquired better qualifications; but the broad effect has been to raise certification thresholds for career achievement without substantially diminishing social inequalities in the competition for economic success (Goldthorpe, 1980; Halsey *et al.*, 1980; Hirsch, 1976). To note that is neither to discount the intrinsic benefits of enhanced average opportunity, nor to deny all scope for reform to compress disparities of opportunity. But were such measures in the future, as hitherto, to leave overall capitalist mechanisms of resource allocation largely intact, they would still – so the tenacity of relative opportunity inequality suggests – require 'positive discrimination' on a scale to engender hard resistance from those vested interests in privilege which are so significant a social by-product of capitalist economics.

A prime ingredient of western public welfare policies is, of course, acknowledgement of a right for all to protection of basic livelihood against the vicissitudes of markets, personal misfortune and old age: the guarantee of some bedrock share in welfare. Whether topped up by reference to previous earnings or not, bedrock provision is intended – if in rather ideal presentation – to take account only of need irrespective of contribution, service or desert on other grounds. There is an echo of notions of equality here: a proposition that all members of a society have rightful claims to sustenance and opportunity – and at a level which, through formalised or irregular index-linking, carries some partial reflection of standards of life common and commonly rising in the society at large. Just for that reason there have been liberal voices to ascribe to the Welfare State progressive replacement of class inequality by common social citizenship: remaining property- and market-gener-ated disparities of livelihood are seen as *en route* to moral neutralisation by the height and universality of guaranteed provision and by an associ-ated parity of status or respect for all through their common member-ship of this welfare-tuned society (Marshall, 1950). There have also been more critical voices to deny this image validity as an account of present trends, but to offer it as a goal for new reform: so, for example, the suggestion that poverty as a target for eradication be conceived as shortage of secure means for participation in common styles of life (Townsend, 1979, pp. 248–62).

The critics are right to deny the image of citizenship empirical validity; and this not just because some large minority of the population are below the threshold of citizenship by one or other version of the latter conception, or because a much smaller but still substantial minority do not achieve even the publicly 'guaranteed' level of bedrock provision.[1] The central weakness of the image of citizenship – whether as an account of where current trends are leading, or as a goal of new policy still set in a 'mixed economy' frame – is that it posits prescriptions for distribution overriding the working rules of capitalism. It assumes effective subordination of those rules to a conception of legitimate need autonomous of them. But definitions of need in public provision for bedrock welfare are not autonomous of the rules. With variations only – though significantly – in relative generosity, western policies for income maintenance define need by reference to the labour market. Minimum benefits must, so far as possible, be kept below the general floor of labour market earnings; and as the markets work that floor is low, well under average earnings. Top-up supplements look to previous earnings of individual beneficiaries. So no more than minimum benefits do they distance themselves from market prescriptions; and they carry the inequalities of those prescriptions – whether modified by some compression, or even by contrast accentuated when account is taken of public support for private welfare provision – into state measures. It is hard to imagine how social policy could be pulled away from such reference to market distribution while the economic context remains capitalist. Even with much technological displacement of labour, pressures for maintenance of commitment and discipline among those actually or potentially in work are likely to require public provision to continue to underwrite – not to undermine – the monetary carrots and sticks of market arrangements.

So neither policies aimed to reduce inequalities of opportunity nor measures for basic income maintenance put independent principles of distributive justice in the place where capitalism has a moral void. The conclusion holds on consideration of most other areas of state activity. As the largest single employer of labour, for example, the cluster of central government, local authorities and public corporations might be thought to gear patterns of pay in its own sector to political prescriptions on occasion different from those set in labour markets of the private sector. But even attempts to do anything of the sort are rare. Swedish social democratic measures to compress differentials both this way and through general incomes policy in the 1960s and early 1970s seem exceptional as well as to little ultimate effect. Commonly two recipes for public sector pay prevail in alternation: comparability with the private sector; and counter-inflationary restraint to 'encourage the others'. There is no autonomy of distributive principle in that; nor is there much plausible scope for it while private sector labour markets, part-fragmented though they are, bulk collectively largest. In some other spheres state policy does or may carry hints of an independent ethic of welfare: in provision, for example, for progression of direct taxation and, at times in recent years, for modification of general pay restraint in favour of the lower paid. But the hints are misleading. For one thing, there are often counter-balancing elements of associated policy: progression of direct taxation is more or less neutered by regression of indirect taxation; if pay restraint in one phase should have narrowed differentials – for which the evidence is weak anyway – another phase will tolerate their restoration (Westergaard, 1978; 1982; Fallick and Elliott, 1981). For another thing, and more central to the conclusion, there is no stated target for such ostensibly redistributive ingredients of public policy. They reflect no doubt a sense that all is not well with a property- and market-led share-out of welfare; so of course does state provision for basic income maintenance. But they do not back up that loose reflection of diquiet by formulation of any distinct set of norms to say how welfare should be shared out.

In one form, however, public policy has by implication asserted an autonomous conception of distributive justice: this not of course for general application, but in a selected area of service regarded as sufficiently essential to warrant insulation from property and market influences on demand. There may be small instances of this in odd corners of welfare provision – free travel for pensioners, for example. But the only instance of broad sweep – significant for its exceptional character – is that of provision for health in the manner embodied in the original objectives of the British National Health Service, and in more recent reforms in the same field in Scandinavia. Shortcomings of implementation, cumulative retractions and restrictions at the hands of successive governments, toleration or encouragement of effectively privileged private service – all these make, at least in Britain, for a gap between initial vision and current reality. But the distributive principle as originally conceived was distinct, and distinctly at odds with market prescriptions for welfare allocation. The aim was full parity of provision according only to medical need, and at a high common level by current standards. Behind this in turn was a vision of equality of condition in health: a vision more radical than that, for example, which in practice has been most influential for expanded provision of free education – equality not of condition but of opportunity, for efficiency as well as equity. The fact that even approximate application of such a notion of equality of condition is effectively confined to the one field of services for health – in implementation rather services for ill-health – has helped to limit achievement even within that field. It has also helped to veil the moral challenge posed by the notion to the normal working rules for distribution. Yet for all those limitations, there is here the sketch of an egalitarian conception of distributive justice open, outside its present economic context, to much wider application.

IV

On this front, then, social policy has ventured some way outside the fences set by capital logic. That fact does not square readily with those recent versions of Marxist theory which have sought to explain, and variously categorise, the activities of the modern western state essentially by reference to their functions for maintenance of the capitalist order (Holloway and Picciotto, 1978). To say that is not to deny strength to theory of this kind. It has offered a challenging schema to account for the sources of twentieth-century governmental growth. By contrast analysis of liberal inspiration has, by and large, had little to give here beyond a picture of continuous development – for good or, in 'new right' eyes, for ill – impelled by no clearly identifiable forces save a progressively widening public conscience, a steady surge of popular demands, or some pluralistic interaction of pressures with less recognised direction and circumscription of character to their outcome than matches reality. Such function-oriented Marxist theory has, moreover, held firm to the necessary distinction between the logical requirements of capitalism as an economic system and the particular, variable and often rival, interests of specific clusters of business. It has, in its general formulations, eschewed the vulgar proposition that governments serve as mere agents of capitalist enterprise. Above all, it has been accurately insistent on the range of support for capital's viability in a changing world which is central among the consequences of the immense expansion of state activity since Marx last put pen to paper.

But there are strengths also in much other Marxist – and some non-Marxist – work on the modern state (Miliband, 1969; 1977; McEachern, 1980; Gough, 1979; Panitch, 1976; Crouch, 1977), while there are patent weaknesses to the school of theory most brightly coloured by emphasis on state functions for capital. The metaphor of 'function' is here – as it was for the quite differently inspired fashion of structural-functionalism in post-war American sociology – a very risky one. It tempts its devotees into neglect of the questions how, in historical practice, needs and interests are defined by those to whom they are ascribed; how they are then translated into policy to serve them; and how far such functional service may in turn be nullified by unintended consequences.[2] Obtrusively abstract in style of analysis, 'state deriva-tion' theory stands at arm's length both from these issues and from the associated questions posed by the wide range of variation in scale, scope and orientation of government action among contemporary capitalist nations: are, for example, the very different mixes of state activity in Sweden and the United States equally of service to capital's long-run progress?

True, objections on some of these scores can be technically dismissed by reference to a frequent feature of the classifications of state functions proposed. This is the inclusion of one category commodious enough to take in any government activity which may seem not to enhance but to inhibit business interests whether long- or short-term, general or par-ticular. That category of function, in common formulation, is main-tenance of capitalism's 'legitimacy' in face of actual or potential opposition from its victims. So the point is taken on board that what the state does in historical fact is shaped by contest not only between common capital interests and the idiosyncratic interests of rival business groupings; but also, and potently, by the larger clash of interests between capital and labour, to the latter of which the former may offer legitimacy-boosting 'concessions'. This, schematically, is realistic enough – if not exhaustive, because it leaves out of account the variable pressures of interest from groups in the class order whose circum-stances attach them firmly neither to capital nor to labour (including many 'middle-class' people dependent for their livelihood on public employment). But the catch-all reference to legitimation, left con-ceptually and empirically undifferentiated, reduces the exercise from a theory open to test to a classificatory system which may be more or less useful. In fact its utility is small because the category of legitimation is so capacious. It is not just that any state activity which seems to detract from capital interests can, for that very reason, be said to prop up the capitalist order's political credibility. It is also that to this heading of legitimation especially will be assigned 'concessions' of a very different kind, with different repercussions for the skew balance of advantage between capital and labour.

There has, after all, to be some substance to some 'concessions', or they will not in aggregate help towards legitimation. Indeed there is substance to them. Taken together, for example, publicly provided benefits in cash and kind do make for some vertical redistribution from richer to poorer, though very much redistribution through state welfare involves only horizontal transfer within broad classes.[3] Modest vertical redistribution does not, of course, herald the dawn of a socialist order: it takes place, by and large, without any challenge to capital's prime working rules for distribution. Even so, it indicates scope for shifts in the class balance of advantages; it can help on that score to raise labour expectations as much as to appease them; and so in turn may, on occasion, feed back into class contest larger questions about distributive justice to which liberal ideology in tune with capitalism has no answers. Very plausibly it was just such a process that gave much of the push towards popular 'ungovernability', 'desubordination' or disenchantment with 'status' which many commentators have noted as a significant feature of the industrial and political scenes from the 1960s (Miliband, 1978; Goldthorpe *et al.*, 1978). 'Concessions' are not then uniformly and unambiguously functional for the order of capital. The balance can tip towards 'dysfunction'. It seems to do so not least when public provision for health – whatever large services this may yield capital by way of support for 'reproduction of labour', and however much else of it is explained as boosting 'legitimacy' – comes in a form that implies principled if tacit challenge to the amorality of capitalism's normal guidelines for distribution.

Insensitivity of function-oriented 'state derivation' theory to these issues reflects in part its abstract formalism. It reflects also an assignment of low priority to concerns with distribution characteristic of a wider range of neo-Marxist analysis. Thus much of the running in recent research and debate on the problem of 'class boundaries' – work that has grappled hard with the need to bring Marxist perspectives to bear fully on the circumstances and prospective affiliations of white-collar employees – has been made by adherents of a distribution-blind proposition. This, variously formulated, is that class boundaries must be seen as set primarily by relations of production (Poulantzas, 1978; Crompton and Gubby, 1977). Relations of production in turn are seen – for all practical purposes of analysis, and notwithstanding occasional reference to their fusion with relations of exploitation – as manifest from work functions. Consideration of rewards is at best subsidiary. Indeed, to take large account of distributional inequality in mapping class contours may be labelled Weberian heresy, out of key with Marx's inspiration. Class locations are assigned in answer to the question 'who does what?' (for example by way of contribution to capital control of production, rather than by way of contribution to the coordination of production necessary irrespective of capital control). The question 'who gets what?' figures little if at all.

The logic is strangely at odds with the thrust of Marxist class analysis, whatever may be read into the fine print of Marx's writings. For that thrust is towards interest formation. 'Class situation' is, in the first instance, shorthand for circumstances and relations of economic position which make for logically ascribable collective interests in maintenance of capitalism or in its replacement by some sort of alternative socialist order – or, where class situation is structurally ambivalent, in neither very clearly.[4] People's productive roles certainly shape their class situations – in part directly, but no less indirectly because differences in productive role give rise to the inequalities which mark the distributive order. It is not least those distributive inequalities themselves – of income, security, opportunity and autonomy in life, as well as of authority and power – which must carry weight for interest formation. Whatever the functions of their work in the larger economic system, employees can the less plausibly be assigned inherent interests in throwing off their chains the greater their relative incomes, security and opportunities: the less evident their subjection to exploitation. This is to put the point crudely, and could be misread to suggest an amorphous class structure of continuous gradations in contrast with the actuality of distinct discontinuities. But it is sufficient for the purpose here: to emphasise that Marxist analysis cannot, for realistic application, push distributional issues to the periphery of its sociological concerns.

V

No more should Marxist theory push distributional issues to the periphery of its moral concerns. Marxism carries a condemnation of capitalism, not just a diagnosis of it; and for both diagnosis and condemnation an explicit statement of ethical assumptions is necessary. Class interests as they are formed within capitalist economies cannot be fully identified without reference to some calculus of gains and losses in prospect from a socialist transformation for people differently placed in the current order. Denial of capitalism's moral legitimacy similarly cannot be sustained without specification of socialist objectives. All that in turn requires Marxists to spell out their prescriptions for distributive justice: to put suggestions for a positive ethic in the place where liberal-capitalist ideology by its nature has a void. With some exceptions, however, western Marxists seem not to have joined to the force and diversity of so much of their recent work in socio-economic analysis arguments of corresponding challenge about principles of distribution.[5]

There is not likely to be any single and obvious set of prescriptions which could command common agreement by virtue of some ineffable logic of Marxist philosophy.[6] My own provisional suggestions are that a socialist order, should it come, must seek 'equality of condition'. By that I mean a state of affairs in which life circumstances would be the same for all in effective outcome, with exceptions only of strictly limited impact and on explicitly stated grounds. Those grounds for deviation from substantive equality could be of three kinds, no more.

First, no means may be available to full equality of condition on this or that score. For example, neither the best intentions nor the most generous compensatory treatment are likely ever to make up for the stultification of human potential associated with mental or physical handicap.

Second, different individual needs and interests can justify varied provision; and concern for cultural diversity, intellectual autonomy and innovation will require it. But provisos are essential. If functional specialisation can hardly be eliminated in all rationality, for instance, recognition of special needs claimed on behalf of specialist groups – say by professionals and academics for protection of *milieux* conducive to their work – could readily lead to cumulative privilege unless protestations of special need were both rigorously scrutinised and met by extra rewards (if at all) only in such form as to minimise the risk. Thus expectations of a continuity of premiums from working life into retirement – in parallel with current public and private provision to carry market inequalities forward to old age – must be firmly resisted. So too all sociological experience suggests that sustained measures of 'positive discrimination' would be imperative to curb tendencies for protected *milieux* to become privileged sub-cultures frustrating both equity of opportunity and efficacy in deployment of talent to full common benefit.

Third, deviations from full equality of condition might be justified by reference to their contribution to other aims of policy expressly awarded priority. For example, some gradation of incentives – to work at all, or to work in particular jobs or circumstances for which the supply of suitable volunteers was short – could prove practically necessary, though special rewards merely to counterbalance negative features of some work situations would involve no departure from the principle of equality in outcome. This is an instance of a more general point. Deviations from the principle might be irresistible if they could be shown to improve the absolute welfare of some with no adverse effect for others, or the absolute welfare of many with only small adverse effect for a few. But to admit deviation under the latter heading especially is to set foot on a slippery slope: the terms 'many', 'small' and 'few' have an elasticity liable to undermine the rule of equality rather than to allow only rationally calculated exceptions from it.

There is room for sharp disputes of principle among egalitarians here. But agreement might not prove so difficult in practice, given acceptance of the premiss that departure from equality of condition would be tolerated only if its utility under any of the clauses of exception were reasonably demonstrated and subject to continuous review. Deviations from the rule would, moreover, run less risk of accumulating into a new structure of inequality because they would have the express status of exceptions. Whatever pattern of differential incentives could prove necessary, for example, the baseline of common equality would limit their range. As things are now, by contrast, low wages at the bottom of the labour market set a very low ceiling on public bedrock provision; and high initial rewards for top management help to pitch demands for extra business incentives very high.

In sum, welfare allocation today is amoral. Save exceptionally, concern for human need enters into it only in subordination to property- and market-oriented prescriptions bereft of concern for distributive justice. If an alternative socialist order were to be geared to equality of condition, it would allocate welfare according to a prime assumption of parity among all in human needs – this in principle irrespective of varying individual contributions, merits or deserts. Exceptions would be strictly utilitarian of purpose. Permitted disparities of condition might bring with them disparities of esteem; but they would not be designed to do so, let alone unnecessarily to add concrete rewards to socially recognised honour. The rule of equality of condition would also reverse the priorities suggested by those – liberal reformers and even some Marxists inclined to fight shy of equality – who offer parity of respect or status as a goal alternative to parity of effective provision. Equality of esteem may be for ever a pipe-dream devoid of sociological plausibility; it is certainly so unless preceded by equality in the substantive circumstances of life.

Notes

1 Cf. Townsend (1979, pp. 278–81). In 1968–9 one-quarter of the population

were assessed as in poverty by a 'relative deprivation' (citizenship threshold) standard necessarily open to conceptual dispute, and 6 to 7 per cent as below the minimum level set for public provision. Changes since then, especially rising unemployment, are likely to have increased deprivation by such indices.

2 Brief illustration may be worthwhile. Public educational provision can plausibly be described as designed to serve some functions for capital – direct and indirect inculcation of discipline; multi-levelled foundation training, identification and selection of talent, for subsequent employment; mollification of socio-political opposition. But even leaving aside the seemingly infinite elasticity of the last category, these functions in any case are not achieved with great efficacy. Much talent, for example, is known to be wasted; and the social processes behind that help also to engender oppositional sub-cultures among many adolescents not obviously conducive to discipline and legitimacy. If, nevertheless, on the latter score experience of successive rejection at school should make young working-class people more willing to accept the stringencies of labour markets and low-grade work because release from school comes as a relief, even such 'cooling out' could hardly be the product of some rational calculation of this imponderable benefit for capital against the costs of talent wastage, indifferent commitment to work and grumbling discontent. The untidy social realities of the outcome are surely part-'dysfunctional' for capital; and this in consequence especially of pressures – from those with privileged vested interests in keeping equality of opportunity at bay, and from translation of class divisions into sub-cultural rifts – which are potent side-effects of inequality of a kind to hamper rather than help capitalism's viability.

3 Thus British Family Expenditure Survey data for 1979 suggested, after standardisation for household composition, a reduction in the aggregate shares of the wealthiest 10 per cent from 27 to 20 per cent of total income through the combined effects of taxes and benefits assignable to individual households; and a rise in the shares of the poorest 10 per cent from 0 to 4.5 per cent ('The effects of taxes and benefits on household income, 1979', *Economic Trends*, January 1981). Income inequality both 'before' and 'after' is almost certainly understated, but the reality of some real vertical redistribution need not be questioned. For further discussion of the general point see, e.g., Westergaard (1978; 1982).

4 The central concern of Marxist class analysis with interest formation has been underlined by, among others, Wright (1976; 1979). But despite this and his cogent associated criticism of Poulantzas (1978), Wright's own emphasis in answer to the problem of 'class boundaries' is on relations of production with little clear reference to distribution.

5 Among exceptions are V. George and P. Wilding (1976, pp. 129–38), who draw on J. Rawls and W. G. Runciman to arrive at egalitarian guidelines similar to my suggestions, except that they allow scope for 'merit' and 'contribution' as criteria for deviation from equality (to match common

fundamental needs) on grounds which appear to be more than merely utilitarian.

6 Marx's own familiar prescription – from each according to ability, to each according to need – is plainly egalitarian in spirit. But left in that bald form it leaves open to doubt, *inter alia*, the relationship between the two component propositions: would individuals fully qualify for the second if they wilfully withhold contribution under the first; and if not, would the grounds for their disqualification be moral disapproval (carrying intentional stigma) or merely utilitarian?

References

Crompton, R., and Gubby, J. (1977), *Economy and Class Structure*, London, Macmillan.

Crouch, C. (1977), *Class Conflict and the Industrial Relations Crisis*, London, Heinemann.

Fallick, J. L., and Elliott, R. F. (eds) (1981), *Income Policies, Inflation and Relative Pay*, London, George Allen & Unwin.

George, V., and Wilding, P. (1976), *Ideology and Social Welfare*, London, Routledge & Kegan Paul.

Goldthorpe, J., *et al.* (1978), 'The current inflation: towards a sociological account', in F. Hirsch and J. Goldthorpe (eds), *The Political Economy of Inflation*, London, Martin Robertson.

Goldthorpe, J. (1980), *Social Mobility and Class Structure in Modern Britain*, Oxford, Clarendon Press.

Gough, I. (1979), *The Political Economy of the Welfare State*, London, Macmillan.

Halsey, A. H. *et al.* (1980), *Origins and Destinations: Family, Class and Education in Modern Britain*, Oxford, Clarendon Press.

Hirsch, F. (1976), *Social Limits to Growth*, Cambridge, Mass., Harvard University Press.

Holloway, J., and Picciotto, S. (eds) (1978), *State and Capital: a Marxist Debate*, London, Edward Arnold.

McEachern, D. (1980), *A Class against Itself: Power in the Nationalisation of the British Steel Industry*, Cambridge University Press.

Marshall, T. H. (1950), *Citizenship and Social Class*, Cambridge University Press (see Part I).

Miliband, R. (1969), *The State in a Capitalist Society*, London, Weidenfeld & Nicolson.

Miliband, R. (1977), *Marxism and Politics*, Oxford University Press.

Miliband, R. (1978), 'A state of de-subordination', *British Journal of Sociology*, vol. 29, no. 4.

Panitch, L. (1976), *Social Democracy and Industrial Militancy*, Cambridge University Press.

Poulantzas, N. (1978), *Classes in Contemporary Capitalism*, London, Verso (first French edition 1974).

Townsend, P. (1979), *Poverty in the United Kingdom*, Harmondsworth, Penguin.

Westergaard, J. (1978), *Social Policy and Class Inequality: some notes on welfare state limits*, Socialist Register, London, Merlin Press.

Westergaard, J. (1980a), 'Distributional welfare and concepts of equality', (unpublished mimeo).

Westergaard, J. (1980b), 'Production versus distribution: some issues in Marxist class analysis', (unpublished mimeo).

Westergaard, J. (1982), 'Income, wealth and the welfare state', in D. Coates and G. Johnson (eds), *The Socialist Primer*, London, Longman.

Wright, E. O. (1976), 'Class boundaries in advanced capitalist societies', *New Left Review*, no. 98 (July/August).

Wright, E. O. (1979), *Class, Crisis and the State*, London, Verso.

Chapter 5
Marxism, the individual and the welfare state
Peter Leonard

Disillusionment with the Welfare State in the 1980s contrasts starkly with the hopes that were invested in its development in the 1940s. One strand in this disillusionment is the suggestion that individuals, within the working class especially, have experienced Welfare State provision in health, education, housing, social security and personal social services as predominantly alien, bureaucratic and remote. A Welfare State which was seen as essentially benign in the mid 1940s has become perceived, it is argued, as overwhelmingly oppressive. Furthermore, some Marxist writers (Hall, 1979; Corrigan, 1979; Leonard, 1979) have suggested that the widespread negative experience of welfare provided a fertile ground of receptiveness to a radical Right politics committed to cutting, dismantling and transferring to the private market substantial sectors of state welfare provision.

Although those who supported electorally an anti-Welfare State programme may have come to regret the political choice that they made, the initial success of right-wing anti-welfare ideology among some sectors of the working class deserves continued evaluation. In particular, it directs our attention to the quality of the individual's experiences of welfare as the foundation against which the authenticity of various ideologies about welfare is ultimately tested. Clearly, there is continuing empirical work to be undertaken here, but this work needs to rest on a theoretical base which effectively connects the individual experience to the wider historical forces which penetrate and form the context of that experience. From what elements can this theoretical base be constructed? While it should be acknowledged immediately that such a base, effectively integrating individual experience with social structure, cannot at present be established, some progress has been made. I am suggesting, furthermore, that this progress has come from the starting-point of a Marxist analysis. To support this contention requires some account to be given of the Marxist approach to the Welfare State at the level of broad structures and processes and the criticisms to which this approach has been subjected, especially because of its lack of a theory of the individual. Then we will need to identify examples of work within Marxism which attempt to begin to establish a materialist theory of the individual. From these elements we will suggest the kinds of theoretical insights which may be gained into the individual's experience of the Welfare State in this precise historical conjuncture in late capitalism in the 1980s.

Marxist approaches to social policy

The emergence of a distinctively Marxist approach to the study of social policy in Britain is of relatively recent origin and signalled by the early work of Saville (1975) and the repercussions created by Miliband's study of the advanced capitalist state (Miliband, 1973), especially his debate with Poulantzas on the relative autonomy of the state and the possibilities of class struggle within it (Blackburn, 1972). From these beginnings a substantial literature has now emerged which confronts other analyses of welfare, especially those within the Titmuss tradition, at every turn (see Donnison, 1979). This is not the place to survey this critical literature (see Wilson, 1981), but at this point simply to note its growing importance as a perspective on welfare in the 1980s, and to identify its material and ideological origins. Most clearly, its origins appear to be partly in the growing crisis in state welfare beginning to emerge in the late 1960s and early 1970s as the world-wide boom in the capitalist economies began to falter and Britain's particularly vulnerable position became evident. Cuts in public expenditure, gradually rising unemployment, falling living standards, especially among the most vulnerable, and the general restructuring of welfare, were all signs that the 'old Welfare State' was probably coming to an end. But what had happened to those idealistic visions of the Welfare State which were forged during the Second World War and emerged as a social demo-cratic hegemony based on Beveridge, Keynes and the Attlee govern-ments? Until the early 1970s this vision of the possibility of achieving social justice through welfare within a 'post-capitalist' mixed economy dominated both the practice of social policy as an instrument of state intervention and also its study within the discipline of social administration. Indeed, the same people – Titmuss, Abel-Smith, Donnison and others – were active both as advisers to Labour governments and in developing their analyses of these government's policies (Rose, 1981). Until the decisive move to the Right within the Conservative party in the later 1970s, the essentially social democratic vision of the Welfare State encompassed, indeed, all the main political parties in Britain.

As the vision fades, the assumptions upon which it is based, namely that it is possible to maintain full employment, rising living standards and increased social expenditures, whilst sustaining capital accumulation and profitability, become increasingly challenged by both the Right and the Left. So far as the Left is concerned, this deepening material and ideological crisis in the social democratic Welfare State was accompanied by very significant and far-reaching changes in Western Marxism itself, changes which have stimulated the growth of the Marxist study of social policy. Briefly, we must identify these changes in Western Marxism as a consequence of an escape (still in progress in many contexts) from the powerful grip of Stalinism and of economic determinism, on the one hand (see, for example, Thompson, 1978, and Anderson, 1980) and its confrontation with feminism, on the other (see Rowbotham et al., 1979). Three specific developments within Marxism, all interconnected, are important here. The first, and most crucial for our purposes, is an increasingly sophisticated analysis of the capitalist state, in which the state itself is conceptualised as relatively autonomous and reflecting a balance of class forces, not in the political pluralist sense, but in the sense of manifesting contradictions as a result of class struggle. Ian Gough (1979), for example, suggests that contradictions within the capitalist Welfare State can be seen in the tendency for state social provision to be both oppressively directed towards control and containment and also progressively meeting some of the needs of the working class; at the same time the capitalist state experiences the increasingly sharp contradictions between the push for the social expenditures necessary for the effective reproduction of an appropriately disciplined, physically efficient and educated labour force, and the vital imperative of a capitalist economy – capital accumulation, profitability and economic growth. The other two important developments within Marxism which have proved significant for the study of social policy are concerned with the nature of class struggle and the crucial importance of ideology. We can take these two together as reflecting in part a move from narrow economism towards continuing attempts to forge a satisfactory analysis of society which is both feminist and Marxist. So far as the Welfare State is concerned, we see a recognition of the significance of women, of public sector workers and of community activists in struggles within and against the state apparatus (London–Edinburgh Weekend Return Group, 1980) together with an acknowledgment, which owes much to the original work of Gramsci (1971; 1977), of the great importance of ideological struggle in an advanced capitalist society.

Responses to Marxist analysis

The outcome of these various trends is the establishment of a vigorous and flexible Marxist strand in social policy analysis to which other work has to respond. The nature of these responses is of some interest. One response is to incorporate some elements of a Marxist perspective into social administration and thereby, to some extent, to neutralise it. Taylor-Gooby (1980), for example, has suggested that different trends in Marxist work provide different explanations for the success of capitalist welfare states in retaining political legitimacy. One trend emphasises the mystifying nature of the social relations of everyday life in capitalist societies: ideology embedded in the material conditions and exploitations of the working class. The other trend places more emphasis on ideology as the successful strategy of the ruling class in persuading the subordinate class of the legitimacy of its power. Now this latter trend, Taylor-Gooby argues, presents a more superficial, idealist critique of the Welfare State and one which may suggest the possibility of considerable welfare advances within capitalism if the ruling class can be defeated in a 'battle for consciousness'. Such a critique is clearly more vulnerable to incorporation within a predominantly social democratic social administration tradition than is one which underlines the fundamentally exploitive nature of capitalist social relations, and the discourse to which these relations give rise and which form the very parameters both of debate about the Welfare State and individual experience within it.

But incorporation is only one possible response. There are, after all, many problems and deficiencies in the various Marxist accounts of social policy and so a continuing and sustained critique is to be expected. Criticism of Marxist approaches to welfare cover a wide range of issues, from which we will select two of the most significant. The most powerful, and one which has been given most attention on the Left, is that mounted by feminist scholarship concerning the absence, in most Marxist analysis, of any recognition of the fundamental significance of gender in the history and present policies of the Welfare State. Rose, from her position *within* Marxism, as well as feminism, criticises Marxism when she writes that '[it] is not sufficient at a theoretical level for a materialist analysis of welfare to posit class relations as central, merely "adding on" the specific oppression of women as a well-meaning attempt to demonstrate hostility to sexism' (Rose, 1981, pp. 478–9). Interestingly, she suggests 're-reading Titmuss' in order to develop an analysis of 'the sexual division of welfare', a proposal for the incorporation of some elements of a dominant strand in mainstream social administration into a feminist and Marxist perspective. But criticism of Marxism from feminism, given the latter's concern to understand the individual experiences of women within a patriarchal social order, connects with the second and for us most significant strand of criticism: the absence of any sustained account of *individual* experience of the capitalist Welfare State and a preference for wide-ranging, general theory. These criticisms range from the more vulgarly ideological accusations that Marxists are not interested in the pain and suffering of individuals compared with the 'imperatives of the class struggle', to the more sympathetic concern that Marxism may be of little use to those who want to help individual welfare clients (Cohen, 1975). There can be little doubt that many of these criticisms are valid, though one would suspect the motivations of those critics who appear, still, to equate Marxism with monolithic Stalinism. There *is* no fully developed theory of the individual within Marxism nor, as yet, any completely satisfactory account of gender oppression. It is also important to acknowledge that concern with wider political and economic forces may produce a distancing effect, as when male Marxists characteristically tend to prefer to discuss women's oppression in terms of theories of domestic labour, surplus value and social reproduction, rather than become engaged in an examination of their own part in the everyday exploitation of women. Of course, Rose's (1981) defence of Titmuss notwithstanding, similar criticisms can be made of mainstream social administration, for although concern about the individual's experience of welfare has been expressed, non-Marxist social science lacks a theory of the *gendered individual* which locates the person in the precise historical context of the state, the economy and the social relations of production and reproduction which create and are created by the person.

The reflexive nature of historical materialism

But if these highly significant gaps are to be found in both Marxist and non-Marxist work, why should we choose on intellectual grounds rather than only political ones, the former in preference to the latter? Although political commitment to a socialist form of welfare may itself lead to a preference for Marxist analysis, there are also, in interaction with this commitment, strictly theoretical grounds for doing so, as the remainder of this chapter will attempt to demonstrate.

Essentially, the intellectual reasons for choosing to develop understanding of the individual's experience of the Welfare State on the terrain of Marxism lie in the nature of historical materialism as a method and in the work being undertaken within this tradition to examine individual experience using materialist categories of analysis. The crucial point about historical materialism, for the purposes of this discussion, is that as a theory of the relationship between ideas, institutions and material existence, it is able to render an account of the historical roots and functions not only of other non-Marxist theories and ideologies, but also of *itself* as created out of a particular historical conjuncture of social forces (Goldmann, 1969). This is the essentially *reflexive* character of historical materialism and it provides the basis for a critique of historical materialism from within itself (see Gouldner, 1980), as well as in response to outside forces, such as feminism. If we are to understand Marxism as developing within the particular historical period of the patriarchal and capitalist mode of production and reproduction, we must also understand that Marxism has been shaped and distorted by this context. It was created from *within* a dominant patriarchal and bourgeois ideology and so it continues to carry the marks of its origins. We cannot here enter into a detailed historical account of Marxism's limitations and distortions, but simply to point to the links between narrow economism and the limited perceptions of political struggle which characterised revolutionary forces under male leadership; to how the necessary work in creating a materialist political economy came to be seen as *sufficient*, thus blocking the development of a theory of the individual; and to how recognition of the historic and hierarchical division between intellectual and practical labour, characteristic of class societies, did not wholly prevent such hierarchical division within Marxist practice, a division which among other things contributed to the neglect of the crucial significance of women's domestic labour in the production and reproduction of past and present societies. It is because of the reflexive nature of historical materialism, then, that Marxism contains the possibility of developing a theory of the individual by transcending some of its own limitations. This may be seen as a rather abstract reason for engaging in work within the Marxist tradition: more important for practitioners in the social policy field is some account of how Marxists are approaching the problem of individual experience.

Marxism and the individual

Rather than make an attempt to provide a wide-ranging survey of Marxist efforts to develop a theory of the individual, we shall select the work of two scholars in the field, Lucien Sève (1978) and Michael Schneider (1975) as representative of different kinds of approach to the problem. Two primary possibilities present themselves to those who wish to begin to fill the gap in Marxism concerning individual experience: one is to turn to already existing 'bourgeois' psychologies, such as psychoanalysis, in an attempt to transform them for Marxist purposes; the other is to start on the construction of a theory of the individual exclusively from within historical materialism itself. Schneider provides us with an example of the former option and is in a long tradition which includes Wilhelm Reich, the Frankfurt School and its divergent successors such as Fromm and Marcuse, and present-day feminists such as Juliet Mitchell. Sève ploughs a lonelier furrow in his attempt, as a philosopher, to establish the foundations of a materialist theory of personality from within Marxist categories.

Although Schneider's work stands within a long tradition of dialogue between Marxism and psychoanalysis, it deserves particular attention because of its combative attitude to some developments within Marxism, which he labels 'Stalinism', and also its deep criticism of Freudianism. From its starting-point of two critiques, Schneider's work makes an important effort to relate the political economy of advanced capitalism to the psychological realities of working-class existence. His attack on 'vulgar' economistic Marxism is familiar within contemporary Western Marxism and feminism; for us his critique of psychoanalysis is especially important. Unlike Mitchell (1975), who presents herself as an uncompromising advocate of Freud, Schneider is deeply critical of the embeddedness of psychoanalytic theory in bourgeois ideology which leads it to an 'ideological blindness' – an inability to recognize the historical and class context of its work. Thus psychoanalysis attempts the impossible task of creating a science of the instinctual nature of men and women *as such*, a fallacy of idealism, rather than locating them historically. Schneider argues that the structure of psychosexual instinctual development, its temporary end result (the Oedipus complex) with its exclusive claims of ownership of the mother and rivalry with the father, is nothing more than the imprint of bourgeois relationships within production – 'owning', 'alienation', 'competition'. What psychoanalysis, because of its ahistorical idealism, fails entirely to understand, Schneider suggests, is that under capitalism, psychosexual development and its accompanying family socialisation functions to anchor, early in the instinctual structure of the child, anal-retentive and aggressive impulses in relation to possessions, to foster a psychosexual disposition towards wage labour (and, we might add, domestic labour depending on the child's gender) and to identify (through the Oedipus complex) bourgeois power and class hierarchy with the authority of the father. Specifically, Schneider attempts to demonstrate, on the basis of Marxist political economy and a historicised psychoanalytic theory of illness and neurosis, that the structure of social instincts and needs becomes, with the historical development of commodity production and of money, equally abstract. The 'abstraction' of use-values and of those useful needs and satisfactions which correspond to them, and which lie at the core of the commodity and money form, lies also at the root of those processes of psychic 'abstraction' which Freud described in his concept of 'instinctual repression'.

Thus Schneider grasps hold of both Marx's theory of commodities and money and also Freud's theory of repression in order to produce an account of the experience of the individual within this specific historical period, which in Britain we might call late and disintegrating welfare capitalism. In such a society the essence of the production of commodities lies in the repression of use values by exchange values, a repression which involves instinctual renunciation for the individual as human needs are loosened from their immediate objects, namely concrete sensuous satisfactions, and attached to abstract satisfactions – money. The personality most appropriate to this pursuit of money, so necessary at a structural level to the accumulation of capital, is the anal-compulsive character delineated by Freud. Such a person might be seen as compensating for the loss of a qualitative relationship with instinctual objects by compulsively quantifying through orderliness, punctuality, calculation and denial or absence of feeling. These 'ideal' characteristics of behaviour based on a 'work morality' were not finally imposed on the working class until the nineteenth century with the establishment of a six-day working week: from then on uniformity, regularity and other necessary traits were developed through family socialisation, later accompanied and supported by schooling, 'curative' rather than preventive health care, social work and other sectors of the Welfare State. The detrimental psychological effects on the individual of massive instinctual repression in the face of capitalist 'rationality' is the subject of much of Schneider's discussion of mental illness.

Class, gender and mental illness

Schneider's approach to mental illness must, if it is to be Marxist, begin not with libido, as Freud's did, but with *work*. Although his argument at this point is severely limited by its absence of specific consideration of women's domestic labour, its strength lies in its portrayal of mental illness as in many respects an extreme form of the same characteristics as those required for commodity production. The replacement of complex and coordinated behaviour by automatic and even stereotyped forms, characteristic of mental illness, is precisely a consequence of the capitalist form of the division of labour, where work processes become more complex and technical, whereas work for the majority of people becomes simpler, more automatic, increasingly de-skilled (see Braverman, 1974). Thus the power of abstract labour over the individual results in many kinds of illnesses, both mental and physical, including, apart from those designated as 'psychiatric', heart, circulatory and stomach troubles. The fact that the working-class population and women generally show a higher incidence of various kinds of mental and physical illness may be taken to suggest that the most oppressed parts of the population experience greatest instinctual repression and, with 'mental illness', the greatest incentive to escape from the intolerable world of capitalist rationality into their own delusionary picture of the world (see Brown and Harris, 1978). Although this brief account of Schneider's attempt to develop a class-linked theory of mental illness does not do justice to the complexity and subtlety of his argument, we need to note here that there are difficulties about Schneider's argument which stem, in part, from his lack of attention to the problem that psychiatric diagnosis may also be class-linked in the sense that different labels may be attached to the same 'symptoms' because of the class position of the patient and the likely treatment that will be offered. Notwithstanding these difficulties, the argument seems a strong one and points to the negative experience for the individual of receiving health and social care which fails even to acknowledge, let alone respond to, the more fundamental social forces which determine mental and physical condition. The Welfare State operates here in an overwhelmingly 'curative' role, ensuring by symptomatic treatment the return of patients as quickly as possible into production and reproduction. Because, predominantly, illness itself is seen as an individual matter, prevention of illness is likewise presented as almost entirely a question of personal action rather than wide structural change. The experience of the individual of these kinds of health policies and practices are that they nowhere connect up with the oppressive reality which is faced daily in both social and domestic labour and are therefore bound, despite the possibility of short-term symptomatic relief, to be seen ultimately as both ineffective and *part* of the oppressive reality itself.

In late capitalism, however, not only is production of central importance, but also, increasingly, *consumption*. Schneider argues that the symptoms produced by the lifelong compulsion to perform wage labour are masked by a specifically capitalist 'pleasure principle' of a totally unfettered mania for buying. Furthermore he maintains that whereas working-class resistance appears in unconscious rebellion against capitalist work pressures (i.e. through illness), resistance seems to have vanished so far as buying and consumption behaviour is concerned. Although there is a rather puritanical edge to Schneider's attack on 'the consumer society', no doubt provoked by his experience of the West German 'economic miracle', which must therefore make us careful in using it in relation to an economy in recession with a very high level of unemployment and lowering living standards, none the less the main point is well made. Although the commodity has real use-value to the buyer, for the seller it is nothing but a means of realising its exchange value in the form of money. Packaging is the *appearance* of use value, an appearance which becomes increasingly detached from its *actual* use value. A new mystification of the commodity develops in late capitalism, Schneider suggests, as the appearance of the commodity assumes gigantic proportions through advertising. At the same time the real value of commodities tends to decrease through their planned deterioration, and their 'ideal value' in a certain sense increases as they assume a fantasy aura. The effects on the individual psyche of this new mystification of the commodity are profound, for it involves a complex process of re-education and re-moulding of the personality. Those features of personality which were so important at earlier stages in capitalism – the classical anal-retentive compulsive character – are now, to some extent, contradictory to capitalist needs. What capitalism now needs is the 'highly variable commodity fetishist', the compulsive buyer rather than the compulsive saver. Women as 'housewives' and sexual objects play a crucial part here as consumer for the family unit as well as themselves. Families living on low incomes including social security cannot continue to buy commodities at the manic level projected by the advertising media, and so women especially may experience major emotional stress including guilt and depression at being 'bad mothers', created from the contradiction between a socialisation to consumption and the lack of the material resources necessary to fulfil their socially constructed 'needs'. Welfare State intervention is of course unable to overcome this contradiction: suggesting that poor people should budget 'more effectively' or lower their expectations simply reinforces the definition of the problem as an individual one.

Having looked briefly at some features of the work of Michael Schneider, work which attempts to connect political economy to the psychology of the individual through an emphasis on the repression of use-values and its consequences in terms of instinctual renunciation, we are able to turn to Lucien Sève for a contrasting approach.

Personality and social labour

Like Schneider, Sève is concerned with the nature of human labour under capitalism and sees this labour as central to a Marxist theory of personality. If, Sève argues, psychology is a science of man (*sic*) and we ask 'what is man?', the answer is 'a being who produces his own means of subsistence and thereby produces himself'. So psychology must be based upon the Marxist analysis of labour and, in particular, on 'social' productive labour and on the relationship between concrete and abstract activity. We shall elaborate on this distinction later: at this point we must note that his emphasis on social labour leads to a critique of psychoanalysis which is more profound than that of Schneider and others of the Marx-Freud synthesis school. Sève admits that under certain conditions psychoanalysis can be assimilated by historical materialism, and reworked critically, within certain limits, on the basis of its own concepts, such as the unconscious. But for Sève, psychoanalysis cannot become the theory of personality required by Marxism because in psychoanalysis the individual does everything *except* social labour! Psychoanalysis has been built up by considering the human being outside the sphere of labour, which is why it interprets the individual's life in the language of childhood. Although in other work he has conceded that psychoanalysis 'is perhaps destined to be integrated into the general theory [of concrete individuality] as a theory of the initial stages of the making of man and of its effects on the later stages' (Sève, 1975, p. 56), in his major work (1978) he appears to be reluctant to use psychoanalysis even in the study of childhood. He suggests that psychoanalysis takes for granted that the infantile structures of the unconscious are the basis of the structure of the psychic apparatus as a whole and throughout life. But historical materialism, he points out, shows us that the adult personality is not the result of the unfolding of a human nature or essence inherent in the individual, but is 'the effect of the singular insertion of an individual in a determinate system of social relations' (Sève, 1978, p. 284). The *objective* changes which the personality has to confront in the transition to adolescence and adulthood result in changing the nature of the preceding infantile experiences by reducing them to a stock of available psychic materials, rather than as determinant. In its pointing to objective material relations Sève's argument is useful in preventing an overemphasis on childhood socialisation as the primary means by which social reproduction takes place. He shows us that the lack of awareness of individuals, under capitalism, of the way in which they are determined by exploitive class relations does not refer back to childhood, nor is it rooted in internal instincts, but is related to the social powerlessness of the individual: escape, Sève argues, is not possible through individual cure, but only through collective struggle. We will return to this point later.

Moving from Sève's confrontation with psychoanalysis to his argument that, within Marxism, the theory of labour must be the basis on which a psychology should be founded, we have noted that this basis centres on the distinction between abstract and concrete labour. The individual's labour power, which s/he sells for a wage, cannot be a manifestation of self-expression, abilities, or needs but is reduced, under capitalism, to a commodity. This labour power, Sève contends, does not therefore create use-values for the worker, but takes on abstract form as an exchange-value. In other words, people's concrete activity, when engaged in commodity production, becomes abstract labour, separated from and opposed to the person; concrete and abstract labour are thus two sides of the same labour which is opposed to itself. Sève's argument becomes clearer if we contrast personal life against social (productive) labour. In personal life (eating, sleeping, leisure) the individual appears to be able to determine freely the kind of activity which is undertaken and relate this activity concretely to his or her needs. But beneath this appearance is the reality that the limits of personal life are in practice fixed by the social relations of production, so that a priority for personal activity must be the reproduction of a person's labour power. Even 'personal life' is not therefore lived primarily for the person, but in order to prepare, sustain and refresh him or her for the tasks of productive labour or, we might add, domestic labour. So the personal 'private' life of the individual becomes, under capitalism, dominated by the requirement to produce and reproduce the system: concrete individual activity becomes an appendage of the abstract form of labour power. But in social labour (the daily work in factory or office) the individual is even more restricted, for individual capacities cannot be properly developed because such development is simply not the aim of productive activity under capitalism except where it contributes to exchange value and thus profit for the capitalist. Understanding the relationship between concrete and abstract labour provides, for Sève, a basis for the analysis of the fundamental contradictions of personal life: between social activity and private activity; between abstract and concrete aspects in the development of personality; and between personal consumption and the reproduction of labour power.

With these elements Sève attempts to construct the foundations of a Marxist theory of personality in the form of 'hypotheses' which psychologists are invited to elaborate and test out. One must acknowledge that Sève's arguments at this point are extremely complex, conducted at a high level of theoretical abstraction, and generally unconnected to empirical examples. To summarise such work in this chapter would be impossible, but it is possible, none the less, to point to some important elements in his analysis and some of its implications for understanding individual experience. On the basis of a theoretical distinction between an individual's *acts* and his/her *capacities* (the ensemble of potentialities necessary to carry out any act) and the significance of the *use-time* devoted to various activities and capacities, Sève constructs a general picture of the personalities which are formed on the basis of capitalist social relations. This 'general topology of personalities' distinguishes between on the one hand *concrete activity* involving both acts of direct benefit to the individual (playing amateur football, reading novels) and also the development of those capacities necessary to carry out these acts (training and learning activity for personal use), and on the other hand *abstract activity* including both the acts of which social labour consists (manipulating a machine, cleaning a floor, writing a report) and also the development of those capacities necessary to carry out these acts (specific skills training). Now, if we ask ourselves what is the amount of time which is devoted to these different activities we find that they vary between individuals. However, if we could calculate the use-time of a particular individual as between various activities over a month, a year or several years, we would be in a position to understand something of the contradictions and restrictions on personality development that the individual experienced. We might find, for example, that like the factory worker, a woman engaged full-time in domestic labour and child care devoted most time to abstract (or in the case of unpaid domestic work, 'pseudo-abstract') activity, concrete personal activity occupying a minor place and being of such a passive kind that little development of capacities and skills was required. By looking at the working-class elderly person or the unemployed young person, we would be able to understand the different ways in which people are affected by the imperatives of capitalist production and reproduction. The use-time between different activities is frequently totally unbalanced, with social labour of the most abstract kind dominating for example the factory worker's time, while little opportunity for the development of new capacities is available for the working-class old person.

This relation of an individual's experience of the world to the social relations of capitalist production and reproduction is effectively hidden from view. Because relations between people are obscured behind relations between things, a positive lack of awareness exists. This is an 'objective illusion' which can only be abolished, Sève argues, along with the social relations which sustain the illusion. But this lack of awareness is also an ideology in so far as it *justifies* alienating social conditions and the corresponding forms of use-time between concrete and abstract activities – conditions and activities which are seen as essentially 'natural' and unchangeable rather than as socially constructed within definite historical periods. Under capitalism, personal growth is essentially determined by a use-time which includes a high proportion of learning activities, a high rate which is probably governed most importantly by the learning activities associated with social labour, which is why intellectual and skilled workers have psychological advantages over others. If an individual is compelled to undertake abstract activity of the most alienating form and is thus prevented from engaging in the 'expanded' reproduction of his/her labour power (the development of new capacities), then the acquisition of new capacities loses its appeal. This loss of motivation, Sève argues, may assume an internal psychological form (such as depression or anxiety) and/or a behavioural form (such as domestic violence or drinking problems) which mask the objective social causes of this lack of motivation. Under these conditions, self-expression is no longer possible, and social labour is reduced to the level of a mere dehumanised means to 'earn a living'. As a compensation, the individual may withdraw into increased concrete consumption, a de-politicised solution much encouraged by capitalist production.

Theoretical problems

We have discussed, in outline, two of many Marxist approaches to the individual. We have suggested that they contain insights into individual experience and personality development which could be profitably worked upon in order to construct an account of the impact of the Welfare State on the individual. But we have also already pointed out the more obvious limitations in the work of both Schneider and Sève; most importantly in their failure to confront the crucial facts of gender structures and social relations. Their analyses are undertaken in terms of class alone and so could not, as they at present stand, meet the need to establish a theory of the *gendered* individual in relation to the state and society. However, even these authors offer some useful pointers to some necessary elements in a feminist analysis: Schneider through his work on consumption and Sève in his proposals for a theory of the domestic economy of the family based on an examination of the *material exchanges* that take place within it. However, we are not proposing that an analysis of gender or an account of the reproduction of patriarchal social relations can simply be added on to these existing Marxist perspectives: they must be subjected to a thorough feminist critique and may then emerge as *one part* of a developed theory of the individual. Our purpose here is simply to suggest that these approaches have a value as part of a broader enterprise.

The conflict between the approaches of Schneider and Sève are quite clear, most obviously in their different critical evaluations of psychoanalysis. They are both concerned however to found their work on the centrality of human labour, on the nature of commodity production and consumption under capitalism, and on the effects of capitalist social relations on personality development and the 'psychological problems' of the individual. Sève's framework, though powerful, is still essentially a philosophical preliminary to detailed psychological work, whereas Schneider has the great advantage of working, in part, on a highly developed psychological theory. At this stage in the development of a theory of the individual within historically specific social relations, we need to draw upon a number of perspectives and not expect the conflicts between them to be resolved. Schneider and Sève are both valuable because they emphasise different but equally important factors in the social reproduction of the individual: both ideology as *intention* in the socialisation of the individual from childhood, and also ideology as *structure* embedded in the actual material relations of commodity production and consumption.

Individual experience of the Welfare State

What emerges most clearly from the foregoing discussion is that an individual's experience of the Welfare State cannot be properly understood except in the context of an historical analysis of the wider social relations of production and reproduction within which the modern capitalist interventionist state emerges. We would argue that the state in Britain, as elsewhere, has intervened in the lives of individuals through 'welfare' provisions in order to further the social reproduction necessary for the labour market, to attempt to ensure control (both repressive and ideological) over dissident and 'problematic' sectors of the population, and also enhance material provision for the working class, depending on the precise historical balance of class and gender forces. The difference between the 1940s and the 1980s so far as the Welfare State is concerned is that at the present time the balance of class forces has moved decisively against the working class. The Welfare State thus contains contradictions which are ultimately experienced as problems and conflicts for the individual. These contradictions at the level of the whole social formation are not, of course, experienced directly by individuals but through various mediating structures, in the case of state intervention in the welfare field through specific local organisations and services, the activities of particular officials and the levels of provision, or lack of it, in the neighbourhood in which the individual lives or works.

Once we focus on the quality and quantity of the local provision of welfare we can see at once that every side of this provision is psychologically problematic for the individual. Where welfare provision functions to ensure social reproduction and control, it is bound to be deeply experienced as alien and oppressive precisely because such provision makes more abstract what was previously concrete activity. Working-class adolescent boys and girls frequently experience school education not as use-value, as concrete activity and the development of personal capacities, but as geared to social labour and social reproduction of the most abstract and de-skilled kind. Youth Opportunities Programmes are even more problematic for the individual in that the abstract activity involved in participating in them does not even lead, for most, to employment, and if it does, is often of the most menial and abstract kind making no demands for personal psychological growth. Women in particularly deprived working-class families, especially if they are single parents, may experience their own previously concrete activity of child care becoming more like abstract social labour (perhaps 'pseudo abstract' would be the best term) under the impact of close monitoring, checking and advice-giving by social workers. What may have previously been experienced as a relatively free, spontaneous, gratifying though deviant relationship, becomes, as a result of state intervention, experienced as more disciplined and calculating, involving increased instinctual 'surplus' repression (Marcuse, 1969). What these examples may be taken to point to is that the opportunity for personal growth is restricted not only by the general material relations of production and reproduction, but also by the specific intervention of state welfare, which may, indeed, further restrict the very *motivation* for personal psychological growth with profound consequences for the individual in anxiety, guilt, frustration and free-floating anger.

Where direct material benefit for the individual is an outcome of welfare provision, the experience may still be predominantly problematic. The benefits of the Welfare State are usually experienced in the form of *passive concrete consumption*, involving very little choice or participation in the process: the individual is at the receiving end of a bureaucratic and professional service, acted upon rather than acting. Although material benefits, such as social security payments or medical treatments, are of use-value to the individual, their consumption is not balanced by the stimulation of those capacities and skills upon which personal psychological growth and satisfaction depends. In spite of the rhetoric about enhancing welfare recipients' capacity to be self-determining, in practice welfare structures such as health care services or old people's homes require passive compliance rather than active, questioning involvement. The detrimental psychological effects of the passive consumption of welfare services is well understood by women's welfare groups, claimants' unions, and community organisations where the activity involved in the demand for services and participation in their delivery is seen as having not only a direct material benefit in terms of improved provision, but also a personal psychological pay-off for the members in terms of the development of specific skills.

Whilst we may be able to increase our understanding of the individual experience of the Welfare State through various key Marxist concepts, and direct our research on the basis of these concepts, we must acknowledge that the individual cannot escape from the effects of structural contradictions though may, depending on precise historical conditions, including the particular balance of gender and class relations, be able to develop capacities and avoid certain kinds of psychological damage through expanding concrete activity. Put another way, although the negative individual experience of welfare can only be fully overcome through a transformation of the patriarchal and capitalist social relations which ultimately determine this experience, participation in the collective struggle towards that change has important consequences for the individual at a psychological level. The Welfare State is one target for that struggle: the struggle to democratise it and make its services and staffs more directly accountable to the population. Such a collective struggle involves the development of a wide range of individual capacities and a move away from apolitical anger and frustration at the Welfare State and passive consumption of its services. From a negative individual experience of the Welfare State a positive commitment to transforming it can emerge.

References

Anderson, P. (1980), *Arguments within English Marxism*, London, Verso.

Blackburn, R. (ed.) (1972), *Ideology in Social Science*, London, Fontana.

Braverman, H. (1974), *Labour and Monopoly Capital*, New York, Monthly Review Press.

Brown, G., and Harris, T. (1978), *Social Origins of Depression*, London, Tavistock.

Cohen, S. (1975), 'It's all right for you to talk: political and sociological manifestos for social work action', in R. Bailey and M. Brake (eds), *Radical Social Work*, London, Edward Arnold.

Corrigan, P. (1979), 'Popular consciousness and social democracy', *Marxism To-day*, vol. 23, no. 12.

Donnison, D. (1979), 'Social policy since Titmuss', *Journal of Social Policy*, vol. 8, pt. 2.

Goldmann, L. (1969), *The Human Sciences and Philosophy*, London, Cape.

Gouldner, A. (1980), *The Two Marxisms*, New York, Seabury Press.

Gough, I. (1979), *The Political Economy of the Welfare State*, London, Macmillan.

Gramsci, A. (1971), *Selections from the Prison Notebooks*, London, Lawrence & Wishart.

Gramsci, A. (1977), *Selections from Political Writings*, London, Lawrence & Wishart.

Hall, S. (1979), 'The Great Moving Right Show', *Marxism To-day*, vol. 23, no. 1.

Leonard, P. (1979), 'Restructuring the Welfare State', *Marxism To-day*, vol. 23, no. 12.

London–Edinburgh Weekend Return Group (1980), *In and Against the State*, London, Pluto Press.

Marcuse, H. (1969), *Eros and Civilization*, London, Sphere Books.

Miliband, R. (1973), *The State in a Capitalist Society*, London, Quartet.

Mitchell, J. (1975), *Psychoanalysis and Feminism*, Harmondsworth, Penguin.

Rose, H. (1981), 'Re-reading Titmuss: the sexual division of welfare', *Journal of Social Policy*, vol. 10, pt. 4, pp. 407–502.

Rowbotham, S., Segal, L., and Wainwright, H. (1979), *Beyond the Fragments*, Newcastle Socialist Centre and Islington Community Press.

Saville, J. (1975), 'The Welfare State: an historical approach', in E. Butterworth and D. Weir (eds), *Social Welfare in Modern Britain*, London, Fontana.

Schneider, M. (1975), *Neurosis and Civilization*, New York, Seabury Press.

Sève, L. (1975), *Marxism and the Theory of Human Personality*, London, Lawrence & Wishart.

Sève, L. (1978), *Man in Marxist Theory*, London, Harvester Press.

Taylor-Gooby, P. (1980), 'The state, class ideology and social policy', University of Kent (unpublished).

Thompson, E. P. (1978), *The Poverty of Theory and Other Essays*, London, Merlin Press.

Wilson, E. (1981), 'Marxism and the "Welfare State" ', *New Left Review*, 129.

Chapter 6
Women and social welfare
Gillian Pascall

Perhaps the most striking claim in feminist analysis of social policy is that it is impossible to understand the Welfare State without understanding the way in which it deals with women. According to Elizabeth Wilson 'only an analysis of the Welfare State that bases itself on a correct understanding of the position of women in modern society can reveal the full meaning of modern welfarism' (Wilson, 1977, p. 59); and '*First and foremost* today the Welfare State means the State controlling the way in which woman does her job in the home of servicing the worker and bringing up their children' (p. 40) (my stress).

If these claims are only half true then most textbooks on social policy are missing something. The lack is perhaps most striking in those volumes which attempt to review theoretical perspectives on welfare; none of the recent texts in this area (Room, 1979; Mishra, 1977; Taylor-Gooby and Dale, 1981) show feminism as a distinct approach to welfare; few social policy texts, apart from specifically feminist ones, have more than passing reference either to issues as they affect women or to the way in which feminists have analysed welfare (Ginsburg, 1979, has half a chapter; Gough, 1979, a few pages; Townsend, 1979, has a section on mothers alone; Jones *et al.* 1978, has a few references to 'sex equality'), though there is a new journal, *Critical Social Policy*, which aims to give space to feminist writing. My point in this paper is not to carp at individuals (because we have all been subject to the same influences), but to examine the various traditions and the ways they are structured, to try to explain why these traditions neglect issues and analyses which are now commonplace in the women's movement; to ask whether approaches to welfare dominant in the 1980s are any more receptive to feminist understandings of the Welfare State than approaches developed in the 1940s; and to try to show in the broadest outlines what feminists have to say which is not being reflected elsewhere.

To some extent the lack of a specifically feminist analysis within the main traditions is a matter of political history. It can be argued that the post-war era started a particularly barren period for feminism, when sociology began to reflect a cosy view of family life and social policy concerned itself with pressing women back into its confines. Traditions of social administration that were born in this climate of the 1940s did not have a vigorous feminist movement to draw on (but as we shall see later there was some critical writing which their exponents failed to notice) and feminism as a political movement did not re-emerge until the late 1960s. However, in its re-emergence feminism has taken welfare issues as a major part of its work. This is true in a practical context, in the refuge movement; in the political context, for example in issues about abortion and cohabitation; and in the academic context, where there is now a considerable feminist literature about women and welfare. The unifying theme of these feminist critiques of social policy has been a critique of the 'patriarchal' family in modern society and an analysis of the Welfare State as supporting relations of dependency in that family. In this paper I will argue that this analysis presents a challenge which none of the major traditions of social administration has been able to meet at all adequately (though each fails for different reasons). Further, Mary McIntosh's injunction that we must 'see the question of women as integral to any analysis of social policy' (1981, p. 41) is far from being realized in practice.

For the purposes of this essay I will take the 1940s as the birth period of two significant traditions in social welfare studies, Individualism and Social Reformism. *The Road to Serfdom* (Hayek, 1944) formed the starting-point for a continuing critical approach to the Welfare State based on individualist assumptions; it was followed by *Individualism and the Economic Order* (Hayek, 1949), and later by more thoroughgoing analyses of social welfare (e.g. *The Constitution of Liberty*, Hayek, 1960). The category Social Reformism links together Beveridge, Titmuss – whose early publications date from this period – and Marshall, whose famous lecture, 'Citizenship and Social Class', was delivered in 1949. The second group will get much the most attention in this essay, forming as they do the backbone to a way of thinking about social administration which was nearly all-embracing, as far as academic practitioners of the subject were concerned, for about three decades.

However, despite the continuing vigour of these traditions, the intellectual going, in social administration departments of the 1980s, has been taken up by a new school, the Political Economy of Welfare. This is represented by such writers as Gough (1979), Ginsburg (1979), Corrigan and Leonard (1978), Taylor-Gooby and Dale (1981).

Before embarking on a discussion of the strengths and weaknesses of these approaches in relation to feminist thinking, it seems worth while to set the context of the 1940s from a feminist point of view. What kinds of empirical information and theoretical analysis did writers of that period have available about the position of women? It must be admitted that radical critiques of the family were not prominent in the intellectual and political climate of the time. However, one can draw together a few strands which suggest that radical interpretations of the family were available, if not common, and that there was sufficient empirical study of the nature of women's lives to give rise to unease about a system of welfare and thinking about welfare that took the harmony and security of family life for granted.

Curious among publications of the 1940s was a new edition of Eleanor Rathbone's major work on *Family Allowances* (1949) with an epilogue by Beveridge himself. While some aspects of Rathbone's work are highly conservative (e.g. her assumption that every man required a woman 'to do his cooking, washing and housekeeping' (1949, pp. 15–16), her denial of allowances to unmarried parents (p. 243) and her position on wages (SPGB, 1943), there are many points in the analysis that speak to feminist thinking of the 1980s. Her arguments derive from a position about equal pay for women; they involve a critique of the idea that women should be dependents ('the very word suggests something parasitic, accessory, non-essential' (Rathbone, 1949, p. x)), an exposure of the nature of power in relationships between men and women, which leads in a 'minority of cases' to violence and sexual exploitation as 'part of the price they [women] are expected to pay for being kept by them [husbands]' (1949, p. 71), and a critique of legal and economic systems which set 'no price on the labour of a wife' and naturally have affected the 'wife's sense of the value of her own time and strength' (1949, p. 61). Beveridge writes in the epilogue that when he read the book 'as soon as it appeared in 1924', he 'suffered instant and total conversion' (Rathbone, 1949, p. 270). However, in the same epilogue one can see how his conversion was tempered; the only justification he cites in 1949 for adopting family allowances is the concern about the relationship between earnings and benefits (Rathbone, 1949, p. 274).

Sylvie Price has written a fascinating account of women's responses to the Beveridge report in the 1940s (Price, 1979), in which she shows that not all women were grateful for the benefits brought to them as house-wives and dependents. The most 'developed critique' of Beveridge which she found came from the Women's Freedom League. The authors, Abbott and Bompass, describe Beveridge's 'error' as 'denying to the married woman, rich or poor, housewife or paid worker, an independent personal status. From this error springs a crop of in-justices, complications and difficulties.' In criticising the lower rate of benefits proposed for married women they wrote:

> This retrograde proposal creates (and is intended to create) the married woman as a class of pin money worker, whose work is of so little value to either the community or herself, that she need feel no responsibility for herself as a member of society towards a scheme which purports to bring national security for all citizens (Abbott and Bompass, 1943, cited in Price, 1979).

Thus these authors identified the way in which the state is involved in the perpetuation of dependency in the home and its connection with low pay in the labour market, an argument which has resurfaced in recent years.

Finally, it is worth remarking on the empirical tradition of investi-gation into women's lives, represented in 1939 by the publication of Margery Spring Rice's *Working-Class Wives*. While the values that inform this work are scarcely radical ones from a feminist point of view, the 'titanic job' of housework and the misery of some women's lives cannot be missed in this painstaking and passionate investigation. While marriage as a whole is supported the results of bad marriages are clear to see; Spring Rice (1939, p. 95) comments ironically on the womens' attitudes:

> Throughout their lives they have been faced with the tradition that the crown of a woman's life is to be a wife and mother. . . . If for the woman herself the crown turns out to be one of thorns, that again must be Nature's inexorable way.

Thus analyses and evidence were available in the 1940s, however fragmentarily expressed, which could have informed the debates in the social administration departments then being established and the developing approaches to welfare. They did not in fact have any detect-able impact on this new body of writing, and the next sections will be devoted to asking why not, and to showing the analyses of women's position which in fact underpinned it.

The individualist position is here represented by Hayek. A trenchant account of the economic discipline within which his approach has its roots is provided by Eleanor Rathbone (1949, p. 10):

> In the work of still more recent economists, the family sank out of sight altogether. The subsistence theory of wages was superseded by theories in which wives and children appear only occasionally, together with butcher's meat and alcohol and tobacco, as part of the 'comforts and decencies' which make up the British workman's standard of life and enable him to stand out against the lowering of his wage.

An analysis which roots freedom in the play of market forces is likely to leave out of account a great deal of the space which women inhabit. While Hayek claims to recognize 'the family as a legitimate unit as much as the individual' (1949, p. 31), it is the individual in the market-place who fills the pages of his main works. Hayek's 'pre-sociological' (Taylor-Gooby and Dale, 1981, p. 69) approach makes sex an inappropriate category of analysis in the market-place (making the individuals appear to be masculine); it also makes the family appear as an occasional appendage to the world of production rather than as the object of investigation. The family's role is specified as being to transmit traditional morality and those qualities which are necessary for success in the market-place; so that there is no justification for denying to individuals advantages 'such as being born to parents who are more intelligent or more conscientious than the average'. This applies to families or to 'other groups, such as linguistic or religious communities, which by their common efforts may succeed for long periods in preserving for their members material or moral standards different from those of the rest of the population' (Hayek, 1949 p. 31). The intellectual heritage of this approach in social policy flows directly to Sir Keith Joseph's transmitted deprivation thesis where poor families (incompetent women) are seen as incapable of fitting their children to succeed in the labour market (Joseph, 1972).

Among the group of 'Social Reformists' to whom I refer next, Beveridge has had much the worst press amongst feminists. Beveridge's misfortune in this respect has as much to do with the clarity of his statements on the subject as it does with fundamental differences of view amongst less maligned authors in this group; it also, of course, has to do with the fact that his proposals for social security were put into practice and have had direct effects on women's lives. Beveridge's most quoted words in this context express his clear view of women as house-wives and mothers: 'In the next thirty years housewives as mothers have vital work to do in ensuring the adequate continuance of the British race and of British ideals in the world' (1942, p. 53, para. 117). This status had practical expression in the separate insurance class given to 'House-wives, that is married women of working age' (1942, p. 10). Most of these married women would make 'marriage their sole occupation' (1942, p. 49) and it was assumed that 'to most married women earnings by gainful occupation do not mean what such earnings mean to most solitary women' (1942, p. 49). Paid work would often be 'intermittent' (1942, p. 50). The married woman's benefits would not need to be 'on the same scale as the solitary woman because, among other things her home is provided for her' (1942, p. 50). Married women, in general, would have 'contributions made by the husband' (1942, p. 11). Thus was the concept of the dependent married woman analysed with singular clarity and encased within social security practice.

There is room for debate about how far Beveridge's assumptions concerning the extent of married women's employment were correct even in their own time (DHSS, 1978, p. 92). It is arguable that Beveridge imposed an out-of-date and middle-class model of marriage and work onto women whose lives were very different (although it has to be admitted that representatives of working-class women at the time were grateful even for the crumbs offered to them as housewives under the Beveridge scheme) (Price, 1979, pp. 10–11). But Beveridge's fundamental assumption was that social security had a secondary role for married women, because of the security offered to them by men in marriage. While he did take some account (not followed up in the schemes) of the possibility that men's security offerings might fail on account of separation, he gave inadequate recognition to the variety of women's situations and relationships and to the variety of possible patterns of work and domestic labour. Inadequate assumptions about marriage and about work both led to schemes that have treated women badly in practice.

While Beveridge was brilliantly clear in his discussion of women, marriage and social security, he has never been taken as a major theorist of the Welfare State. One of the most influential theoretical papers of the period was T. H. Marshall's 'Citizenship and social class' (1949). The main theme was an understanding of the Welfare State in terms of the development of citizenship rights and a discussion of their relationship with social class. Of course the social class theme was not one that was likely to lead Marshall into an explicit consideration of women, and the paper belongs to its period in the use of examples referring to men and children except in relation to the vote (Marshall, 1949, p. 81). While Marshall asserts the rights of citizenship, nowhere does he analyse the problematic relationship between citizenship and dependency in the family as he does between citizenship and social class. However, the concepts of citizenship and of social rights could be seen as theoretically open to use in analysing women's position in the Welfare State; and they can also be seen as useful in setting targets for people to achieve, or in defending existing institutions (Mishra, 1977, p. 32). There is, of course, a distinctive liberal branch of the women's movement which finds these concepts useful in this political way. However, the notion of rights has its limitations. As Eisenstein remarks 'Liberal rights are structured via the inequalities of man and woman' (1981, p. 344), and the rights specified in Marshall's analysis do not offer any challenge to the prevailing orthodoxies about relations between the sexes.

Titmuss has already had some attention from the point of view of feminist analysis, and I owe a lot to Hilary Rose's article (1981) both for the original idea behind this chapter, and for her work on Titmuss himself. Titmuss has played such a key role in the development of social administration, and the hegemony of the Titmuss school was so complete (Rose, 1981, pp. 482–5) that he acts as a useful hinge for discussing the work of this social administration school more generally. There are three main points that I would want to make about the openness of this approach to the understanding of women. The first is to agree with Hilary Rose that the empirical tradition and the sensitivity of Titmuss's perception do make it harder to be blind to the ways in which women's lives are lived and the effects of the Welfare State on them. The second is that the view of the family usually assumed within this paradigm derives essentially from functionalism and is thus in practice often neglectful of power relationships and the possibilities of conflict within the family. The third is that while the strength of this approach in analysing the shortcomings of the way the Welfare State operates in practice have been repeatedly demonstrated, so has its unfortunate inability to explain these shortcomings. Thus while the detailed accounts of the way Welfare State agencies operate in practice are useful in a feminist analysis, it is insufficient as a way of understanding why women should receive such short shrift at the hands of welfare agencies.

To turn to Titmuss after searching the social policy literature of the 1940s is to see new doors opening. Women populate his pages in the way that they do not those of Marshall or Tawney (1952, pp. 220–1), for example, and there are accounts of the lives and deaths of women in all the publications of the era. One can refer, for example, to the chapter on Maternal Mortality in *Poverty and Population* (Titmuss, 1938, pp. 139–56); to a powerful defence of people's right to choose in matters of population and the need 'to obtain a balanced harmony between the productive, cultural and political activities of women and their function as mothers' (Titmuss and Titmuss, 1942 p. 115); and to the justly regarded account of the evacuation of the war period in *Problems of Social Policy* (Titmuss, 1950). Later essays in the 1950s show some sensitivity to the changes in women's lives brought about by a reduced period of child-rearing and lengthened period of marriage, in particular the change towards greater dependence on men (Titmuss, 1958 pp. 93 and 110) and the potential for women to find alternative fulfilment in work (p. 102).

The question to raise from this is just how far the empirical method is responsible for the insights of the analysis and how far those insights can be attributed instead to the qualities of Titmuss himself as a social observer. If one examines the work of people of the Titmuss school, it is possible, I think, to find some case for the first of these possibilities. A very good example can be found in Dennis Marsden's work on *Mothers Alone* (1969), where careful interviewing and observation revealed women's painful experiences of dealing with the DHSS, especially their experiences of the cohabitation rule. But unfortunately it is also possible to find works where women are mentioned only in passing, if at all. Empirical investigation of itself does not guarantee that observers will see what is there to be seen; the categories of analysis can as easily exclude phenomena from vision as include them. In Titmuss's own work, the virtual exclusion of family conflict is a case in point, and the reasons for this will now be addressed.

While Titmuss was suspicious of theory he was obviously not innocent of it. His eclecticism and wariness about committing himself to the higher reaches of sociological theorising make it difficult to pin him down to any one theoretical vision, but his absorption of the main currents of contemporary thinking is none the less evident. It would, given Titmuss's rejection of an explicit theoretical approach to the family, be unfair to describe him in too simple terms as a 'functionalist'; but I want to argue here that his thinking about the family was influenced by that body of theory, and that this influence goes some way to explaining some silences in his work.

The essay on 'Industrialization and the Family' (Titmuss, 1958, pp. 104–18) is mainly an account of the threat to family stability that comes from rapidly changing circumstances in the economic world and a plea for the need to protect the family through social welfare. One of the frameworks that he adopts in this essay seems to be a homely version of the sociological account of universalistic values appropriate to the economic sphere and the particularistic values that belong in the family. He begins: 'What society expects of the individual outside the factory in attitudes, behaviour, and social relationships is in many respects markedly different from what is demanded by the culture of the factory' (1958, p. 111), and he goes on to discuss the difficulties that a state of mind encouraged by the industrial world has for family life. This concern with relations between the two spheres is entirely characteristic of functionalism and it gives a clear indication of where Titmuss's thinking about the family begins. The rest of the argument suggests tentatively that the family in Britain is accommodating to these changes in a satisfactory and democratic way (fathers are pushing prams), but that we need to 'see the social services in a variety of stabilizing, preventive and protective roles' (1958, p. 117).

The picture of the contemporary family that emerges is ultimately a cosy one, in which the strengths and values of family life are holding out successfully against the 'gales of creative instability' (1958, p. 117) from the factories. Functionalism's assumption that the family is a 'solidary unit' where the 'communalistic principle of "to each according to his needs" prevails' (Parsons, 1955, p. 11), and whose function is 'the stabilization of the adult personalities of the population' (Parsons, 1955, p. 16) underlies Titmuss's thinking. Unsurprisingly one finds a similar blindness to that which Elizabeth Wilson describes in the empirical sociology of the 1950s: 'Where were the battered women? Where was the cultural wasteland? Where was the sexual misery hinted at in the problem pages of the women's magazines? Where was mental illness? Young and Willmott banished it to a footnote' (Wilson, 1980, p. 69). It was the women's movement, not social administration, which much later brought to light the miseries of many housewives and the extent of family violence. The assumption that all was well within the family is a legacy which survives in social administration.

Finally I should like to comment on the lack of explanatory power in the Titmuss paradigm. The detailed investigation of people's lives and the impact of state welfare upon them has enormous strengths (and the political economy of the Welfare State could not have been built without it); but there is a gulf between exposures achieved in this way and the ability of exponents to explain why welfare provision so often fails. Titmuss's own explanation, in terms of the ever-increasing needs generated from technological change, bows before the evidence collected by his intellectual offspring. The Welfare State has been found so often to be not merely inadequate, not merely short of resources and short of vision, but often inhumane in its treatment of those to be 'helped', and unresponsive to the changes suggested by the careful arguments of its critics. Feminists would be unwise to look to this tradition to explain, for example, the response of welfare agencies to homeless women or the continued operation of the cohabitation rule.

While the traditions so far described survive, the social administration field is now dominated by the Political Economy approach. Concerned with the lack of explanatory power of the Titmuss genre, its isolation from broader theoretical perspectives, and with 'crises' in the Welfare State which existing literature seemed ill-equipped to understand, a number of writers turned to Marxism and wrestled with the attempt to bring Welfare State analyses under its umbrella. Emblem of the 1980s is a new journal, *Critical Social Policy*, which is intended as a forum 'to encourage and develop an understanding of welfare from socialist, feminist and radical perspectives' (*Critical Social Policy*, 1, 1, 1981, p. 1). The political economy school makes clear gestures in the direction of feminist writers, as will be seen from this rubric, but there remains the question of how open the approach is in practice. Criticism of the 'sex-blind' categories of Marxism has come from Heidi Hartmann (1981a, pp. 10–11) and Hilary Rose (1981, p. 501) amongst others, and feminist theorists are much preoccupied with questions about the uses of a Marxist analysis in understanding patriarchy in capitalist society (e.g. Hamilton, 1978; Sargent, 1981). The gestures of the political economists of the 1970s and 1980s could be seen as a matter of fashion as much as a matter of theory, given the intervening rise of an active Women's Liberation Movement and the unwillingness of radicals to be seen to deny its existence. On the other hand it could be argued that Marxism does give fruitful openings both to analysing women's position and to explaining their oppression.

There are two areas where these openings have been used in the political economy texts. The first is in the analysis of the industrial reserve army, and women's place in it; the second is in the analysis of women's role in the reproduction of the labour force. Both Gough and Ginsburg have something to say in both these areas. Thus Ginsburg writes: 'The social security system not only reflects but strengthens the subordinate position of women as domestic workers inside the family and wage workers outside the family' (Ginsburg, 1979, p. 26), and he has a rather more extended section in which he characterises the Welfare State as 'the use of state power to modify the reproduction of labour power and to maintain the non-working population in capitalist societies' (1979, pp. 44–9).

Women's relationship to the labour market is, of course, a matter of considerable interest. Marxist analyses of the labour market (particularly the one by Braverman, 1974, pp. 386–402), shed a lot of light on employed women's relation to capital, their use as a growing army of cheap labour, and capital's capacity to jettison them into dependent family relationships when required. The part the Welfare State plays in maintaining dependent relationships within the family can then be seen as support for capital's exploitation of women in low-paid and insecure work. This is a revealing account in so far as it locates the employment of women within larger economic trends and sets a context for their experience of paid and domestic employment. To understand the experience from women's point of view, of course, we have to look elsewhere (perhaps to Hilary Land's illuminating piece *Parity begins at Home* (1981), written for the Equal Opportunities Commission).

The category, reproduction of labour, provides the second space for Marxist interpretations to locate women. In Marxist terms the reproduction of labour is seen as primarily benefiting capital. Children are brought up and workers are 'serviced' in the cheapest possible way by using the unpaid labour of housewives. Housewives are thereby seen as having an indirect relationship to capital, but as nevertheless performing crucial labour which enables greater exploitation of male workers. This analysis at least has the merit of directing attention to the fact that housewives do significant work (though this should not be a new discovery), and it puts that work in a respectable position within an analysis of the economic system (Hartmann, 1981a, pp. 3–11). However, the economistic concern with the reproduction of labour, rather than the production of people, is unacceptable from a feminist point of view. The framework offers no explanation of why women do such an overwhelming share of domestic labour, even when they are also employed. And neither, as Hartmann points out, is the possibility that men benefit from that labour (as distinct from capitalists) given any attention (Hartmann, 1981b, pp. 377–86). However, here at least is opened the door on the realm where a large amount of women's work and lives are spent; and, furthermore, on the realm where the Welfare State's chief activities lie.

What is, of course, unsatisfactory about these accounts from a feminist point of view is that they treat women's relationship to capital at the expense of women's relationship to men. Occasional references to 'patriarchal families' are set within a framework of class and the families themselves are not approached directly. The political economy of welfare makes relations in the realm of production the key to under-standing; everything else is a reflection of productive relations and is of secondary importance. This is shown in a very simple way, by relative lack of attention to reproduction, and it is also shown in the way that political economy has been able to address the two topics mentioned above, which involve women's relation to capital, but has been unable to address many other areas of concern to the women's movement.

Finally, then, we come to the question of what feminism has to offer in understanding the Welfare State that can not easily be absorbed by the approaches so far discussed, or at any rate, has not been absorbed so far. None of what follows is intended to suggest that social administration should neglect its traditional concern with poverty and inequality or its newer concern with the Welfare State and the relations of production. What is suggested is that feminism offers new insights which should not just be put on one side as 'women's studies'. The first issue is the one I started with, the claim that male/female relations are a central concern of the Welfare State and not a marginal one. What the approaches so far have in common is a strong tendency to bring women in as a secondary and separate topic, almost as a 'minority group'.

Feminists have to do two things here. One, much the hardest, is to find ways of demonstrating the centrality of the Welfare State's concern with male/female relations. The other, the main subject of this essay, is to look at ways in which the structures of dominant trends of thought are conducive to excluding this possibility from view. It is difficult, of course, to disentangle the effects of the male dominance in publications (most of the texts referred to have been written by men) from the structure of the ideas that they promote. But it does seem to me that all the approaches so far discussed would find it difficult to conclude that male/female relations were in fact a central concern. Individual liberal-ism's concern with the market-place, social reformism's functionalist assumptions about family life, and political economy's economic reductionism all find such an idea difficult to accommodate. This is not to say that it is not very useful for feminists to engage with these approaches; much of the best work on women and the Welfare State has come from socialist feminists wrestling with their twin histories.

Feminist analysis has to begin with the family, and feminist analysis of the Welfare State has to begin with the relations between social policy and the family. This section, then, will sketch three main themes in feminist analysis that are not accommodated in the alternative approaches already discussed, and that form the building-blocks of a feminist case for taking relations between state and family more centrally and more critically. The first is discussion within feminism about the nature of the family; next is the subject of the support given by social policy to dependent relations within the family; and last is the characterisation of the Welfare State as the ideological face of patriarchy.

The family is the focus of many and varied debates within feminism which I shall have to skim over here. The key point in this context, however, is that 'Far from being "natural" and unproblematic, family relationships create and sustain the dependency and inferiority of women' (Wilson, 1981, p. 30). Thus, in contrast to all the alternative approaches the nature of family relationships and the concern of the family with production of people become central subjects for debate. To offer these as subjects does not necessarily mean that we have to conclude that everything about the family is negative (although some feminists do). My own inclination is to stress the ambiguity of the family, as political economists stress the ambiguity of the Welfare State. The family is an arena for caring and loving relationships, and it is in some degree a shelter from capitalist relations; on the other hand it is where women's dependency is nurtured, it is the focal point of exploitative relationships between men and women, and it may be a place of misery and violence.

That social policy sustains a particular form of family relations, and that it plays its part in keeping women within unsatisfactory relationships has been documented quite extensively. Hilary Land's work on social security and taxation is important here (Land, 1976, 1978, Land and Parker 1978), and it is a continuing theme in a growing literature about women in the various social service sectors (e.g. EOC, 1981). And in an example from the Women's Liberation Movement, Women's Aid, while it has been mainly concerned with violence in the family, can also be seen exposing in a very dramatic way the dependency of women in relation to housing. Only a feminist perspective puts these concerns of social welfare in the centre of the stage.

Lastly, and most difficult of all to accommodate with other approaches to welfare, is the Welfare State's ideological force as a representative of patriarchal relations. As Elizabeth Wilson puts it 'The Welfare State is not just a set of services, it is also a set of ideas about society, about the family, and – not least important – about women' (Wilson, 1977, p. 9). So the Welfare State reinforces a particular kind of family and a particular view of femininity, not just through its detailed practice but also through the ideas that it generates. According to Wilson its ideology is best expressed in the social work literature, for 'social work, even more than education, has played, since the War, an expanding and highly ideological role. Its emphasis has been directly on the reinforcement of traditional forms of family life' (Wilson, 1977, p. 83), and Wilson's book draws revealingly from that literature in demonstration.

For the women's movement, the Welfare State has been the focus of many of its political battles, and it is increasingly the subject of much of its literature. While the movement and the literature are increasingly making themselves felt, it can hardly be said that women and the issues raised by feminism have been satisfactorily accommodated within social administration's other perspectives. Moreover, the feminist perspective has more to offer than a place for women and a more accurate understanding of the Welfare State's role. Its concern to relate the detail of personal relations and emotions to broader theoretical analysis is a concern of social administration too. While one branch of social administration has been concerned with detail at the expense of theory, the other has been concerned with theory at the expense of human relations; the effort to build bridges between the macro and the micro is a continual intellectual struggle, in which feminism has a lot to offer. 'The personal is political' is a good slogan for social administration, as well as for Women's Liberation.

References

Abbott, E., and Bompass, K. (1943), *The Woman Citizen and Social Security*, London, Women's Freedom League.

Beveridge, W. (1942), *Social Insurance and Allied Services*, Cmd 6404, London, HMSO.

Braverman, H. (1974), *Labor and Monopoly Capital: The degradation of work in the twentieth century*, New York, Monthly Review Press.

Corrigan, P., and Leonard, P. (1978), *Social Work Practice under Capitalism: A Marxist Approach*, London, Macmillan.

DHSS (1978), *Social Assistance, A Review of the Supplementary Benefits Scheme in Great Britain*, London.

Eisenstein, Z. (1981), 'Reform and/or revolution: towards a unified women's movement', in L. Sargent (ed) *Women and Revolution*, London, Pluto Press, pp. 339–62.

Equal Opportunities Commission (1981), *Behind Closed Doors*, A report on the public response to an advertising campaign about discrimination against married women in certain social security benefits, Manchester.

Ginsburg, N. (1979), *Class, Capital and Social Policy*, London, Macmillan.

Gough, I. (1979), *The Political Economy of the Welfare State*, London, Macmillan.

Hamilton, R. (1978), *The Liberation of Women*, London, George Allen & Unwin.

Hartmann, H. (1981a), 'The family as the locus of gender, class and political struggle: the example of housework', *Signs*, vol. 6, no. 3, pp. 366–94.

Hartmann, H. (1981b), 'The unhappy marriage of Marxism and feminism: towards a more progressive union', pp. 1–41 in L. Sargent (ed.) *Women and Revolution*, London, Pluto Press.

Hayek, F. A. (1944), *The Road to Serfdom*, London, Routledge & Kegan Paul (reprinted 1976).

Hayek, F. A. (1949), *Individualism and the Economic Order*, London, Routledge & Kegan Paul.

Hayek, F. A. (1960), *The Constitution of Liberty*, London, Routledge & Kegan Paul.

Jones, K., *et al.* (1978), *Issues in Social Policy*, London, Routledge & Kegan Paul.

Joseph, Sir K. (1972), 'The cycle of deprivation', in E. Butterworth and R. Holman, *Social Welfare in Modern Britain*, London, Fontana, 1975, pp. 387–93.

Land, H. (1976), 'Women: supporters or supported?', in S. Allen and D. L. Barker, *Sexual Divisions and Society*, Cambridge University Press.

Land, H. (1978), 'Who cares for the family?', *Journal of Social Policy*, vol. 7, no. 3, pp. 257–84.

Land, H. (1981), *Parity Begins at Home; Women's and Men's Work in the Home and its effects on their Paid Employment*, Manchester, EOC/SSRC.

Land, H, and Parker, R. (1978), 'Family policies in Britain: the hidden dimensions', in S. B. Kammerman and A. J. Kahn, *Family Policy: Governments and Families in Fourteen Countries*, New York, Columbia University Press.

McIntosh, M. (1981), 'Feminism and social policy', *Critical Social Policy*, vol. 1, no. 1, pp. 32–42.

Marsden, D. (1969), *Mothers Alone*, Harmondsworth, Penguin.

Marshall, T. H. (1949), 'Citizenship and social class', in T.H. Marshall (ed.) *Sociology at the Crossroads*, London, Heinemann, 1963, pp. 67–127.

Mishra, R. (1977), *Society and Social Policy: Theoretical Perspectives on Welfare*, London, Macmillan.

Parsons, T. (1955), *Family, Socialization and Interaction Process*, Chicago, The Free Press.

Price, S. (1979), 'Ideologies of female dependence in the Welfare State – women's response to the Beveridge Report', British Sociological Association Conference, mimeo.

Rathbone, E. (1949), *Family Allowances*, London, Allen & Unwin. (An enlarged edition of *The Disinherited Family*, London, 1926).

Room, G. (1979), *The Sociology of Welfare: Social Policy, Stratification and Political Order*, Oxford, Basil Blackwell; London, Martin Robertson.

Rose, H. (1981), 'Re-reading Titmuss: the sexual division of welfare', *Journal of Social Policy*, vol. 10, pt 4, pp. 477–502.

Sargent, L. (ed.) (1981), *Women and Revolution*, London, Pluto Press.

SPGB (1943), *Family Allowances: A socialist analysis*, London, Socialist Party of Great Britain (date estimated).

Spring Rice, M. (1939), *Working-Class Wives*, Harmondsworth, Penguin (reprinted, London, Virago, 1981).

Tawney R. H. (1952), *Epilogue 1938–1950 to Equality* (new edn, 1964), London, George Allen & Unwin.

Taylor-Gooby, P., and Dale, J. (1981), *Social Theory and Social Welfare*, London, Edward Arnold.

Titmuss, R. M. (1938), *Poverty and Population*, London, Macmillan.

Titmuss, R. M. (1943), *Birth, Poverty and Wealth: A study of infant mortality*, London, Hamilton Medical Books.

Titmuss, R. M. (1950), *Problems of Social Policy*, London, HMSO.

Titmuss, R. M. (1958), *Essays on the Welfare State*, London, Allen & Unwin.

Titmuss, R. M., and Titmuss, K. (1942), *Parents Revolt: A study of the declining birth-rate in acquisitive societies*, London, Secker & Warburg.

Townsend, P. (1979), *Poverty in the United Kingdom: A study of household resources and standards of living*, Harmondsworth, Penguin.

Wilson, E. (1977), *Women and the Welfare State*, London, Tavistock.

Wilson, E. (1980), *Only Halfway to Paradise: Women in Postwar Britain: 1945–1968*, London, Tavistock.

Wilson, E. (1981), 'Feminism and social policy', *Critical Social Policy*, vol. 1, no. 1, 1981.

Chapter 7
Policy making: a case of intellectual progress?
Adrian Webb

Introduction

Interest in social policy making has burgeoned in recent years. Once state welfare was well developed it was likely that attempts would be made to explain its origins and its contemporary dynamic and an understanding of policy making is relevant to both. The intellectual effort devoted to these tasks has begun to produce a considerable volume of studies of social policy making and a quantum leap in the apparent sophistication of our questioning, if not always in our understanding.

Of course it was not always thus. No area of writing has more clearly revealed the changing nature of the intellectual environment within which social policy has been studied in Britain since the last war. The advent of the 'Welfare State' in its 1940s form and conception aroused only limited interest within the main social science disciplines and the partial intellectual vacuum was filled by the rapid development of Social Administration. But the study of policy making, which might have provided the subject with one distinctive body of analytical theory, was not an early priority or preoccupation. The nearest approaches to such a development were the historical treatments of 'the coming of the Welfare State'; case studies of particular policies, services and institutions; and the study of the 'machinery of government' as it applied to issues of social policy.

The notable exceptions to these rather tangential routes to a body of explanatory theory were by no means negligible, however. Marshall's treatment of Citizenship (1963), Titmuss's analysis of the impact of war (1958), and the development of variants of functional necessity (Goldthorpe, 1962), all contributed to an overtly theoretical tradition –

which nevertheless was slow to take off in the field of policy formation. The order of the day, and the bedrock on which Social Administration was founded, was the analysis of social problems and the advocacy of social policy responses.

The magnitude of the change in the intellectual environment and in the approach taken to policy making is best illustrated by the transformation wrought in a single, influential, work: *Social Policy and Administration* (Donnison, 1965). The empirical base for the book provided by Donnison and his colleagues, then as now, was a mixture of case studies of primarily local examples of the working of the machinery of government in the social services; the enterprise was essentially one of studying social *administration*, with the latter term being broadly interpreted. The individual case studies were micro histories of particular social issues and services welded together by the underlying perception of them as exemplars of a particular phenomenon, or more accurately of two closely related phenomena: public service governance and administration; and the development and modification of social policy. But neither social policy nor the governance of public services was explained in terms of a systematic theory or model. Instead, Donnison adopted two rather different methods of painting in the backcloth in the original and the 'Revisited' edition (1975) of the book. In the first a 'historical-descriptive' account of the development of state welfare policies was provided; in the second a categorisation and critique of theoretical perspectives on policy making served a similar purpose. In each case the setting for the case studies mirrored the intellectual climate of the time; but what, precisely, does this tell us about the fate and productivity of studies of policy making – and of Social Administration?

In common with many other retrospective critics (Mishra, 1977), I have in effect characterised the early Social Administration tradition, and writing on social policy formation, as ideographic (essentially descriptive writing – especially in the form of case histories of policy change). By comparison, recent developments seem to represent a surge towards a nomothetic approach (theory building for the purpose of understanding and explanation). Is this a fair approximation? Has intellectual progress been made?

Divergent perspectives on policy making

Why are we interested in policy making? It is a question which goes some way towards exposing the reasons for the range and complexity of the relevant literature. The natural assumption may be that the purpose of studying social policy making is to explain the origins, and determinants, of social policies. In practice, however, at least three different emphases can be detected: the study of specific policies without reference to a broader theoretical framework; the exploration of social policy forma-tion within the wider context of public sector policy studies; and the analysis of state welfare as a phenomenon in its own right. Let us consider each of these in turn.

In the first the purpose is to understand changes which have taken place in a particular social service, social issue, or policy – to the virtual exclusion of a wider framework. The focus of attention is housing policy, or child endowment, or policies towards ethnic minorities. This approach sits comfortably with the applied, issue-centred, reformist tradition of Social Administration, but the wood is lost sight of while examining the trees.

In the second approach emphasis is placed on a broader framework beyond the detail of particular cases: that of public sector policy and administration. Public administration initially provided a model and sympathetic 'cognate discipline' for social administrators interested in studying state social services as public services. The machinery of government was studied by adopting a descriptive-analytical approach to the *institutions* of the public sector. However, the emphasis has shifted from the institutional to a *processual* one and the analysis of policy making and implementation processes have therefore come to the fore. The rapid growth of 'public policy studies' has transformed the field. Writers with a primary allegiance to the study of social policy making now locate their interests within the broader public policy framework, while those more rooted in the latter see social policy as an important substantive component of public policy. For them, however, the wood is studied without close questioning of its role or relationship to the wider topography; there is no necessary assumption that state welfare exists either as an identifiable entity or as a unitary objective.

This assumption is the distinctive starting-point for the third approach. Social Administration has largely taken for granted the existence of the 'Welfare State' as an ideological, or political and administrative, entity. The assumption has been that individual examples of state welfare do, or should, amount to more than the sum of the parts – in the sense of having compatible and mutually reinforcing effects on society, in the sense of being underpinned by a cohesive set of values and objectives, or both. A key intellectual task has therefore been to explain the origins of this phenomenon, to explain the barriers to its full realisation, and in doing so to defend it. Even without adopting this prescriptive commitment to the 'Welfare State', however, it is perfectly possible to regard the widespread development of state welfare as a phenomenon which is unlikely to be understood merely by examining the processes surrounding individual policies. The outcome is similar in both cases; questions about policy formation become subsumed within a broader concern with the origins, roles and functions of state welfare. It therefore makes sense to look to theories operating at higher levels of generalisation than those appropriate to the study of public policy processes: in particular to sociological theories operating at the societal level.

It may be argued that of the three emphases noted, only the second can truly be said to be about policy making and that the last raises altogether different questions. If this proposition were accepted, however, the study of social policy formation would be the purview of a policy studies approach rooted in political science and organisational sociology and our search for understanding would be confined to the study of policy processes; it would neglect some of the wider issues. It is the coexistence of all three perspectives which underlines the ways in which social administrators have experienced the need to develop a more theoretical orientation and to become more open to the base disciplines of the social sciences and to the intellectual currents within them. If intellectual progress is to be seen as movement from the ideographic to the nomothetic, progress is what we seem to have been experiencing.

What has been achieved?

Merely to begin to state the case for intellectual progress, however, is to emphasise the need for caution, and there are three good grounds for such caution. The first is that the contrast between the volume and apparent sophistication of present and past attempts to explain the forces which shape social policy can all too easily conceal the real merits of earlier writings. The second is readily summarised in the pointed question: does our present knowledge really amount to much despite the effort involved – are we really much wiser? The third, closely related to the second, is that the rich harvest of work relevant to social policy formation forces us to recognise the true scale of the challenge implied in the notion of Social Administration as a 'field of study'. In losing its intellectual insulation – the unity of belief and purpose of the post-war Fabian tradition – has it subsequently been exposed to more heat than light? Has Social Administration begun to acquire the strengths associated with the idea of a multi-disciplinary field of study, or is this notion a mere delusion?

Let us take the first of these caveats and avoid doing an injustice to the post-war pioneer writers on social policy. Their contribution can easily be denigrated, or underestimated, if they are characterised as a-theoretical and pragmatic, as crypto-functionalists beneath their a-theoretical skins, and as naïvely optimistic about the beneficence of the state and the triumph of a progressive liberalism – in the form of a consensual welfare capitalism engineered by the persuasive force of Fabian rational argument. This extreme characterisation may be a straw man of my own making, but there is none the less a danger of repudiating the past by dismissing an earlier generation of writers as men *of* their times, rather than understanding them as men writing *for* their times. Far from removing the need for historical studies of change, for example, theoretical controversy within sociology has underlined the necessity of historically located understandings of policy makers', bureaucrats', professionals' and, indeed, clients' own views of the world they inhabit and of their actions. Policy debates, as much as the organisations which mediate them, demand the skills of 'social action archaeologists': values, perceptions of problems and commitments to social responses are historically layered – they do not merely have their existence in the present and in timeless definitions of interests (Kogan, 1975).

Similarly, while it is true that neither Marshall nor Titmuss, for example, developed a systematic statement of the significance of social class for social policy, both expressed the critical awareness of the limitations of welfare capitalism which has come to be a hallmark of most recent writing. Titmuss, in particular, was an early and persistent critic of the impact on policy and implementation of capitalist institutions (e.g. the insurance industry), of 'bourgeois' values (individualistic materialism and competitiveness) and of organised middle-class and professional interests (e.g. the medical profession). At the same time, however, he underlined the violence done to historical understanding if medical doctors, for example, are simply regarded as members of an undifferentiated social class.

The limits of ideational explanations

The second and third caveats to the proposition (that we have made intellectual progress) direct our attention from the past to the present and future state of the art. One of the major changes in the intellectual climate of the post-war period has arisen from the exploration of the limits – in theory and practice – of 'ideational' theories of change in social policy. By this I mean explanations of social policy formation which emphasise shifts in values, as well as the role of ideas in an intellectual sense. Explanations of this kind have taken a variety of forms and have been developed with varying levels of sophistication. They range from the identification of 'great men' (e.g. Bentham, Mill, Beveridge), through the specification of philosophical and intellectual movements (e.g. Utilitarianism, Fabianism, Keynesianism), to propositions about linkages such as those between elite opinion, legislation and mass opinion advanced by Dicey (Goldthorpe, 1962).

However, the ideational perspective has also enjoyed other and equally powerful manifestations. Two of particular note are rationality and social learning. The notions of rational policy making and social learning can be found in isolation and in tandem; a linking, but often subterranean, theme is that of social progress. Marshall's citizenship thesis implies social learning and rational policy making without specifying them as processes, while Titmuss specifies a number of processes by which ideas and values may change without explicitly bringing them together (e.g. the 'discovery' of social need, shared objectives and the preconditions of concerted action in the context of war as sources of policy making and the impact of policies and institutions in turn on values – especially altruism). Indeed, the entire tradition of socialist gradualism is strongly rooted in the conviction that policies will change values and mass opinion as well as in the conviction that rational argument backed by empirical evidence will help to create the political will and mass support to initiate such policies in the first place.

Beyond these generalised expressions of support for rationality and social learning as sources of policy change lie some examples of more specific formulations. Heclo attempted, rather unconvincingly, to deploy a social learning thesis based on basic concepts borrowed from learning theory (Heclo, 1974). More ambitiously, Ford advanced, in a less frequently cited work, an explanation of policy development in which he suggested that the critical event which triggered major advances was the confluence of empirical evidence, developed theories which attracted widespread support, and effective administrative instruments (Ford, 1968).

The advent of policy analysis and policy studies

It was the post-war development of policy analysis which most clearly harnessed rationality as the motive power of systematic social learning. This was the pivotal concept in what Heclo identified as the prescriptive branch of policy analysis (Heclo, 1972). Comprehensive rational planning was the apparent apotheosis of social learning, although in concentrating on policy processes it tended to lose sight of the broader movements of values and intellectual thought which earlier writers had highlighted.

The deficiencies of rational planning have been rigorously exposed in practice and in critical appraisal and have contributed as much as other changes in the intellectual climate to puncture the appeal of the ideational line of thought. Yet the demolition of this well entrenched and strongly optimistic theme of much social policy writing leaves a difficult question: if not ideas, rationality and social learning, what are the primary influences on policy? The pursuit of this question has become the *leitmotif* of the rapidly expanding body of positive theory in policy studies. The main contenders tend typically to be organisational processes, incrementalism, and partisan mutual adjustment. Although some writers would not necessarily distinguish them in this way, each has its merits.

An emphasis on organisational processes as constraints upon the exercise of rational choice, and as productive of 'policy', underlines one source of 'decision-less decisions' or 'policy-less policy' (Bachrach and Baratz, 1970). It is also a useful counterpoint to 'conspiracy' theories of why desired, radical and rational changes are so often 'subverted'. Perhaps the most valuable lesson to be learned from this viewpoint, however, is that it is all too easy to exaggerate the significance of policy. Much of the impact which organisations have on their environment is neither the manifestation, nor the subversion, of a policy and, moreover, most organisational processes are not specifically designed to give life to policies. Since most social policy is nominally the product of, or pursued through the medium of, large organisations, to put policy in its place is more than wise.

A second valuable, but distinctly unresolved, question has emerged:

what do we mean by 'policy' and how far does it make sense to distinguish it from 'policy implementation'? (Webb and Wistow, 1982); (Barrett and Fudge, 1981). To do so is to accept the constitutional principles which underpin the theory of democratic political control and conveniently to divide a process which translates intentions into outcomes between existing academic domains: political science and organisational studies. To refuse to do so is to recognise the fictional nature of the supremacy of politics over administration, but at the risk of losing sight of the fact that the concept of policy is precisely a means of buttressing political (and hierarchical) control as the precondition of legitimate action in a representative democracy.

Whichever way one proceeds, the ambiguous and problematic relationship between policies and organisations remains. It is well revealed by two examples: the centrality of discretion in areas of public policy where professionals and 'street-level bureaucrats' are key (Hill, 1972); (Adler and Asquith, 1981); (Lipsky, 1980); and the mismatch between organisational processes and an ideal policy process (Webb and Wistow, 1982). In the first case, policy is stated chiefly in broad 'banner goal' terms (e.g. 'to heal the sick and promote a healthy society'). Control over action through policy is willingly attenuated. The importance of workers' individual and group interests, values, perspectives and paradigms in shaping the impact of an organisation or service illustrates the merit of studying the 'assumptive worlds' of key actors (Young, 1977).

The mismatch between organisational processes and an ideal policy process, however, is an example of an unwilling attenuation of policy as a source of control. If organisations really were to exist to fulfil a policy, or set of policies, organisational processes would be designed and continually redesigned specifically to ensure that this ensued. In practice, however, resource allocation, financial control, personnel management and performance evaluation are all shaped by convention, legal and resource constraints, whatever body of theory of good organisational practice may be brought to bear, and by diverse interests. The tensions and conflicts between these processes are in turn resolved, or not, according to standard operating procedures and the internal distribution of power, skill and status within the organisation. At best, these organisational processes are orchestrated in the pursuit of the organisations' founding, or especially crucial, policies; more typically, they will operate with a 'life of their own' and in only spasmodic harmony.

What is true of single, complex organisations is no less true of governments. As Titmuss (1958) first argued in highlighting the social division of welfare and as Heclo and Wildavsky demonstrated in discussing the role of the Treasury, outside the pages of election manifestos a central strand of social policy – egalitarian redistribution – is little more than a pious fiction (Heclo and Wildavsky, 1974). The policy processes which would be needed to give it life as an explicit and pivotal policy are not the existing organisational processes of our central government system. While the dominant interests and power distributions in our society ensure that this particular failure is not merely organisational, the limits of large-scale organisation remain as a set of constraints in their own right. Despite the crucial role of formal organisations to public policy, however, the interface between political science and organisation theory is still not well developed, as Jenkins argues (Jenkins 1978).

Incrementalism as an explanation of policy formation is popularly conceived as the antithesis of comprehensive rationality. This is to do the concept violence, while highlighting the need for a closer analysis of its various meanings – not least in social policy. Understood as a strategy for coping with uncertainty, incrementalism is an alternative and, prescriptively, a superior form of rationality to that advocated in comprehensive rationality. Its essence is the containment of change within the confines of knowledge and experience. Like comprehensive rationality, it is a means of social learning: based on the empirical testing of a course of action by 'doing', rather than by exhaustive analysis prior to action. But other sources and forms of incrementalism are worth exploring.

The switch from the psychology of comparative plenitude to that of scarcity in publicly funded services has thrown rationing procedures into relief and it is now more possible to see incremental changes in service outcomes as an equitable and rational political response to excessive unmet demand (Judge, 1978). A major impact may be made through rational planning on a narrow front, but a defensible sharing of scarce resources inhibits the selection of such options, especially in democratically controlled public services. It is therefore necessary not merely to distinguish between incremental modes of *analysis* and incremental *changes in policy*, but also between incremental changes in policy and incremental *changes in service outcomes*. For example, rational planning as a mode of proceeding may produce an incremental mouse or a dramatic shift in policy, but demand, and supply, pressures may ensure limited changes, or sudden shifts in service *outputs* in either case.

What has been hinted at in reference to incrementalism is made explicit in the notion of partisan mutual adjustment (PMA): namely, that *outcomes* are the product of divergent interests (of varying degrees of organisation) interacting one with another. The notion of PMA is most useful if seen as a way of looking at policy; it suggests that far from being a 'top–down' process, policy making must also be seen as a 'bottom–up and all over the place' process. Presented in an extreme, but logical, form, policy must now be seen as the *output of interaction* between interests, rather than as the *input of intentions* into public organisations. In short, PMA can do for policy studies what 'informal organisation' did for organisational studies. Its strength is that it challenges not only prescriptive approaches to policy making based on comprehensive rationality, but also 'constitutional' approaches which assume that a 'top–down' model is not only the legitimate, but also a realistic, statement of where power lies.

The idea that organised interests 'negotiate an order', rather than that constitutionally approved orders prevail unchallenged, can be seen to be applicable at all levels of public policy studies: within public organisations; in the field of interorganisational interaction (e.g. between government departments, between tiers of government such as central government and local authorities); in the field of interaction between 'politics' and 'administration' (e.g. between ministers and civil servants); within the field of 'politics' (e.g. between parliament and government, or party activists and parliamentary leadership); and between the constituent parts of the state (e.g. government and judiciary). Hill's categories of ideological politics (e.g. 'real' politics), administrative politics (e.g. intra-organisational) and bargaining politics (external pressure-group action) are designed to make the same point (Hill, 1972). However, his is not a complete list of the arenas and it assumes differences in the 'style' of politics in each arena. Perhaps it is sufficient merely to argue that organised interests do seem to interact in a variety of arenas of importance to policy making, that these arenas are at least partially insulated one from another, and that constitutional 'fictions' about the order within and between these arenas need to be viewed sceptically.

Indeed, the argument can be underpinned by noting the divergent theses about how 'politics' relate to policy making which have held sway in post-war social policy. The first, representative (party) democracy, placed political control at the policy core and focused the discussion of power and conflict on ideological party politics. Its inadequacy is revealed by the constraints placed on a governing party by the opposition party which lead to bargaining and a negotiated and often ritualised conflict, but also by the inadequacy of equating ideology and power conflicts with party politics. The second, pluralist democracy, emphasises the multiple interests which possess and exercise power throughout the political system: interests external to the party system; interests within the parties themselves; and interests within the state. Pluralism is seen to involve independent bases of action, divergent interests, values and views of the world, and uncertain and shifting patterns of power. By way of contrast, the elitist model emphasises the limited value of the party and pluralist explanations of policy making arising from their neglect of systematic concentrations of power, of dominant views of the world, and from their preoccupation with a behavioural methodology which emphasises the overt *use* of power in determining policies.

Before drawing the obvious conclusion that the elitist, or radical, view of power throws the whole notion of policy making into doubt, let us return for a moment to partisan mutual adjustment – which was where we embarked on this consideration of organised interests. What began as a liberating perspective has shown signs of degenerating into something less productive of late. To say that the real world of politics and organisations consists of interests interacting is of little theoretical merit unless explanations of that interaction are offered, and one recent tendency has been to use the labels 'bargaining' and 'negotiated order' so liberally as to drain them of meaning: 'bargaining' merely becomes synonymous with 'interaction'.

What is needed is a classification of how organised interests interact and an explanation of why. The distinction in literature on interorganisational relations between bargaining (understood as interaction through bilateral exchange) and power-dependency relations is vital. If one adds to it the possibility of non-interaction, a simple classification of modes of interaction is readily available. The reference to non-interaction also raises another key dimension: that of the boundaries of the polity. Not all interests in society are organised and not all organised interests interact on any particular issue. Processes of selection and exclusion (including self-selection and self-exclusion) have to be explored if we are to understand the composition of the polity of interacting interests surrounding any particular issue. The key tasks pinpointed by the framework adopted are: to understand more fully the ways in which interests are defined internally by a group and externally by other groups (definitions which determine the potential for consensus, mutual indifference, or conflict); the implications of these definitions for the domains and strategies (e.g. resource gathering strategies) of organised interests; the factors which are crucial to the structuring of polities; and the dynamics of interaction in the power-dependence and bargaining modes.

The theoretical labyrinth and the need for intellectual maps

In moving from a discussion of rationality in policy making to a consideration of interests and power, we have illustrated the emerging strengths – and limits – of policy studies. If we concentrate exclusively on policy making and policy processes we run the risk of ignoring wider perspectives on the determinants of social policy. For example, contingency theory has offered one systematic theory of power at the organisational level and political science has generated debates on the distribution of power in political systems, but a broader sociological viewpoint is needed to relate these to issues of social structure (Lukes, 1974). The problem of power illustrates the issue, but it is only one example of the general dilemma.

To admit that a rounded view of policy making must be located within the broader context of the origins and functions of state welfare, however, is to invite problems. The complexity which ensues is well illustrated by even a cursory glance at key books. The major perspectives and theories identified by the authors of popular 'texts' are as follows:

(i)	Goldthorpe (1962)	Functionalist
		Action frame
(ii)	Marshall (1963)	Anti-collectivist
		Non-socialist collectivists
		Genuine socialists – Fabians/Social democrats
		– Marxists/Revolutionary socialists
(iii)	Hall *et al*. (1975)	Systems theory
		Pluralist
		Elitist
		Bounded pluralism
(iv)	Donnison (1975)	Institutional, policy oriented
		Systems/pluralist
		Structuralist
		Neo-Marxist
(v)	George and Wilding (1976)	Anti-collectivist
		Reluctant-collectivist
		(Fabian) collectivist
		Neo-Marxist

(vi)	Mishra (1977)	Pragmatic (a-theoretical social administration)
		Functionalist
		Industrialisation/convergence thesis
		Neo-Marxist
(vii)	Carrier and Kendall (1977)	Positivist – universal psychological forces
		– non-social forces
		– reified social constructs
		Interactionist
(viii)	Higgins (1978)	'Great man' thesis
		Evolutionist – social betterment
		Rational economic man
		Political expediency/conspiracy
(ix)	Room (1979)	Liberal – Political liberal
		– Economic liberal
		– Social democrat
		– Marxist
(x)	Taylor-Gooby and Dale (1981)	Individualist
		Institutional reform
		Structuralist
		Conflict theory
		Marxist

This seems to illustrate an almost bizarre lack of agreement about the intellectual map required in a systematically theoretical approach to the study of state welfare and social policy formation. The only obvious point of widespread agreement evident is the identification of a neo-Marxist perspective as both distinctive and comprehensive in its theoretical ambitions (though this agreement, in itself, contains the danger of concealing the many rooms which go to make up the neo-Marxist mansion). How then, can we begin to discuss social policy formation other than by operating narrowly within a single perspective, or by adopting our own idiosyncratic categorisation of the perspectives which we recognise?

The first and simple approach is merely to recognise that, relocated within a disciplinary framework, there is something approximating a 'complete set' of theories and perspectives from which authors have simply chosen sub-sets according to their disciplinary allegiance or personal predilections. The 'complete set' draws on sociology, political sociology, political theory and policy studies – with important contributions from other disciplines along the way (see table). What the social administration textbook writers tend to neglect most consistently is the explanation of individual and small group behaviour – the realm of decision theorists and of psychology. As Self (1972) has argued, integrating the human actor into theories of political and policy process remains one of the almost unmet challenges. The impact of non-positivistic sociology on policy studies has at least yielded a groundswell of interest in the assumptive worlds of actors in the policy process, but the problem has been identified rather than tackled.

Frameworks from sociology	Frameworks from political sociology	Political ideologies
Functionalist	Pluralist	Classical liberal (anti-collectivist)
Conflict	Bounded pluralism Structuralist	Social democratic (non-revolutionary socialist collectivist)
Neo-Marxist		Non-socialist collectivist
Interactionist	Elitist	Neo-Marxist revolutionary socialist

The problem of moving beyond the sorting of the theoretical cards into suits is, of course, that of the underlying differences between the disciplines in what is recognised to be problematic, what are seen to be the essential components of a good theory and, therefore, the level at which such a theory operates. What we emphatically do not possess is a means of spanning these theoretical disjunctions; neo-Marxists alone would claim to have moved far in the direction of creating an integrated body of theory. Have we in fact progressed, or have we merely entered a blind alley of competing and fundamentally irreconcilable theories and 'paradigm candidates'?

The problems of a 'field of study'

What has happened, in fact, is that the growth and diversification of interest in social policy formation has revealed the inherent problems of a 'field of study'. Once a theoretical orientation is sought there is a choice of strategies: the development of a distinctive body of theory and the pursuit of 'discipline status'; the adoption from a base discipline of a single paradigm or perspective within which to work; the search for a genuinely 'multi-disciplinary' blending of compatible perspectives or paradigms; or the acknowledgment that incompatible perspectives and epistemologies prevent such an accommodation and entail a continuing 'agony of choice'. The last of these seems to be the only realistic and defensible choice. It is not helpful to work blindly within the narrow confines of a view of policy making which excludes wider issues, but it is equally pointless to deny the gulf between writers who work from different ideological standpoints and theories of social order.

Nevertheless, there are themes which can be pursued across these barriers and at several levels of generalisation. I have, for example, used five sources of, or barriers to, change – ideational, organisational, bargaining behaviour, power and core assumptions – to structure this review, but there are also discernible points of convergence between the perspectives which are worth closer scrutiny. Let me mention three. One is the nature and role of the state – especially the abandonment of the view of the state as beneficent, neutral, or as 'above the battle'. This points to the necessity of beginning with interests and exploring their exclusions or representation throughout the key processes and institutions (private or public) which bear on policy making. A major issue becomes that of how the different components of the state (national and local) filter, reflect and structure interests. The structuring of polities and the interaction of interests within them may or may not vary from one component of the state to another, and by policy process. In short, the state may be monolithic and systematically biased in particular directions, or not; the crucial step is to pose the question rather than assert the answer either way.

A second theme is that of the importance of core assumptions, as well as structural formations, as key to the nature of power. It is central to any exploration of the *limits* of social policy, which is a negative but fundamental role for the study of social policy formation. Personally, I would emphasise the value of examining the core assumptions which appear to echo through all industrial societies (the inculcation of a work ethic, the pursuit of economic growth, the dominance of economic over social systems of valuation, the dependence on bureaucracy and hierarchy). But whether the emphasis be on core assumptions rooted in political culture, the capitalist system, or the 'assumptive worlds' of practitioners, we are directed to factors which effect the differential success of interests.

A third and final illustration of such points of convergence is the significance of legitimacy to the operation of the state. It arises in two senses. The first, and more commonly noted, is the need to clothe state policies in legitimacy and the tendency for this to become a factor in policy making. But the second is that policy has itself traditionally been a means of legitimating administration and 'control from the top'. For Social Administration, the concern is both to discover to what extent and in what circumstances public service outcomes are the result of such a conventional view of how policy is 'made and implemented' and to ask which interests benefit from conformance with or departure from this, by now rather passé, view of how the world works.

References

Adler, M. and Asquith, S. (1981), *Discretion and Welfare*, London, Heinemann, 1981.

Bachrach, P. and Baratz, M. S. (1970), *Power and Poverty: Theory and Practice*, New York, Oxford University Press.

Barrett, S. and Fudge, C. (1981), *Policy and Action*, London, Methuen.

Carrier, J. and Kendall, I. (1977), 'The development of welfare states: the production of plausible accounts', *Journal of Social Policy*, 6 (3 July).

Donnison, D. V. (ed.) (1965), *Social Policy and Administration*, London, Allen & Unwin.

Donnison, D. V. (ed.) (1975), *Social Policy and Administration Revisited*, London, Allen & Unwin.

Ford, P. (1968), *Social Theory and Social Practice*, Dublin, Irish Universities Press.

George, V. and Wilding, P. (1976), *Ideology and Social Welfare*, London, Routledge & Kegan Paul.

Goldthorpe, J. (1962), 'The development of social policy in England, 1800–1914' *Transactions of the Fifth World Congress of Sociology*, vol. 4, pp. 41–56.

Hall, P., Land, H., Parker, R. H. and Webb, A. L. (1975), *Change, Choice and Conflict in Social Policy*, London, Heinemann.

Heclo, H. (1972), 'Review article: Policy analysis', *British Journal of Political Science*, vol. 2, pp. 83–108.

Heclo, H. (1974), *Modern Social Politics in Britain and Sweden*, New Haven, Yale University Press.

Heclo, H., and Wildavsky, A. (1974), *The Private Government of Public Money*, London, Macmillan.

Higgins, J., (1978), *The Poverty Business*, Oxford, Basil Blackwell; London, Martin Robertson.

Hill, M. (1972), *The Sociology of Public Administration*, London, Weidenfeld & Nicolson.

Hill, M. (1976), *The State, Administration and the Individual*, Glasgow, Fontana/ Collins.

Jenkins, W. I. (1978), *Policy Analysis*, London, Martin Robertson.

Judge, K. (1978), *Rationing Social Services*, London, Heinemann.

Kogan, M. (1975), *Educational Policy Making*, London, Allen & Unwin.

Lipsky, M. L. (1980), *Street Level Bureaucrats*, New York, Russell Sage Foundation.

Lukes, S. (1974), *Power*, London, Macmillan.

Marshall, T. H. (1963), *Sociology at the Crossroads*, London, Heinemann.

Mishra, R. (1977), *Society and Social Policy*, London, Macmillan.

Room, G. (1979), *The Sociology of Welfare*, Oxford, Basil Blackwell; London, Martin Robertson.

Self, P. (1972), *Administrative Theories and Politics*, London, Allen & Unwin.

Taylor-Gooby, P. and Dale, J. (1981), *Social Theory and Social Welfare*, London, Edward Arnold.

Titmuss, R. M. (1958), *Essays on the Welfare State*, London, Allen & Unwin.

Webb, A. L., and Wistow, G. (1982), *Whither the Welfare State? Policy and Implementation in the Personal Social Services, 1979–80*, London, Royal Institute of Public Administration.

Young, K. (1977), 'Values in "The Policy Process",' *Policy and Politics*, 5 (3) (March).

Chapter 8
Development and disengagement – social policy in Scandinavia and Britain
John Greve

On superficial examination social welfare policies in Britain and the Scandinavian countries appear to have developed in broadly similar ways since the war.[1] Moreover, some major innovations or changes, particularly in social security – such as the introduction of two-tier wage-related schemes – have occurred at roughly the same time. In reality, however, each country's unique combination of historical, cultural, demographic, political and economic factors has shaped significant – even fundamental – differences in social policies and in the levels and organisation of provision.

The influence of values is clearly of crucial importance in social policy, notably as they affect the attitudes and expectations of the public and the attitudes and behaviour of those responsible for promoting or hindering activities impinging upon the welfare and well-being of individuals – whether those responsible are employers, administrators or managerial staff in private or public enterprises, their equivalents in central or local government, and, not least, national and local politicians. The communications media also play an important role in shaping the climate of values. Like politicians, they can either retain and reinforce prejudice and conflict, or attempt to foster understanding, rationality, tolerance, and constructive behaviour.

The Scandinavian countries have strong historical and, with the qualified exception of Finland, cultural and linguistic ties. Political and economic relations have been progressively strengthened, the more so since the establishment of the Nordic Council in 1952 – despite some complications associated with Finland's special relationship with the Soviet Union and Denmark's membership of the EEC. Overriding any difficulties is a resilient determination to work together on political, economic, social and cultural matters to the mutual and cumulative benefit of the people in the Nordic group of countries – Denmark, Finland, Iceland, Norway and Sweden.

In the social policy field, as in others, Sweden has been a major influence on developments throughout Scandinavia – especially in Norway and Finland, but to a lesser extent in Denmark. The adoption and adaptation of policies and measures across national boundaries has a long history in Scandinavia, but the traffic has increased since 1952 as the activities resulting from the setting up of the Nordic Council have multiplied and become institutionalised with an extensive framework of intra-Scandinavian co-operation and exchange in several fields. Nevertheless, there is no single Scandinavian model of Welfare State, and although the countries hold some major social values and objectives in common, there are national differences in the ranking of priorities, methods of financing, and machinery of implementation.

For about the first ten years after the Second World War the nascent welfare states in Britain and Scandinavia bore a strong family resemblance – from a distance, at any rate. But the superficial similarities have become increasingly misleading since the late 1950s – and, with growing maturity, the manifestations of underlying 'character' have become more evident in the past decade or so.

The differences between Britain and the Scandinavian countries which have become more pronounced over time relate to three linked dimensions: the level and quality of provision; the philosophy, objectives and scope of socially-oriented policy; and the concept of welfare.

The Scandinavian countries have deliberately sought to be more generous across the whole range of social policy, pursuing a philosophy which is essentially more creative and less mean-spirited than that which has motivated successive governments in Britain.

In the first decade or so after the war, the dominant economic objective in each Scandinavian country was to build a strong and expanding modern economy. The broad objective in social policy was to secure reasonable minimum standards for all – with regard to income, health care, welfare, housing, education and employment – while creating the foundations and framework of a Welfare State.

Thereafter the Scandinavian countries were readier to abandon the ambulance wagon and safety net ideology – in contrast to Britain – and from the mid 1950s were transferring a growing share of the increasing national product to the retired, children, families, handicapped and unemployed. High priority was given to simultaneous investment in the economic and social infrastructures. The indexing of the 'social wage' was introduced earlier and with less controversy than in Britain where the practice is under renewed attack from influential circles both inside government and in the higher levels of the private sector.

In order to achieve the objectives listed above, private consumption was accorded lower priority in Scandinavia than it has been in Britain. A comparison of statistics for industrial countries shows that over a long period of time a substantially larger share has been taken out of the national product in Britain for wages and salaries, with correspondingly less for spending on industrial investment, communications, and social policy. Capital expenditure on housing, education, the health sector, and public and environmental services has been relatively poor. Meanwhile, national insurance and supplementary benefits are notably low by comparison with those in other countries, and key benefits have scarcely, if at all, improved their relative position as against average earnings since 1948. It is significant both from the point of view of social justice and as an indicator of the adequacy of the national insurance scheme, which is at the core of the Welfare State services, that a complicated and stringently means-tested system of 'supplementary benefits' has become, as a matter of deliberate policy, a major feature of income maintenance in Britain.

In Scandinavia the aims and scope of social policy have broadened since the 1950s with growing emphasis on preventive measures and on positive social and economic development affecting society as a whole. Social unity has become a major theme of policy. The evolution of social policy aims since the 1950s has involved a growing co-ordination and integration of economic, social and environmental objectives and measures.

The ethical values motivating and guiding social policies in the Scandinavian countries – and, indeed, informing the comprehensive vision of the tasks and responsibilities of central and local government – are now more explicitly stated. Official committee reports, white papers, and the preambles to statutes are likely to define equity, freedom of choice, democracy, individual fulfilment and personal dignity as overriding goals of social and related policies – concepts which rarely find their way into comparable documents in Britain. And if they do, nowadays, as recent government consultative documents, white papers and circulars show, the patent motives are to effect a reduction in government spending – at least on the budget of the department issuing the document – and to transfer greater responsibility for help and support to the family and the local community. It is axiomatic, however, that public resources will not be made available which will enable families and neighbours to discharge adequately the increased responsibilities placed upon them. There are clear and disturbing signs of 'social disengagement' by government in Britain.

Consensus, planning, and decentralisation

The political parties and the public in Scandinavia have reached a high degree of agreement on societal objectives and social policies. Various factors have contributed to this, including the small population size and relative social, cultural and ethnic homogeneity of each country – and across the region; geographical and climatic conditions and the nature and distribution of natural resources; the political tradition – influenced by the circumstances of climate and natural resources – of searching for areas of constructive agreement; the strength of organised labour and the social democratic parties – which are themselves manifestations of economic and social factors; and the adaptability and productivity of the economies – for it should not be overlooked that social policies can be expansive and optimistic when economic growth is part of normality.

But while the rapid rise to prosperity in the past generation has created more favourable conditions for the emergence of consensus in the Scandinavian countries, political and administrative institutions and practices which have encouraged and facilitated collective effort have been functioning for a very long time. The place of local authorities in the political system and the active role of *ad hoc* committees and com-missions in the making of policy are important features of the machinery of political representation and decision making.

The pursuit of consensus – and a propensity not to rush major reforms in policy – typically lead to a painstaking and detailed analysis of circumstances by a committee and its secretariat, involving open and widespread consultation at all stages from consideration of the terms of reference of the committee, through the submission of evidence and opinions, to discussing the draft report before the final version is delivered to the government.

Central government undoubtedly plays a key and dominant part in the Scandinavian countries – and there have been, and still are, strong centralising tendencies of the kinds which are associated with modern urban-industrial societies but, in general, governments have not been as autocratic in behaviour or as unresponsive to local government pressure as in Britain. Trends in Britain and Scandinavia are now clearly in opposite directions. In Britain, central government, notably through the inner cabinet and the highest echelons of the civil service, is unilaterally annexing power while dismantling or disregarding the channels and institutions of consultation and accountability which were constructed over a long period in a struggle to create a more democratic and responsive system of government.

In Scandinavia, on the other hand, since the late 1960s, governments in each of the four countries have set in motion processes of decentralisation of responsibilities and decision making to regional and local government, accompanied by some transfer of resources. The declared aims of these measures are to reinforce local self-government, encourage greater involvement by local organisations and individuals in activities which affect their daily lives and the local environment, and to create scope for wider discretion and choice in the conduct of government and administration at local and regional levels. It would be facile to exaggerate the extent to which a real shift in power or resources has taken place, but what is significant is, first, that central government in each country has explicitly drawn attention to the desirability of reversing centralising tendencies and, second, that processes designed to attain that end have been set in train.

One feature buttressing the autonomy of local authorities in Scandinavia is that they levy the taxes, passing on a predetermined share to central government. And it is noteworthy that governments have enabled this important source of local power to continue.

All the Scandinavian countries have adopted comprehensive long-term planning as the most effective way of managing national affairs, but the degree and extent of prescriptiveness and regulation varies from one country to another. National planning is most highly developed in Norway – originating in 1946 – and is in its most formative phase in Finland.

The national plans or programmes combine social, economic, infrastructural and environmental dimensions. Typically, they are formulated in detail for the next four years and are outlines for the ensuing fifteen to twenty years. Implementation and adjustments are made through the annual budgets, together with mid-term reviews, and the programmes proceed on a rolling basis.

The scope of government forward thinking and programmes in Scandinavia has broadened progressively since the 1950s and the relative emphasis in objectives has changed. Increasing priority has been given to social and environmental improvement and development – and with it a growing share of GNP.

The progressive and fundamental change in emphasis in central government priorities is most clearly illustrated in the evolution of the Norwegian four-year programmes. The first two programmes, from 1946, focused on economic reconstruction and capital formation, while social policy was given a lesser place – and consumer spending was explicitly given a residual priority. The two most recent programmes – for 1977–81 and 1982–5 – give pre-eminence to 'the human environment', and 'a qualitatively better society' involving

- greater solidarity and equality
- strengthening the family and the local community
- employment for everyone
- a better working environment
- sound management of natural resources and the environment
- freedom, democracy and protection through the law
- international solidarity.

The opening chapter of the 1977–81 programme points out that

Freedom to choose a life-style and the opportunity to influence decisions relating to oneself are of fundamental importance for well-being and welfare. Our society should be based upon a *decentralised decision-making system*. The government is planning a further development of economic democracy and continued decentralisation within the public sector.

Questioning the effects – defining 'welfare'

The main purpose of this chapter so far has been to highlight the divergence in the approach to social policy as between Britain and the Scandinavian countries. No attempt has been made to assess how effective the Scandinavian policies have been. It would be absurd to portray the Scandinavian countries as having found the secret of eliminating social or individual problems and difficulties. Indeed, there is no lack of evidence to the contrary. The *material* disadvantages and deprivations have been largely overcome for the mass of people in Scandinavia, but other 'problems' have either persisted – for all the dazzling economic and social advances of the past generation – or have been generated by them. 'Adjustment' difficulties and 'deviancy', including profound psychological symptoms, excessive drinking or drug-taking, delinquency, opting out of education or employment – these are the kinds of problems which figure prominently in public debate in Scandinavia. And it is difficult to achieve a perspective about such matters. For, as long as human beings are involved, and humanitarian sentiments are evoked, or civic norms apply, what percentage of drug addiction, alcoholism, asocial or 'anti-social' behaviour, is tolerable in the population?

Apart from Denmark, where the levels and causes of unemployment are closer to those of the Western European mainland, the Scandinavian countries have continued to sustain high economic growth and full employment over the past twenty years or so, even during the oil price inflation of the 1970s. But Norway, Sweden and Finland have all managed to do so for reasons that are peculiar to each of them. Whether they can continue to do so in the face of secular changes and recession in the world economy and escape the looming shadows of unemployment, remains to be seen. What is salutary, from the point of view of both proponents and opponents of comprehensive Welfare State policies, is that the studies referred to below – and evidence from a variety of other sources in Scandinavia, Britain and elsewhere – is that improvements in levels of living have come overwhelmingly through economic growth, that the changing structure of the economy and occupational change have been more important than social policy in redistributing personal material resources and life-chances, and that many of the key social and economic differentials have survived egalitarian policies.

A dilemma lurks behind the civilised aims and the consensus of views which have found increasing expression in Scandinavian social policies. The crucial question is how much equality can be achieved in complex urbanised industrial society when inequalities have been shown to be largely determined by social origin, education, occupation, sex and, ironically, by policies seeking to widen the range of access to social and economic goods and services and to effect a more egalitarian distribution. Inequalities are being sustained and multiplied by the nature of the modern economy and by the unintended consequences of social policies.

There is a nagging concern in radical and liberal circles in Scandinavia – notably among academics, politicians, administrators, and labour organisations – over the manifestations of social dysfunction and the continuation of inequalities to which reference has been made. But the questioning of the effects of policies and the 'success' of the Welfare State is not recent, it was gaining in strength and volume in the mid 1960s. The questioning stemmed from different kinds of reasons, prominent among them being what the Finnish sociologist Uusitalo called 'the sacred status of economic growth as a supreme goal of public policy'. In the late 1960s criticism of the priority given to economic growth was associated with attempts to formulate alternative or complementary goals, and terms such as 'quality of life', 'welfare', 'well-being' and 'level of living' became common currency in academic and public debate and influenced policies to an increasing degree.

But two other sources of questioning of policies were of greater political importance, and the government-sponsored studies of the distribution of 'welfare' and the impact of policies in the Scandinavian countries originated in spreading concern and scepticism over the persistence of low incomes and social and economic inequalities.

Criticisms about economic growth were directed primarily, but not exclusively, at the goals of policy. The questioning about low incomes and inequalities related to the effects or inadequacies of social and economic policies. And in some significant respects the studies have strengthened the ground of the critics and reinforced the urgency of questions about the respective functions of economic and social policies in modern 'welfare democracies' (Castles, 1978).

The studies

The first of the comprehensive studies into the nature and distribution of welfare was launched in Sweden in 1968 by the government Commission on Low Income which had been set up by the Social Democratic government three years earlier, following mounting political pressure from academics, journalists and, not least, party members and the trade union movement.

The Swedish initative had effects throughout Scandinavia which still continue to flow, influencing the philosophy and methodology of social enquiry, relations between social scientists and government, and the formulation and content of social policy. The contributions of Sten Johansson, and later his colleagues at the Institute for Social Research in Stockholm, have been of seminal importance. The work of Johansson and the institute, which was set up by the Swedish government for the purpose, has been theoretical, methodological and empirical, focusing on 'conceptualising and measuring welfare'. Their pioneering work gave stimulus and shape to debate and social enquiry in all the Scandinavian countries.

The Finnish government appointed a committee in 1968 to investigate the circumstances of low-income groups, finally reporting, somewhat inconclusively, in 1975. Meanwhile, several other bodies were investigating social and economic conditions. For instance, the Ministry of Social Affairs and Health began regular studies of the incidence and effects of social transfers. In 1973 the State Research Council published a research programme indicating the priority sociopolitical areas for research. These included health; the maintenance and improvement of living conditions; and research into ways of increasing democracy and equality. The government-funded Economic Council established a research group which produced a seven-volume report in 1972 on the 'quality of life'. A main conclusion of this report was that rapid economic growth had not led to commensurate improvements in the quality of life for all groups in society – the 'benefits' had been distributed unequally. Moreover, economic growth had produced detrimental side-effects, many of which had not been foreseen. Significantly, the undesirable consequences and problems were most marked in health, education, and the field of social planning. The research group argued that economic growth and social development should be regulated in ways which gave priority to fulfilling human needs and aspirations.

The Norwegian Government commissioned a comprehensive investigation into living conditions in 1972. A broadly representative committee was formed to 'support a research group in its work'. The investigations were carried out by teams from universities and research institutes with help from government departments. Among the chief aims of the investigations, as defined in the official terms of reference, were: 'to analyse the causes of such inequalities as may be found', 'to illuminate the situation of low income groups relative to those of other groups', and to formulate a comprehensive definition of 'living standard'. The distributive and redistributive effects of government policies, not only in the social sector, were also to be examined.

With regard to defining and measuring individual, family, and community 'living standards' the government considered that certain components were important and should be taken into account. These were: economic resources, income and wealth, health, employment, working environment, housing, education, consumption, leisure and recreation, political participation and resources, and circumstances experienced while growing up.

The work was completed in 1976, producing nine major reports and fifteen shorter publications. The government accepted most of the findings, but found difficulty in accepting that some 'egalitarian' policies, particularly in education and district development, had actually widened social and economic differentials. Nevertheless, the results of the investigations have influenced the two four-year programmes since 1976, and in 1978 the Central Bureau of Statistics was given the task of mounting 'level of living' studies on a regular basis in co-operation with other government departments.

In 1972 the Norwegian government set up a commission of enquiry to investigate the distribution of power in society. It had some overlapping membership with the steering group of the studies described above, and has produced a series of reports.

The Norwegian approach to 'components of welfare' borrowed heavily from the Swedish model which used nine components in the earlier surveys, but later added five more. In Sweden, surveys were carried out on a continuous basis and the results have been used increasingly widely within government, by employers and trade unions, the media, academic and research institutions, and market research.

In 1978 the Central Bureau of Statistics (SCB) reaffirmed the purpose of the surveys in the following terms:

> The principal aim of the SCB's statistics on living conditions is to illuminate continuously the distribution and development in the central components of welfare as a basis for social debate and the work of reform.

A document produced by the SCB a year earlier reported that 'all the Swedish political parties have moved that continuous surveys of living conditions should be carried out'.

Denmark came later into the field of policy and welfare studies – although the government-financed Institute for Social Research has conducted numerous investigations into different aspects of 'welfare' in the broad sense employed above – but there are major similarities between Denmark and the other countries in the approach and the issues selected for investigation. A Low Income Commission was set up in Denmark in 1976, with explicitly egalitarian terms of reference. It was charged with indicating whether education policy, labour market policy, social policy and housing policy, together with income transfers, can be altered in such a way as to bring about a more equitable distribution of the proceeds accruing to the community from production.

The scope of the welfare concept

Defining 'welfare' in operational terms, without at the same time being excessively restrictive or normative, is a central problem in welfare theory, welfare research, and social policy. Indeed, it may be said that the problem is one of ascending difficulty as we move from theory to research and from either or both to the formulation and implementation of policy. For, in the real world, policy has to have regard to feasibility, the constraints imposed by material resources, time, and public acceptability.

As noted earlier, much of the academic and political discussion of welfare which spread in Scandinavia from the late 1960s received its impetus and raw materials from the Swedish national studies of 'levels of living' led by Johansson.

In the theoretical presentation of the case for the levels of living or distribution of welfare studies, and in justifying the approach adopted, Johansson was adamant about political considerations and the objective of feeding the results of theoretical and empirical work into the processes of policy making. Enquiry and research are to serve as instruments of change and reform.

Thus Johansson's working definition of welfare was seen by him as an 'objective' one combining three elements:

Resources – 'welfare' involved the possession of or access to material and other resources; the latter including political power.
Consensus – Johansson argued that there was general agreement (shared values) in Sweden on what was harmful or undesirable in living conditions.
Public policy – the components of welfare (of which nine key ones were initially identified) must be capable of modification through policy measures.

Johansson asserted that his nine components of welfare met the criteria postulated by the three elements just listed. His theoretical and pragmatic approach has been criticised by some of his academic colleagues in Scandinavia. In practice, however, his group of components has been accepted – with additions and modifications – and formed the core of the studies in Denmark, Finland, Norway and Sweden. In little over a decade the multi-dimensional and dynamic concept of 'welfare' has become a major feature of welfare theory, policy studies, and debate about social policy in Scandinavia.

Acceptance of such a conception of welfare, involving a perception which is essentially responsive and dynamic when applied to social relations, or to the interaction between an individual and his social or physical environment, means that it cannot be restricted to a narrowly defined operational field of social policy. The holistic perception and concept of welfare which has gained ground in Scandinavia did not materialise in a philosophical vacuum. Widely shared social and political values and the evolution of more comprehensive policies – seeking to place economic, social and environmental measures within a co-ordinated framework – influenced the shaping of welfare theory. That theory, in turn, has tended to suffuse economic and environmental policies as well as 'social' policies. In the sphere of public policy, welfare is indivisible.

British disengagement

While trends in Scandinavia have been towards progressive development in the scope and richness of social policy and in the direction of more comprehensive social and economic management and planning, opposite tendencies are evident in Britain. The test of social benefit has been increasingly applied to economic policies in Scandinavia. In Britain, the test of economic advantage – but narrowly defined – is increasingly applied to social policies. And these tendencies are not altogether out of character.

Support for Welfare State policies has always been uncertain and qualified in Britain, and the kind of social and political consensus which has been forged in Scandinavia has never been achieved here – not even in wartime.

The united front which was presented to an external enemy during the war masked a deeply divided class-ridden society with a profoundly authoritarian political system. The chilling degree of disinterest and lack of empathy which large sections of the well-to-do population demonstrated towards their social inferiors – who happened to be the large majority of people – survived the bloody slaughter of the Great War (the first 'people's war') and the economic desolation of the 1920s and 1930s. It would be historically naïve to expect a massive spiritual conversion to have swept through England as Big Ben tolled eleven on Sunday morning, 3 September 1939, and Britain became a nation at war. The country did not unite that year, and only partly the next. There were still two million unemployed at the time of Dunkirk – five years after economic recovery had started – and there would have been more had it not been for the thousands who had joined the armed services.

Despite the Beveridge Report and the wartime coalition government, white papers – all in 1944 – on a post-war National Health Service, Employment Policy, and Social Insurance, and the 1944 Education Act, agreement on social priorities and measures proved not to be deep-rooted or durable. Within five years or so after the end of the war Conservative ideologues, economists, politicians, and employers' pressure groups were pressing for changes, some of them of funda-mental significance, in the objectives, scope and nature of social policies. In general, these pressures were for a reduction in state involvement, a larger and growing role for private sector institutions, and a wider use of means-testing.

British attitudes to social policy – collective provision, mutual and therefore reciprocal acceptance and discharge of social responsibilities – reflect the long-established and resistant class divisions. The nature of political differences and the institutional forms which have evolved around them are part of the broader social and cultural system. The adversarial, or conflict, approaches to the conduct of government at central and local levels, and to industrial relations, have not emerged by chance. They are products of what many thousands of people see as the most effective way of protecting their interests and of extending their command over material and power resources. The rigidly hierarchical organisation of the political and administrative arms of government, and the obsession with secrecy by both, are seen as essential to the protec-tion of these arrangements. And they have their parallels throughout the fields of employment – that is to say in other major social institutions – including the so-called liberal professions and the universities.

Ambivalence and antipathy towards comprehensive social provision or planning through the medium of public agencies is strikingly wide-spread in Britain. Apart from a brief euphoric period in the aftermath of war, social and economic policies have been disjointed and erratic – this can be seen in relation to housing, physical planning, state retirement pensions, employment, the management of the economy, and the organisation of local government and the National Health Service. The most consistent feature in relation to pensions and other social security benefits has been their low level by comparison with earnings. And in the past two years their real value has been reduced still further.

Full employment – one of the key and, in 1944, bi-partisan elements of social and economic policy – has been abandoned by both Labour and Conservative governments. Indeed, governments have gone further in using human material as an economic regulator, as a factor of production (and consumption) and governor of price inflation. In almost unparalleled dedication to implementation of a monetarist policy the Conservative administration elected in 1979 has used manpower as a regulative commodity; 'de-stocking', discharging into unemployment, as a means of attaining the declared supreme goal of reducing inflation.

Since around 1973 there has been an increasing tendency for policies in Britain to be regressive and socially and economically dysfunctional in their effects on the organisation and levels of output of the economy and on industrial and social relations. In contrast to trends in Scandinavia, the incipient negative view of social policy, which has always been widely held in Britain, has grown in strength and influence since the early 1970s. Social policies are seen as being about 'problems' and 'poverty'; housing policies are about council tenants and subsidising people who do not need it; supplementary benefits and unemployment pay encourage sloth, 'scrounging', and act as a disincentive to work, despite successive reports to the contrary from the Supplementary Benefits department and numerous independent studies. Social services and, indeed, the public sector as a whole are regarded by large numbers of people as being parasitic on the body of the economy. These negative perceptions of the effects of social and public services are given respectability and credence by the utterances of government ministers including the Prime Minister.

The positive view of the place and role of social policy has faded. It is not seen or promoted as being unifying, socially and economically developmental, creative, expressing and seeking to diffuse and reinforce civilised values and standards, as being concerned to liberate individuals and enable them to find greater fulfilment, and to create conditions for the enrichment of social and personal relations. Least of all is the provision and development of social policy seen as a principal goal of economic effort and growth.

The most striking and profound difference that has emerged over the past twenty years between Britain and the Scandinavian countries is manifest in the contrast between the regressive policies of the former and the more developmental and integrating policies of the latter. Strong and, so far, effective political forces in Britain appear bent on relegating social policy and its institutions to a more peripheral and residual role rather than perceiving them as an essential and desirable part of the main structure and fabric of society. At present the virtues of the market are eulogised and impressive claims made for the social and personal benefits which, it is argued, the market can provide more effectively and economically than any other system. The evidence of history and the experience of other advanced economies – including some of the richest – does not support these assertions.

In the 1970 edition of his book *The Welfare State* David Marsh said 'all political parties seem to be committed to maintaining the Welfare State'. Ten years later, in the 1980 edition of the book, although his account was still generally optimistic, there were also more indications of anxiety and, significantly perhaps, the focus of the book was narrower in that the explanations and preoccupations were now exclusively with Britain. Did this mirror the change of mood in Britain which had become more apparent in the 1970s?

In reviewing recent historical developments, the Finnish sociologist J. P. Roos observed in 1978 that the 'Welfare State is one part of the image of the developed capitalist State, the most public, but simultaneously the most illusory'. It might fit neatly into some *post hoc* explanation of cyclical historical development, or of historical determinism, if Britain, the first industrialised nation, were also the first to move through the Welfare State phase under the influence of a pre-industrial political philosophy. But it would be ironic and, for many, the outcome could be tragic.

Notes

1 For those interested in Scandinavian social policy the following are recommended:

International Council on Social Welfare (ICSW) (1974), *Development and Participation*, Helsinki.

International Council on Social Welfare (ICSW) (1980) *New Directions in Social Policy*, Paris.

Johansson, S. (1972), *Conceptualizing and Measuring Welfare*, Stockholm, Institute for Social Research (Mimeo).

Johansson, S. (1976), *Towards a Theory of Social Reporting*, Stockholm, Institute for Social Research (Mimeo).

Ringen, S. (1981), *Hvor går velferdsstaten?* (Whither the Welfare State?), Oslo, Gyldendal.

Scandinavian Sociological Association (1978), 'The Nordic Welfare States' (Special issue of *Acta Sociologica*), Oslo, Universitetsforlaget.

Norway

Ministry of Finance (1977), 'Langtidsprogrammet, 1978–81' (Long-term programme), Oslo.

Ministry of Finance (1980), 'Langtidsprogrammet 1982–85', Oslo.

Universitetsforlaget (1976–8), 'Levekårsundersokelsen' (Reports of the living conditions surveys), Oslo.

Sweden

Ministry of Economic Affairs, Medium Term Surveys (various). The Swedish Economy (Annual).

Social departementet (Ministry of Social Affairs) (1977), 'Socialtjänst och socialforsakringstillägg' (Final report of the Commission on Social Welfare), Stockholm.

Central Bureau of Statistics (1975–80), 'Levnadsförhållanden' (Reports of the level of living surveys), Stockholm.

References

Castles, F. G. (1978), *The Social Democratic Image of Society*, London, Routledge & Kegan Paul.

Marsh, D. (1970), *The Welfare State* (2nd edn. 1980), London, Longman.

Chapter 9
Social assistance and social welfare: the legacy of the Poor Law
Richard Silburn

Introduction

'There is always an unmapped area of dangerous fallibility between a policy and its pursuit' (Mr Srinivasan in Paul Scott, *The Raj Quartet*, vol. 1). The study of welfare policy since the Second World War is not an entirely unmapped area, and it affords many examples of the 'dangerous fallibility'. The Social Security system was intended to replace the Poor Law, which formally and institutionally it did. Perhaps it was naïve to suppose that the animating spirit of the Poor Law would be abolished along with the institution itself. But it is possible to detect, almost from the beginning, a counter pressure to the vision of an unstigmatising and compassionate system of relief for the poorest; the gradual but relentless intrusion of a meaner and more suspicious spirit, and the parallel development of more inquisitorial procedures which in their more extreme forms evoke a chilling reminder of the world we have not, regrettably, lost.

II

Between early February 1946 and March 1948 a series of Commons debates led to the passing of Acts to establish the National Health Service, the National Insurance Scheme, and the National Assistance Board. The most important of these debates, in terms of parliamentary time and interest, were the first two. The Second Reading of the National Insurance Bill lasted for three days. During both the Debate and the Committee proceedings there were numerous points of disagreement between the major parties. Many of them, however, were on relatively small, albeit important, points of technical detail. On 30 May 1946 the Bill was passed without a formal division of the House. Only one member, Sir Waldron Smithers (Orpington), is reported as expressing loud and sustained dissent, which in his case was not confined to detail, but was more the expression of a rooted distaste for the Bill in its entirety.

The National Health Service Bill was given its Second Reading between 30 April and 2 May 1946. This debate was a rowdy and bitterly divided one. The Minister of Health, Aneurin Bevan, made a long, powerful and at times pugnacious speech. His pugnacity was understandable because it was no secret that the Conservative spokesmen felt intense hostility towards the Bill. The tone of this debate contrasted with the earlier one by its bitterness and the rancour that members of both parties displayed. On 20 July 1946, after a five-hour Third Reading, the House divided and the Bill was passed by 261 to 113 votes.

In contrast, the passing of the National Assistance Act was a tranquil affair. The Second Reading took place on 24 November 1947 and was concluded within the day. The tone of the debate was set in Bevan's opening speech. He spoke for only half an hour, his manner quiet and thoughtful. It was a powerful and moving speech but in a low key. He reminded his audience that 'this occasion marks the end of a whole period of the social history of Great Britain' (Hansard, 444/1603). The Poor Law was to be replaced with a clearly separated responsibility for the maintenance of the poor from responsibility for their other welfare needs. Most people would have their income maintenance needs covered by National Insurance. Any residual groups were to become the responsibility of the state nationally, a responsibility to be vested in the semi-autonomous National Assistance Board established under Part 2 of the Act. This body would be governed by regulations which would apply consistently over the whole country. In this way inconsistencies that had arisen under the separate Poor Law Authorities would be removed.

But cash was only one part of the problem. Bevan went on to identify especially vulnerable groups of people with special welfare needs, such as the blind, the tubercular, vagrants and above all the aged. The National Assistance Board might provide for their maintenance, but it must be the local authorities who would provide for their other needs, because it was at local level that need could best be assessed, and services provided that were direct, personal and caring. Thus, Part 3 of the Act laid upon local authorities the responsibility for the provision and management of residential accommodation for those unable to make provision for themselves.

'These', he concluded, 'are the main provisions of the Bill – simple to state in this House of Commons, detailed to carry out in practice, but bound to have a profound effect upon the welfare and the well-being of large numbers of people in the country' (Hansard, 444/1612).

What followed that afternoon and evening can hardly be called a debate at all. One after another Labour members rose to express their elation that they were witness to a truly historic Parliamentary decision. 'Today we are burying the Poor Law', declared Alice Bacon (Hansard, 444/1667), while Mrs Braddock clearly had this in mind when she opened her speech with the remark, 'I think of what we are repealing, more than of what we are proposing', (Hansard, 444/1631). Some members recalled their own experiences of prolonged opposition to the Poor Law, in one case going back as far as the 1909 Royal Commission. But most recollections were of the inter-war period and the years of the Depression. Mrs Braddock spoke of her anger at the past and hope for the future. 'I am very bitter about what has happened in the past to those people who have found themselves in need of assistance . . . people have come in and asked for a pair of boots and have had to stand in a corner and show the soles of their boots before another pair could be given to them . . . I am pleased that today we are ending all that' (Hansard, 444/1635).

Conservative Party speakers were more muted. Their Front Bench spokesman seemed uncertain what tone to adopt; his speech was criticised later in the debate as carping and mean-spirited. Other Conservatives were anxious to emphasise their party's longstanding commitment to social welfare measures, while yet others paid tribute to the public service rendered for so many years by the much maligned Poor Law Guardians. But no one spoke against the Bill, nor were there any substantial criticisms of it.

One or two speakers added a gentle word of warning, striking a cautionary note that seems to have gone largely unheeded at the time, but which, thirty-five years on, seems very far-sighted. In a noticeably thoughtful speech, Mr Albert Evans (Islington West) expressed his lingering anxiety very plainly.

It has been claimed for this Bill that it will finally sweep away the last remnants of the Poor Law. . . what does this claim amount to? . . . If it means anything, it must mean that we shall clear away the essence of the Poor Law and the stigma that goes with it. If this Bill is successful in removing that stigma from the minds of the poor, then it will indeed go down in history as a great measure. But if that stigma is to go, it will need something more than this Bill, or an Act of Parliament, or regulations. It will need a different attitude of mind on the part of the administrators of outdoor and other relief for the poor. They have a difficult job if they are to remove the stigma of the Poor Law. They have to humanize the relationship between the poor and authority – a difficult and complex task, and one which cannot be done merely by passing legislation (Hansard, 444/1674–5).

In general, however, anxieties such as these were submerged in the euphoria of the moment. The Bill was given its unopposed Third Reading on 5 March 1948, just four months before it was to come into operation.

The establishment of the National Assistance Board was evidently not a contentious issue. It was seen as a simple and necessary measure to round off the social security programme. For the rest of the 1940s and on into the 1950s, National Assistance was regarded as a minor appendage to the major welfare institutions.

III

For the first fifteen years of its existence the work of the National Assistance Board attracted little public or parliamentary attention. Each year the Board published a report on its activities; they make dull reading. The numbers claiming benefit is noted; that the numbers tended to increase each year is likewise noted. Some of the major difficulties encountered by the Assistance Officers in the course of their duties are spelled out. But the overriding impression is of a relatively minor service operating on the periphery of public concern. During the 1950s there were a number of welfare issues that aroused passionate commitment; from time to time there were set-piece debates in the Commons on problems of the Welfare State. But they seldom involved the work of the Board except in passing.

An examination of parliamentary questions concerned with National Assistance gives one a glimpse of the worries that were expressed, and of the preoccupations that lay behind them. For a start there were not many questions at all, often no more than twenty in an entire parliamentary session. Many of these were intended to draw attention to the alleged inadequacy of the scale-rates of assistance, inadequacy that led to considerable individual hardship, particularly among the elderly. Indeed concern about National Assistance almost invariably derived from a prior concern about the circumstances of the aged. The more persistent critics of National Assistance usually declared their affiliations with the powerful groups and lobbies concerned with the elderly.

Front-bench spokesmen had relatively little difficulty fobbing off critical questions. Governments found the autonomy of the Board a considerable convenience, and parried criticisms about the levels of assistance by pointing out that it was the Board's responsibility to make recommendations about these, and that the government was always ready to listen to the Board's advice.

There were some other themes that emerged at question time, though with less regularity. One was the alleged reluctance of many to apply for assistance to which they would be entitled. This reluctance was attributed sometimes to misplaced pride; sometimes it was suggested that there was still a stigma attached to National Assistance; and very occasionally an outspoken member would hint that some might be deterred from applying because of the way they were treated by the Assistance Officers. Here again the normal response from the front bench was bland complacency, tinged with irritation that anyone could doubt that all was well.

A few examples will catch the prevailing tone of the parliamentary discussion. In general, the front bench was reluctant to accept that National Assistance could be improved, and were at pains to stress how well the system was working. On 19 March 1951 Edith Summerskill was told by one Captain Duncan that pensioners were reluctant to apply for National Assistance. She replied, 'I am sorry that the honourable and gallant gentleman has said that, because we try to encourage people to go to the Assistance Board. My experience is that once they have been they are never reluctant to go again' (Hansard, 485/2074). In December 1955 Mr Ernest Marples urged his colleagues to 'encourage their constituents to call upon and ask National Assistance officers to go into their homes, because these officers are their friends and not their enemies' (Hansard, 547/388). This point was picked up later in the debate by Mr Hughes-Young, who said, 'I was glad to hear my Hon. friend the Parliamentary Secretary say that the National Assistance Officer will in time come to be regarded as the old-age pensioners' best friend, and I hope that this is true, in the same way as the policeman is today the small child's best friend'. He then referred to a conversation he had recently enjoyed with one such officer: 'She said it was remarkable how people who at first are worried and frightened when applying for National Assistance, when they realise how much they can get and the kindness of the Board's officers, are overcome with gratitude and send the most pathetic letters to the Board' (Hansard, 547/408–9).

Very occasionally a questioner implies that the Board's officers are not invariably open-handed. In November 1955 Mr W. T. Williams asked:

Is the Minister aware that almost all Hon. members can give him endless examples of people who come to them at 'constituency clinics' and on other occasions with stories of very real hardship? Is the Minister also aware that, when questioned, many of these people say that when it comes to questions of real hardship the officers of the Board exercise their discretion with extreme strictness, if not harshness? (Hon. members: No).

The Minister, Osbert Peake, was having none of it. 'On the contrary,' he declared, 'the Board has been granting discretionary additions more freely, both in spirit and amount, for every year which has gone by' (Hansard, 546/1038).

What was very unusual in the 1950s was the criticism that the Board was being too generous in its treatment of claimants, or that there was widespread abuse of the system. Occasionally some question provoked a back-bench outburst, but these were usually based upon a wholesale repudiation of welfare provision. For example, Sir Waldron Smithers (Orpington) seldom overlooked an opportunity to confide to the House his conviction that 'the Socialistic concept of a comprehensive Welfare State is squandering public money, killing initiative and ruining character, and that that is why our prisons were never so full as they are today' (Hansard, 511/4); a view that Sir Waldron repeated in almost identical terms on numerous occasions.

From time to time a question was asked that is a fore-echo of the 1960s. Was it right to pay National Assistance to people on strike? How many foreigners or, even worse, how many overseas immigrants were receiving Assistance? But accusations of systematic abuse, of widespread fraudulent claims, or dark allegations about feather-bedding the work-shy were very infrequent. It seems to have been generally accepted that National Assistance was essentially a service concerned with elderly people, a group who command widespread public and parliamentary sympathy.

But the tone of press and parliamentary discussion changes markedly from the mid 1960s onwards. A renewal of concern, about widespread hardship that the welfare institutions do not confront, is matched by assertions that social security frauds are easily perpetrated, and commonplace. News stories which claim to expose these abuses become a staple of the popular press. Front bench spokesmen become noticeably more defensive; the blandness and complacency of the 1950s gives way to a more worried response, insisting that the scale of abuse is being greatly exaggerated, but that none the less the Board is ever vigilant. Despite, or perhaps because of, these protestations, outbursts of 'scrounger-mania' have now become a regular, recurrent feature in British public life.

IV

The relationship between public policy and public opinion is complicated and obscure. But it is possible to note some of the ways in which the common currency of political discussion in the mid 1960s started to change. The apparent optimism of the 1950s slowly gave way to a more cautious and anxious mood which finds its reflection in social policy debates and preoccupations.

The resignation of Harold Macmillan in 1962 and his replacement by Lord Home seemed to many to be symptomatic of both a crisis of leadership and a loss of direction in the Conservative Party. Meanwhile the Labour Party was enjoying a period of commanding political leadership under Harold Wilson, so that the election of 1964 seemed to offer the electorate a clear contrast of policies and political styles. But if Labour's landslide victory in March 1966 indicated an acceptance of technocratic, interventionist and growth-orientated government, the crisis measures of July 1966 sowed the seeds of doubt in the minds of many. And as passing time made clear to all, the goal of sustained economic growth, upon which the government's social programme crucially depended, seemed to become ever more elusive. The hopes of 1964 were slowly replaced by a wariness, even a cynicism as, first, anxiety about inflation grew and, later, as the number of unemployed slowly but remorselessly increased to reach, by the mid 1970s, levels unimaginable even a few years earlier.

The election campaign of 1970 was an ideologically sharper one than either that of 1964 or 1966. The Conservative Party was showing a new abrasiveness, and after the Selsdon Park conference espoused the cause of the vigorous entrepreneur who would set the economy free. Each party claimed to represent so-called 'middle opinion', and each represented the other to be a party of extremists. This tendency was to become more marked throughout the 1970s.

Something of the same process of polarisation can also be detected in the social policy discussions of the time. New and highly effective forms of pressure group developed, concerned to draw attention to unacceptable social conditions. Organisations such as Shelter and the Child Poverty Action Group revealed a genius for arresting publicity, so that both housing and income deprivation were more widely discussed than had been the case for many years. But the more persuasive these groups became, the more they seemed to provoke a backlash of contrary opinion and argument. As Shelter and its supporters argued the case of families trapped in the slums of the inner city, so others conjectured (as they had a hundred years earlier) that slums are created by those who live in them. And as CPAG highlighted the cycle of family poverty, so the attacks on welfare scroungers seemed to intensify. Here again we see the comfortable tones of the 1950s become more urgent, but more abrasive.

There were a number of important social policy developments which reflected the changing public mood. As far as National Assistance was concerned, by far the most important was the replacement of the Board by the Supplementary Benefits Commission in 1966. This was more than a simple cosmetic change of title. The work of the Commission, although still formally separate, was to be integrated much more closely with the National Insurance system. Originally the establishment of the SBC was intended to be one element of a much more comprehensive reshaping of social security provision. In the event it became more significant than was originally anticipated. For a start, the notion of social assistance as a temporary and last-resort service for small numbers of people unprotected by social insurance was finally abandoned. It was clear that National Assistance had never in fact been like that, and grew less like it every day. Instead it was now acknowledged that means-tested benefit had become and would remain an institutionalised and permanent feature of social provision – hence the title Supplementary Benefit. One consequence of this reliance upon means-tested benefit was to increase the numbers claiming and receiving benefit. In the first three months of its operation, the number of claimants rose to very nearly 2.5 million, an increase of over 400,000, the bulk of new claimants being old-age pensioners seeking a supplementary pension.

But from the outset, the categories of SBC claimant started to change too. Rising unemployment forced more and more people of working age on to benefit. From 1948 to 1966 the proportion of claimants who were unemployed had hovered around 5 per cent of the total. It increased to 19 per cent by 1975, and to 27 per cent by 1980. Another group of claimants which has also grown steadily in recent years is the single parent (usually a woman) with dependent children. This group of claimants now accounts for about 10 per cent of the total.

But figures which relate only to the number of claimants are misleading. First, it is still the case that pensioners are the largest group of claimants; but many of them are living alone or as one partner in a couple. The unemployed or single-parent claimant is usually a younger person at a different stage of the family cycle; many will have dependents whose needs must form part of the claim, so that the total number supported by the SBC is always much greater than the number of claimants. Second, most pensioners become long-term clients of the Commission. But the unemployed and other client groups may only need help intermittently or for short periods. Consequently it is the case that most new claims for benefit are from non-pensioners. This means that to a greater extent than was the case under the NAB, the SBC is concerned with family poverty, and with hardship among children.

A final point can be made about the 1960s. The years of the Labour administrations were marked by a succession of experiments with incomes policies; moreover, in response to the deteriorating economic situation, these policies were usually restrictive, attempting to hold down the level of wage settlements. To its credit, the Government tried to safeguard and improve the value of pensions and other benefits, but this created a situation where there could be an embarrassing overlap between the levels of benefit income and the lower range of earned incomes.

To summarise: the period between 1965 and 1970 was one of political and economic expectations aroused and then, in some cases, disappointed; of a more vigorous and critical public awareness of problems within the Welfare State; of policy decisions which actually increased the number entitled to claim means-tested benefit; of social and economic changes which altered the nature of the claiming groups;

and a growing awareness and resentment of the 'poverty-trap'. Issues of this kind, and others which were widely publicised, were argued about with a new belligerency and commitment.

V

The Supplementary Benefits Commission was born into, indeed was a product of, a rapidly evolving social and political climate. If the first commissioners imagined that they would be permitted to carry out their responsibilities in the calm tradition of the Assistance Board, they were soon disabused. From the outset the Commission's activities were the object of persistent and vigilant public scrutiny. The so-called 'poverty-lobby' maintained a constant, critical and expertly publicised pressure upon the Commission. The publication list of CPAG includes not only a quarterly bulletin, but a stream of pamphlets and short research monographs which document the difficulties facing poor families, and the impact upon them of Supplementary Benefit policies and practices. Moreover, although the actual readership was probably confined to a relatively small group, the close links that were established between CPAG's London staff and the more serious newspapers and journals, as well as with the broadcasting media, ensured that the CPAG viewpoint was quickly and widely disseminated.

But at the same time the opposing lobby was also extremely vigorous, and erupted regularly with strident allegations about fraud and abuse by claimants and lax administration by the Commission.

The great organs of state, no matter how powerful they are, are surprisingly sensitive about criticism from the outside. This sensitivity may explain the extraordinary secrecy that surrounds so much of British public life, and the reluctance with which public bodies become involved in public discussion, even to defend themselves from misplaced attacks. The Commission was perhaps more exposed than many official and quasi-official bodies, but its initial, almost instinctive, reaction was to try to ignore those criticisms it could not smother.

Behind the scenes, discreetly, the Commission tried to counter the criticisms. Successive chairmen struggled to ensure that the Commission's viewpoint was (as they saw it) fairly presented in the media. But they were cruelly caught between the two main but mutually-opposed thrusts of complaint. Rereading the press cuttings of the early 1970s we see the Commission trying to cope on the one hand with an onslaught from the CPAG about the Wage-Stop, or the policing of the co-habitation rule, while on the other hand they attempted to rebut periodic bouts of scrounger-bashing in the popular press, and to argue that their control procedures, while neither harsh nor oppressive, were nevertheless effective.

In the summer of 1968 the Minister, Mrs Judith Hart, tried to head off precisely such an attack by a public display of Commission energy and vigilance. In a widely reported speech she lashed out at the work-shy, and hinted that much stronger measures were to be introduced to deal with a small but troublesome minority of people she referred to as 'lead-swingers'. Far from reassuring her critics, her remarks seemed to refuel them, and were seen as a vindication of their viewpoint, leading to ever more melodramatic 'revelations' about welfare abuse.

This episode seems to point up one of the difficulties facing the Commission. Any account of the care taken by officers in reaching a decision, or of the control systems to expose fraudulent claims, seemed to provoke rather than allay criticism. The extra emphasis given after 1968 to the policing of the system by the deployment of Unemployment Review Officers, or by recruiting additional Special Investigation Officers, was seen as proof of the need for still firmer action. Meanwhile those very measures were seen by others as intensifying the oppressive aspects of the system, leading to the harassment of the innocent and making the needy even more reluctant to apply for benefit.

The Commission's dilemma is nicely demonstrated in the columns of *The Times*. News stories, feature articles, or correspondence about Supplementary Benefit, becomes much more common after 1968 than it was before. The usual news story is a Court Report of a prosecution for a fraudulent claim; normally rather dull cases of what amounts to little more than petty pilfering by people who are often under very severe personal pressures. Very occasionally there is a more lively case of sustained and premeditated deception involving multiple imposture. But from 1970 onwards there starts to appear another kind of story; of the harassment of claimants by SBC staff, of bullying and threatening tactics by visiting officers, of squalid prying into people's private lives by Special Investigators; stories of families unjustly deprived of benefit, and of a series of administrative malpractises collectively known as 'mucking the claimant about'. The ambiguity of the public's interest and the conflicting demands made upon the Commission is evident. As the Fisher Report on Abuse of Social Security Benefits put it,

The Departments have been assailed by public criticism from two sides: some critics say that they do not do enough and are not tough enough in dealing with abuse, others say they are too tough and intrude too much into the private lives of claimants . . . . Nobody can walk a razor's edge without sometimes falling off, but we believe that in intention and (for the most part) in execution the Departments do their best to tread a sensible and balanced middle course (HMSO, 1973 par. 488).

During the early years the Commission struggled to find ways of walking the razor's edge. Slowly and uneasily (and understandably so given that this was to cut across the conventions of British public administration) the Commission tried to become somewhat more open about the details of its policies and their implementation. It never agreed to the publication of the 'A' Code, but it did prepare and, in 1970, publish a Handbook which explained its policies in greater detail than ever before. Similarly the Commission made an attempt at redesigning its leaflets and forms in ways that made them more comprehensible to a layman.

In 1975 Professor David Donnison became the chairman of the Commission, and during his five-year term of office he consolidated and vastly extended this process. He re-emphasised the independence of the Commission by insisting on the publication of an annual report which would go beyond descriptions of the Commission's daily work to discuss in detail the problems and difficulties of the system; he reserved the right to criticise and comment, including the right to criticise government policy. He insisted that he should be free to make suggestions and recommendations about the development of policy. This perhaps was the most interesting aspect of Donnison's chairmanship; from the outset he made it clear that he felt the need for urgent reform of the whole system, and the annual report was to be one vehicle for canvassing change. Altogether five annual reports were published; these form a series of sustained and deeply serious discussion documents, spelling out the difficulties, exposing rather than glossing over the problems, and initiating suggestions for change.

As chairman, Donnison positively invited critical and informed discussion. He himself was tireless in these efforts, attending meetings and conferences, convening or participating in gatherings big and small in all parts of the country. Seldom has the holder of so important a public office made himself so accessible. The personal strain of such a relentless programme (while at the same time reassuring the Commission's own staff, coping with the anxieties of his own officials, and dealing with the politicians) was evident. None the less he clearly felt that real progress was made, public and professional opinion became better informed, and alternative policy options were being discussed constructively and fruitfully.

In the first report two particular areas were identified as giving rise to especial difficulty. The first arose where there was more than one public body with the statutory authority to make cash payments, and where there was confusion about which of them should have the prime responsibility. Bureaucratic overlap could lead to double payment; but what was more normally the case was that neither body would make a payment, each referring an applicant to the other. Examples of such 'frontier problems' are the powers that a social service department has to make payments (so-called Section 1 payments) to a family where children are at risk; powers that a local education authority has to give grants to help with the purchase of school clothing; and the complex system of rent and rate rebates that the local housing authority administers. From the point of view of the Commission, such overlap of authority sorely tempted the local authorities to abdicate their responsibilities and leave it to the Commission to make the payments. Here was an area where the proper division of responsibility between local and national agencies needed to be clarified.

The second major difficulty had to do with the place of discretionary powers within the supplementary benefit system. Ever since 1948 Assistance and Benefit officers had been given wide powers to make extra payments over and above the basic scale-rates. These could be either regular weekly additions, or single lump-sum payments. The law laid down few restrictions to the exercise of this discretion. In practise the exercise of these powers at local level was severely circumscribed by the detailed guidelines laid down in the 'A' Code, which the officer was expected to follow. Some indication of these guidelines was given in the Handbook, but none the less the exercise of discretion seemed to many to be an arbitrary business. Claimants were unsure of their rights, and unable to establish whether any particular claim had been properly determined.

The Commission was worried about the increasing number of successful claims for these additions. They argued that they were intended to deal only with exceptional needs or circumstances, but that in practice they were becoming commonplace. In the first annual report it was noted that 'the replacement of National Assistance by Supplementary Benefit in 1966 was intended to simplify administration and clarify civil rights by reducing the number of discretionary extra payments' (SBC, 1976, para 2. 16). But this intention was never realised. Both regular and single payments increased with each passing year. Between 1968 and 1979 regular additions rose from 540,000 to 2,252,000, and lump-sum payments from 470,000 to 1,134,000 (SBC, 1980, pp. 147–8).

Gradually the discussion centred upon a number of themes which would be important elements in any reform of the scheme: the simplification of the rules and regulations for easier and more consistent administration, and a substantial reduction of the scope for and reliance upon discretionary additions. A new suggestion was that the regulations should be published so that everyone would know their rights and entitlements, reducing uncertainty and removing the cause of many disputes and disagreements. All of these points were stressed in the report of an internal review of Supplementary Benefit carried out by officers of the DHSS. *Social Assistance* was published in 1978 and distributed in the spirit of a Green Paper, as a discussion document (DHSS). The DHSS encouraged and promoted meetings of interested parties to discuss the proposals, and invited written and other comment. The Commission itself took part in this process, publishing its own reactions to the report. There is no doubt that the Social Security Acts of 1980 reflected parts of this prolonged process of consultation and argument; but there is equally no doubt that they were profoundly influenced by the new approach to welfare issues of the recently-elected Thatcher administration.

VI

The Social Security Acts of 1980 represent the most far-reaching reform of social assistance since 1948. The legislation was prepared in the first few months of Mrs Thatcher's administration, and was an early attempt to arrest the growth of the Welfare State, and to put new and stringent limits to the growth of public expenditure. It was also to end the Donnison experiment in open administration, as the Commission was to be abolished as an autonomous agency and its work was to be absorbed into the Department, subject to day-to-day ministerial control from the headquarters at the Elephant and Castle.

It is too soon to hazard a final judgment on the revised scheme; but it is not too soon to trace the clear drift of policy, and to be keenly aware of some of its consequences. It is also possible to give a preliminary evaluation of how closely the new system fulfils its stated intentions. Are the rules and regulations simpler to understand and to administer, and has their publication meant that claimants now understand their entitlements more clearly than before?

The main thrust of the change has been to make the Supplementary Benefit scheme much more legalistic. In place of very general powers, the Department is now bound by detailed regulations which have the full force of law. The Acts and regulations are to be found in a loose-leaf file, known as the Yellow Book. The revised Yellow Book was published in late 1980; by March 1982, barely fifteen months later, it had been added to and amended by no fewer than nine substantial supplements (HMSO 1982). In all it amounts to several hundred pages of text. Many of the regulations are extremely complex, and they are all couched in a legal jargon that is often, for a layman, quite impenetrable. Experienced welfare rights advisers have difficulty in mastering the regulations; an untutored or unrepresented claimant would find them unintelligible if he had ready access to them, which he has not. Rather as before, claimants and their advisers must rely upon the Department's own Handbook, DHSS leaflets, or upon the one or two guides and Handbooks prepared by independent organisations. As an exercise in administrative simplification, the new system has largely failed; as an exercise in the clarification of citizen's rights it has entirely, and cynically, failed.

The shift from policy to law has helped to erode, but not to abolish, the exercise of discretion. Here the biggest change is in the area of lump-sum additional payments. Such payments are still possible, but now they are governed by a set of regulations which attempts to specify with maximum precision just what needs may be met and subject to what conditions. These regulations are in general restrictive; they narrow considerably the scope for payment. Moreover it is clear that in many local offices they are being interpreted as narrowly and as restrictively as possible. No statistics are yet available for 1981, but it is to be expected that the number of single payments (half of which in 1979 were for necessary items of clothing and footwear) has been sharply reduced.

The problem of the 'frontier areas' has been clarified. There is now one categorical regulation which indicates that no matter how great the need, nor how serious the consequences, the Supplementary Benefit Officer may not make a payment wherever another authority has the power to do so. In many cases these powers are permissive rather than mandatory, and often the authorities concerned will not, as a matter of policy, make payments. In such cases, where before there might have been some confusion about whether a payment would be made, there is now the certainty that it will not.

In short the quest for clarity has led to complexity and the desire to be specific about entitlement has restricted and confined benefit. For the claimant, the going has got rougher, and without expert help his chances of any effective redress have been (in practice) reduced.

And all of these changes have been made in the context of marked and mounting official suspicions about abuse, and some striking changes in the procedures for rooting it out. In the months before the 1980 Acts there was a fresh and prolonged outburt of 'scrounger-mania', but this time much of it was Government-inspired. Mr R. Prentice made it clear that part of the process of 'breaking the mould' required the establishment of over 1,000 new Civil Service posts, as Special Investigators.

The development of this function says much about the opposed forces of welfare and control within the benefit system. Special Investigators were first appointed by the National Assistance Board in 1953, although there is no mention of them until the annual report of 1957 when there were 27 of them. By 1965 there were 107, and in 1972 the Fisher Committee noted that there were 329 such posts (HMSO 1973). By 1980 there were over 400, and the number was still growing, but the creation of over 1,000 new posts is a striking indication of the high priority to be given to this work.

In addition to the increased numbers, there were to be innovations in the methods of investigation. Traditionally the investigators were attached to the regional office, and they were called out when the local office had reason to suspect abuse. But some of the 1,000 new officers operate differently, as the secret but widely-leaked instructions make clear.

> These documents reveal the setting-up of 'special exercise teams' and the creation of a non-prosecution interview, which can result in benefit being withdrawn on the basis of allegations or evidence which the DHSS knows would not hold water in a court of law (Moore, 1981, 138–9).

Squads of these officers move from area to area in a series of intensive operations which include the investigation of randomly-selected claimants, as well as more systematic probing of a number of clearly identified 'target-groups'. The Department's instructions urge investigators to show a proper concern for correct procedure. But there is a consider-able and growing weight of evidence that these instructions are not always followed scrupulously. The Society of Civil Servants, for example, is concerned that 'investigators are being asked to conduct interviews with the aim of persuading the person concerned to withdraw their claim to benefit', and we know about some of the methods of persuasion.

Examples of the kinds of pressure being put upon claimants at the moment include, the destruction of order books in front of the claimant, the promise of 'no further action' in return for admissions, the promise of emergency payments in return for admissions. There is disturbing evidence that techniques very close to 'entrapment' are being used (CPAG 1981: 3).

There is also considerable unease about the way in which interviews are sometimes conducted; claimants have been subjected to prolonged and aggressive cross-examination by pairs of investigators in locked inter-view rooms. All of these methods are prohibited in the Department's instructions. The only fair conclusion that one can reach is that the Department cannot control its own staff, who in turn are responding to strong pressures to achieve results from the Department itself. The only people to suffer are many blameless and vulnerable people who are humiliated and frightened, and all too often wrongfully deprived of benefit.

In 1948 they hoped to create a humane and dignified scheme for helping the poorest, and to abandon once and for all the mean-spirited parsimony of the old Poor Law and the Unemployment Assistance Board. But with the passage of time, and as the needs for assistance evolved in unexpected ways, we have seen the gradual weakening of the welfare resolve and the reassertion, in modern guise, of attitudes and assumptions about the poor that derive from an earlier and harsher tradition. Mrs Braddock hoped that the time was passing when men must 'show the soles of their boots before another pair could be given to them'. One can imagine her robust reaction had she lived to read in the Notes of Guidance of the Chief Benefit Officer that claimants requiring an item of replacement clothing 'should be asked to produce the item which should be examined to see whether it has been damaged to the extent that replacement of the item, rather than repair, is necessary' (DHSS 1981). It would seem that, despite earlier reports to the contrary, Mr Bumble, the Beadle, is alive and well, and lives near the Elephant and Castle.

References

CPAG (1981), *Welfare Rights Bulletin*, no. 41. (April).

DHSS (1978), *Social Assistance*, HMSO.

DHSS (1981), *Notes of Guidance of the Chief Supplementary Benefits Officer*.

HMSO (1973), *Report of the Committee on Abuse of Social Security Benefits*, Cmnd 5228.

HMSO (1982), *The Law relating to Supplementary Benefits and Family Income Supplement* (known as the Yellow Book).

Moore, P. (1981), 'Scroungermania at the DHSS', New Society, 22 January, pp. 138–9.

SBC (1976), *Annual Report 1975*, HMSO.

SBC (1980), *Annual Report 1979*, HMSO.

Chapter 10
Social welfare and the education of social workers
Robert Pinker

For many years the relationship between social administration and social work possessed all the qualities of a marriage of convenience in which a prolonged courtship was taking place. Quite recently the private life of this household was interrupted by the arrival on the doorstep of a sociological lodger who wanted to join the family and reorganise its domestic arrangements as well. A once orderly and respectable household has now become a tempestuous *ménage à trois*.

The growth of social work education

During the 1950s and 1960s most social work courses were specialised. Apart from a few generic applied social studies courses, the majority of students specialised in a particular field of practice – child care, mental health, probation, or almoning, as it was then called. The first generic course was established at the London School of Economics in 1954 with a grant from the Carnegie Foundation. Genericism was then a principle rather than practice of social work education. It was based on the assumption that there was a body of skills, methods and knowledge common to all social workers, irrespective of the settings in which they were employed or the clientele they served (Donnison *et al.*, 1975, ch. 11; Younghusband, 1978).

Throughout the 1960s this model became steadily more popular among the growing number of social work courses. Other pressures towards the unification of social work gave added momentum to this trend. The establishment in 1970 of the British Association of Social Workers brought together representatives from all the various specialist areas of social work, with the exception of the National Association of Probation Officers. The future pattern of social work practice in England and Wales was anticipated by the recommendations of the Kilbrandon Committee in 1964, and the subsequent establishment in 1968 of unified social work departments (including probation and after-care) throughout the Scottish local authorities (HMSO, 1964). In England and Wales, in 1968, the Seebohm Committee also recommended the creation of a single social services department in each local authority, and this was implemented by the Local Authority Social Services Act of 1970 (HMSO, 1968). The probation and after-care service remained separate. Coinciding with this reorganisation of social work practice, the establishment of the Central Council for Education and Training in Social Work (CCETSW) in 1971 was a further stage in the trend towards unification at a national level.

Shortly afterwards CCETSW introduced a single professional qualification, the Certificate of Qualification in Social Work (CQSW), which was based on generic principles and focused on the burgeoning needs of the new local authority multi-purpose social service and social work departments. CCETSW assumed responsibility for validating all social work courses, including those for the professional education of probation and after-care officers. The probation and after-care service insisted, however, that their students should receive some specialist academic and practice teaching. Throughout the 1970s the number of non-graduate, undergraduate and post-graduate social work courses and students continued to grow.

CCETSW did not attempt to impose a uniform syllabus on the colleges, but it did begin to insist that courses should be based on generic principles and it also encouraged them to draw more heavily on the contributory social science disciplines. Over the years CCETSW has formulated a set of rules and guidelines which colleges are expected to observe, but even so the heterogeneous nature of its courses is still one of the distinctive features of British social work education (CCETSW, 1981 and paper 15.1).

The growth of social work was greatly stimulated by the generous funding of these courses. In the case of students, the majority received grants from either the DHSS, the Home Office or a seconding local authority, but in 1974 a significant change occurred in the funding of the courses. Before 1974 the colleges received a separate grant for social work education. Since then the grant has been absorbed into the total UGC budget. Consequently social work no longer enjoys the *apparent* distinction of bringing additional funding to the colleges. It has to bid for internal resources like any other subject. The costs of education in social work are higher per student than those in other social science subjects. Until recently this was offset by the fact that social work attracted a sizeable number of fully funded post-graduate students, but that advantage is melting away because of the reduction in grants. Since its introduction by CCETSW in 1975, the new Certificate in Social Service (CSS) has grown in popularity with the local authorities because CSS training courses are cheaper to run than CQSW courses.[1] And there are other reasons why this is happening. In effect the growth years of CQSW training courses are probably over, partly because roughly 70 per cent of all field social workers are now professionally qualified, and further recruitment has been drastically curtailed because of the cutbacks in public expenditure. The majority of residential workers are still untrained, but the CSS is likely to absorb some of this demand in the years ahead, and the most that the CQSW courses can hope for is a 'steady state', although even that looks doubtful.

The growth in the number of social work courses and students was complemented throughout the 1970s by a remorseless extension of syllabuses. In both social work theory and practice and the contributory disciplines the trend towards genericism demanded an increased range of skills, methods and knowledge from both staff and students, but the duration of the courses has remained constant, and 50 per cent of every course is allocated to supervised practice teaching.

CCETSW's revised 1981 guidelines give some idea of the range of subject-matter in social work courses which are expected to include social work theories and practice and relevant aspects of social policy and administration; central and local government; the social functions of law and the courts; processes of human development, socialisation and functioning; the nature of moral behaviour; and social institutions and theories of social change. In addition students must be able to demonstrate 'a capacity to transfer learning and apply it to practice in respect of either a particular client group or a particular context of practice' (CCETSW, 1981). The guidelines state that not all the various items have to receive equal weighting, or be separately assessed; none the less their implications for teaching and learning are formidable.

The commitment to genericism is a primary cause of the expansion in syllabus content. In principle, students are required to become at least familiar with the three main methods of social work intervention – social casework, group work and community work, in the context of several agency settings and client groups, and with some specialisation in one of these groups. In addition CCETSW periodically draws attention to special issues which are said to be neglected, for example child abuse, the needs of the elderly or the problems of ethnic minorities. Setting aside the normal constraints of time and resources, it is true to say that every social work course chooses to 'neglect' some aspect of this vast requirement – if only to preserve the well-being of its staff and students. On top of this, generically orientated courses call for a high input of social science teaching, and this is another reason for the growth in syllabus content.

Developments in sociology and social administration

Between the early 1950s and the late 1970s there were significant changes in the relationship between social work, social administration and sociology. In the early 1950s social administration began to develop as an undergraduate subject in its own right. Social administration teachers started to assert their own academic identity, and to play down the historical association between social administration and social work. Sociology was already several decades ahead in this respect, and its own relationship with social administration was at best ambivalent throughout the 1950s and the 1960s, when both subjects were gaining in student popularity. By the late 1960s – although there were some important exceptions – the subject fields of sociology, social administration and social work had virtually drawn apart and become separate academic entities.

It is not easy to make generalisations about the processes of change that began in the late 1960s, or to give precise dates to what was an overall, but uneven, trend. In social administration and to a lesser extent in sociology, major research enquiries into subjects like poverty, educational disadvantage, urban deprivation and housing policy drew increasing attention to the social rather than the personal causes of need. The considerable expansion of sociological studies was characterised by a general emphasis on theory, and various types of 'critical' theory deriving from Marxism and phenomenology added a radical edge to the reformist implications of social administration in both teaching and research.

An increasing proportion of new social work students were graduates in sociology or social administration or some combination of the social sciences. A new generation of teachers with the same sort of background was recruited to the growing number of social work courses. As the expansion of social science courses slowed down, it became easier to staff social work courses with teachers from the contributory disciplines.

Social work staff and students alike were becoming more critical of what they perceived as the narrow preoccupation of an older generation with psychodynamic theories and the personal causes of need. Casework became almost a reprehensible practice, associated with political 'quietism', 'blaming the victim' and 'sustaining unjust systems of social control'. These were the beginnings of 'radical' social work, in which the social worker is intended to become an 'agent' of social change, primarily concerned with meeting the material needs of his clients, and challenging the 'system'.[2]

This was the motive force of the sociological deluge that swept through social work and social administration in the mid 1970s, shifting the focus of the debate about social welfare from micro to macro issues. For different reasons both social administration and social work were partly susceptible and partly resistant to invasion by highly ideological forms of normative social theory (Mishra, 1981; Room, 1979; Parry *et al.* 1979; Gough, 1979; Hadley and Hatch, 1981; Ginsburg, 1979; Jones *et al.*, 1978; George and Wilding, 1976).

Social administration has always attracted academics who are committed to social reform and eager to put social science knowledge to practical use. For many years normative debate within the discipline was dominated by a broadly collectivist and reformist consensus, but that was sharply challenged in the 1970s by both Marxist and free-market critiques of the Welfare State and the mixed economy. These attacks coincided with the deterioration of Britain's economic performance and the introduction of new policies of welfare retrenchment.

Unlike the more theoretical traditions in the social sciences, however, social administration has its focus in a specific set of social institutions and the practical application of theories to issues and policies of social welfare. The various theoretical critiques of social administration coincided with a growth of interest in comparative studies within the subject (Higgins, 1981; Rodgers *et al.*, 1979; George and Manning, 1980; Pinker, 1979; Madison, 1980). This development of comparative studies is now beginning to generate a great deal of *evidence* about what happens to the welfare of ordinary people when theories of radical change are converted into actual policies. In the contexts of social policy it is not so easy to dismiss the outcomes of these political experiments –

either Marxist or free-market ones – as aberrations attributable to bad leadership, bad timing or unpropitious economic circumstances.

Comparative research in social work is less developed – for several reasons. Major problems arise in any attempt to hold definitions of the personal social services and social work constant in cross-national studies. There is a high degree of substitutability within the personal social services, and between these and other services. In some countries there are no social workers; in others they are deployed in different settings, under different titles. In these respects at least, social work is more exposed to the influence of macro theories of social change, despite the relatively modest scope of its own activities.

Social administration and sociology are no longer contingent on social work, having become scholarly enterprises in their own right. On the other hand the contribution to social work education from both disciplines is far more substantial than it was twenty years ago, partly because of the growth of genericism and partly because there were plenty of social scientists looking for academic careers in the applied social sciences. It is therefore vitally important that social work clarifies its own educational objectives in what has become a multi-disciplinary activity.

Some writers such as Davies (1981, pp. 194–5) consider that the positive contribution of sociology to social work has been negligible. There is no doubt that some of the sociological literature on social work agrees with this assessment, but takes the view that the solution lies in changing the nature of social work in such a way that sociological knowledge will become more relevant. Another way of interpreting this argument is to say that social work ought to become a contributory discipline to applied sociology.

The effectiveness of social work and the authenticity of its knowledge base have been the subject of continuous criticism since the mid 1950s. The 'legitimacy' of social work intervention is currently under attack from both political extremes. The universalist promise of the Seebohm reforms is not being fulfilled. Conflict is said to exist between the 'managerial' ethos of the new departments and the claims of professional autonomy and discretion. Demand continues to outpace the supply of personal social services. It is not surprising that social work is suffering much uncertainty about its own identity and purposes.

The rapid and continuous growth of social work overrode any attempt to identify and determine its proper limits. The absence of settled objectives in social work was part of a wider failure to define a sensible mandate for the personal social services.

The origins of the problem can be traced back to the Seebohm Report which, having failed to agree on specific objectives, achieved consensus by extending the potential scope of the personal social services to the whole community. The report drew too vague a distinction between welfare needs and other needs in terms of the primary functions of key personnel such as social workers and home helps; it espoused the concept of need without defining it; in the name of 'prevention' it licensed the new social services departments to seek out needs wherever they might be found; and all this was done without specification of the resource implications (HMSO, 1968).

From the start the new departments were burdened with universalist expectations, but not supplied with the necessary resources. On the basis of very cursory discussion, Seebohm had endorsed the generic principle, which is essentially an expansionist concept. The narrower concept of social casework no longer fitted the 'community-orientated' activities of the new departments. Genericism challenged what seemed to be the pre-eminence of social casework, and offered the prospect of equal partnership to group work and community work.

It was forgotten for a time that genericism is a method of teaching social work to individual students as well as a method of practising social work on the basis of multi-specialist teams. Even in training it is impossible to do more than give the student a limited degree of familiarity with the overall range of methods and skills. In practice the distinctive method of social work intervention is social casework on a one-to-one basis. Admittedly, since most individuals live in families, there cannot be a clear-cut division between social casework and group work, but the latter is only a logical extension of the former. Both types of intervention mainly take the form of direct work with individuals. Community work, by its very nature, is largely indirect work with extremely varied groups of people. It has affinities with social work, but it is essentially a different kind of activity. There is a place for community workers in generic teams but, in my view, specialisation ought to be given more emphasis in generic social work education, and there should be a clearer division of labour in area team practice.

The importance that was given to the concepts of community, prevention and genericism – with all their universalist pretensions – left social work with an expansionist outlook which became less and less appropriate as resources began to shrink. Government policies reflected this basic inconsistency between declared ends and available means. From 1969 onwards major legislation affecting the personal social services continued to reach the statute books, either with important sections delayed until resources became available, or without the resources needed for local authorities to meet new and ill-defined responsibilities. The gap between universalist promises and selectivist realities grew steadily larger, not only in the personal social services but in the other major sectors of welfare provision. An increasing proportion of social work was taken up with trying to cope with the referrals and failures of other social services, and many social services departments, in the struggle to conserve inadequate resources, imposed stricter limits on the autonomy and discretionary powers of social workers.

These policy trends partly explain why the times are propitious for those who stress the social causes of need and believe that the social services are no more than one of the controlling instruments of an oppressive society, and that the social workers should cease to be agents of control and should become agents of change. However, the point at issue is not the causes of need, but whether social workers ought to be more concerned with social issues, and who would assume responsibility for personal issues if their priorities were changed.

Genericism has become the other part of the problem. The term 'genericism' was taken to describe a body of knowledge and skills which would be common to all social workers and which would give social work its distinctive identity as an occupation. But no consensus emerged within the profession as to what that identity might be; genericism simply flowed into and took its form from the channels left by the currents of social and economic change.

Under conditions of sustained growth relatively generous funding of more and more activities was added to the remit of social work, in a mood of buoyant and unreflecting optimism. Social work was always being redefined by reference to the last pot-pourri of roles and tasks it had acquired, or the next miscellany it was about to incorporate. Under conditions of deepening economic recession and retrenchment the emphasis shifts towards advocacy, welfare rights and community action. The options have become almost limitless in an occupation which has happily pre-empted every known kind of social intervention in the personal social services. In these ways genericism holds on to the 'identity' of social work by an act of perpetual motion. Growth and thought in social work are inversely related; the more we have of one, the less we get of the other.

Retrenchment has given social workers an opportunity to make use of adversity by having to carry out a realistic reappraisal of the true identity and basic purposes of social work, and of how they can best serve the community. This search for occupational identity ought to lead us back to the relevant skills and tasks of practice. Theories can be useful in the search, if we take care to avoid those which have defined *in advance* what those skills and tasks should be.

Social work is an activity of compromise and reconciliation which is no more compatible with a conflict model of society than it is with a model of society based on assumptions of consensus. It takes account of all kinds of theories, but its function is to help people whose problems frequently defy theoretical explanation. Social work intervention takes place on the disputed frontiers of the personal and social worlds within which people have to order their lives.

CCETSW encouraged the expansion of social work curricula during the early 1970s. More recently it has stressed the need to achieve a greater degree of 'integration' between the various parts of college-based teaching and between college-based and agency-based teaching. In 'The enterprise of social work' I argued that 'integrated knowledge is dead knowledge', and there are several aspects to my argument. First, I think that

> There is no simple way of reconciling the determinism of certain social and psychological theories with the moral theories which uphold the principles of free will and self-determination. Every probation officer (for example) has to weigh the evidence of mitigating circumstances against the claims of personal accountability. If this sort of dilemma could be easily resolved, we would not need to train professional workers to exercise personal judgement (Pinker, 1981).

Second, in a professional course you cannot actually 'integrate' the sort of theories which challenge the very legitimacy and utility of the profession concerned. In the case of social work education you either have to change the definitions and aims of the whole enterprise of social work to accommodate the new theories or you have to expose the fundamental discrepancies between social work practice and the practical implications of the new theories. The first option will lead to 'integration' by takeover and metamorphosis, and the second rules out integration in every sense of the term.

Third, you cannot introduce radical changes in the aims and content of college-based teaching without reference to the aims and content of agency-based teaching and practice. Since there are a number of agencies associated with every college, such changes are unlikely to encourage 'integration'. Unless there is a working consensus between the colleges and the agencies, it is difficult to imagine how anything worth while can be achieved. We must bear in mind that agencies are responsible to their employers, the local authorities, which are bound by a whole range of statutory obligations. Nearly every social work student is grant-aided by authorities which are directly or indirectly his future employers.

A social work course therefore needs to maintain a balance between various educational objectives which are not entirely compatible. Within the college-based part of the curriculum there must be enough consensus for students to develop confidence and competence as future practitioners, and for agency-based supervisors to feel that they are part of a common enterprise. This leads me to my fourth point, namely, that integration must not be taken to the point at which the roles of college teacher and agency supervisor become indistinguishable. In the first place CCETSW licenses the colleges and not the agencies to assess and examine students. Agency supervisors have a part to play in this process, but the final decisions are taken by a properly constituted Board of Examiners.

There is another necessary limit to integration between colleges and agencies. The emphasis in agency supervision rests on the application of knowledge to a range of accepted skills which the student must acquire. College teachers must be able both to complement and reinforce this learning, and to take a broader and a longer view. It is part of their job to investigate the state of knowledge in their field, and to advance knowledge, sometimes by challenging existing practices. If this does not happen, social work education will either become an ossified form of apprenticeship regulated by guilds of practitioners or a diverse set of activities without general structure or regulation. This is not to draw a sharp distinction between original academics and conventional practitioners. Practitioners ought to have more opportunities for innovation and for further formal learning, and some of them do in fact undertake research. The point I am making is that original research is an essential part of the academic vocation.

None the less the broader issues and the long-term perspective in professional education still have to be contained within certain limits of institutional tolerance, but this should not interfere with academic freedom in social work education any more than it does in medical education. Both professional activities are partly regulated by legal imperatives, although the analogy is not an exact one. There are certain tasks which only doctors are allowed to perform. In social work there are certain tasks which only statutory authorities are allowed or required to perform. In the context of the local authorities the law does not specify that only qualified social workers will be allowed to undertake certain statutory duties.

Nevertheless statutory duties absorb a great deal of the time and energy of social workers. They include supervising children and young persons who are at risk, or who are the subject of care proceedings; making enquiries in connection with fostering and adoption; making recommendations to courts; administering probation orders and parole licences; making pre-release reports with reference to mental health, penal and other residential settings; allocating scarce resources in cash and kind; and arranging admissions into psychiatric care and other kinds of residential provision.

Given this and all the other aspects of social work, it would go beyond the limits of tolerance and credibility if a large proportion of social work courses were to be devoted to a sustained critique of the nature of social work itself. There are other parts of academic life in which such issues can be explored at length. The first duty of a professional course is to produce capable practitioners. Who would want to be treated by a doctor, most of whose professional training had been taken up with a critique of existing medical knowledge and practice, and with learning a new and untested approach to medical care?

Social work will always be open to distraction and demoralisation unless it establishes a firmer and more realistic consensus about its roles and tasks. Its basic strengths derive, like those of social administration, from its direct access to a field of practice. In both disciplines the average social theory has the frontline life expectancy of an infantry subaltern in the First World War. Theory of any kind should be treated with caution in applied social science activities. If a theory is deficient or if it is misapplied, clients are the ones who suffer.

Prescriptive theories of social change are governed by a higher law: the scale of social change is proportionately related to the number of social casualties resulting from that change. If social workers have a vested interest in theories of radical social change, it is surely limited to the purely professional sense in which doctors and undertakers can be said to have a vested interest in epidemics.

Defining social work

What kinds of knowledge and skill do social workers need in order to do their job, and how should the job be defined? This essay was written a few weeks before the publication date of the Barclay Committee's Report on the Role and Tasks of Social Workers, so I can only quote from my own contribution to the report. Many social work skills, I suggested,

> are the normal skills of sociable living, although it would be misleading to labour this point. The crucial difference arises from the distinctive use to which social workers put these skills, the type of clientele they serve, the type of context in which they work and the nature of the mandate by which their work is authorised. These are the factors that shape the role and tasks of social workers, and accordingly the skills of social work are informed by a great deal of specialised knowledge.

I went on to argue that

> Social work and social casework are virtually synonymous, but my definition of social casework is a broad one, which includes counselling and various practical tasks. The counselling part of social casework is carried out through the use of a professional relationship between the social worker and the client (and other people who are immediately affected), as the means of helping the client to manage his own life (Barclay Committee Report, 1982).

The above quotations are part of a more developed argument which can be read elsewhere. I then pointed out that the responsibilities and powers – some of which are mentioned above – are vested in the social worker by an employing agency, and that they cannot be 'brushed under the carpet of egalitarianism' or made subordinate to other less precise community-based activities. I concluded that a great deal of social work is necessarily and properly a task of 'maintenance, containment, control and support', so it is inevitable that social workers will find numerous examples of misery and injustice in the course of their work, but this does not justify switching the focus of social work from personal to political objectives. They already have at their disposal the normal channels of communication and influence in their agencies through which to get a better deal for their clients, and they have their professional associations through which to inform public opinion about the shortcomings of social policy. Social workers have to accept the fact that demand for their services is connected with the failures rather than the successes of social policy, whatever type of society they may work in. Their view of social life is both a special and a partial one.

> Because of the enormous complexity, variety and range of needs calling for social work intervention, the case for specialisation is self-evident. The important question is, can specialisation be developed in such a way that appropriate attention will be given to each individual client as a whole person rather than as a collection of separate problems? It is my contention that the demands of generalist and specialist social work can be reconciled within a properly organised system of care based on adequately staffed generic area teams in which there is a sensible division of labour (Pinker, 1981).

These views express my opposition to any further dilution of the tasks of social workers, especially those which would involve them further in ill-defined community-based activities. I unreservedly accept the need to make better use of volunteers and informal care networks, but I do not see why social workers should be extensively used on work of this kind – or how they could be used in this way, without causing local authorities to default on their statutory duties. I am especially critical of the current enthusiasm for the patch-based systems of social work. In my view it is likely to lead to serious inequities in the allocation of resources, breakdowns in systems of accountability and a general decline in the quality of social work practice.

It does not surprise me that the patch model appeals equally to left-wing and right-wing radicals. Each group of advocates hopes for a completely different outcome. Those who hope that patch systems can be used to shift the burden of responsibility and financial cost from the formal to the informal networks of care at least have logic and *realpolitik* on their side. By contrast it is a romantic illusion of the left to suppose that populist sentiment can be harnessed and channelled by social workers through local communities to bring about radical change in the structure of a society. It is clear, however, that some left-wing radicals have learned very little from the recent history of other community-based initiatives. Their enthusiasm for community-based models indicates how easily, as Kipling once wrote, 'the burnt Fool's bandaged finger goes wobbling back to the fire'.[3]

My whole concern is that social work should continue to provide a service of the highest possible quality to people who are needy, vulnerable, damaged, delinquent or unhappy. The idea that community-based activities can create a basis for radical social change in a complex industrial society is political fiction; the idea that social work can be adapted to this end is political science fiction. The essential concern of social work is maintenance at a personal level, not change at a societal level. All societies undergo change in the normal course of events, and in all societies which employ social workers – or their equivalent – the job of social work includes helping the inevitable victims of social change.

The future relationship between social work, social administration, sociology and the other related social sciences ought to be one in which each subject has access to what it needs from the others. They are complementary, but different undertakings. Social work education requires an explicit definition of its own scope and limits if it is to enjoy – and deserve – parity of respect within the social sciences.

Notes

1 For a useful discussion of this form of training see CCETSW, Paper 9.4, *The certificate in social service,* a Progress Report to the Council from the Staff, 1979. The decision by Council to start these courses was taken in 1974, and the first three schemes began in September 1975. See p. 18.

2 See Trevor Pateman, *Counter Course: A Handbook for Course Criticism.* This interesting set of papers illustrates the growth in the range and variety of Marxist critiques of teaching in the social sciences which had taken place by the early 1970s. The preface begins by stating that 'We have produced this handbook for the use of students in higher education who find their courses boring, cramped by exams, methodologically unsound or with content politically obnoxious in its only possible real-world uses. In short, for students who find that their education consists of being processed for a particular niche in the class structure of society' (p. 7). The chapter on 'Social Workers: Training and Professionalism' by Crescy Cannon indicts both 'casework' and 'community' as 'reactionary', but argues that 'community work' is 'a better alternative to traditional casework' because it is a potential 'foundation for militant action' (p. 261).

3 The best up-to-date reviews of trends in radical social work are Mike Brake and Roy Bailey, *Radical Social Work and Practice,* and Steve Bolger, Paul Corrigan, Jan Docking and Nick Frost, *Towards Socialist Welfare Work.* In 1981 a new journal, *Critical Social Policy,* was set up to 'serve as a forum to encourage and develop an understanding of welfare from socialist, feminist and radical perspectives', and it invites support from 'the academic social

science community' and from 'workers and practitioners in the Welfare State, particularly social workers, advice workers and the increasingly wide range of activists in all social services' (*Critical Social Policy*, vol. 1, no. 1, Summer 1981, p. 1).

References

Bolger, S., *et al.* (1981), *Towards Socialist Welfare Work*, London, Macmillan.

Barclay Committee Report (1982), *Social Workers: Their Roles and Tasks*, London, NISW, Bedford Square Press.

Brake, M., and Bailey, R. (1980), *Radical Social Work and Practice* (2nd edn.), London, Edward Arnold.

CCETSW (1979), *The certificate in social service*.

CCETSW (1981), *Guidelines for courses leading to the certificate of qualification in social work*.

Davies, M. (1981), *The Essential Social Worker*, London, Heinemann.

Donnison, D., *et al.* (1975), *Social Policy and Administration Revisited*, London, Allen & Unwin.

George, V., and Manning, N. (1980), *Socialism, Social Welfare and the Soviet Union*, London, Routledge & Kegan Paul.

George, V., and Wilding, P. (1976), *Ideology and Social Welfare*, London, Routledge & Kegan Paul.

Ginsburg, N. (1979), *Class, Capital and Social Policy*, London, Macmillan.

Gough, I. (1979), *The Political Economy of the Welfare State*, London, Macmillan.

Hadley, R., and Hatch, S. (1981), *Social Welfare and the Failure of the Welfare State*, London, Allen & Unwin.

HMSO (1964), Report of the committee on children and young persons (Scotland), Cmnd 2306 (Kilbrandon Report).

HMSO (1968), Report of the Committee on local authority and allied personal social services, Cmnd 3703 (Seebohm Report).

Higgins, J. (1981), *States of Welfare: Comparative Analysis in Social Policy*, Oxford, Basil Blackwell; London, Martin Robertson.

Jones, K., *et al.* (1978), *Issues in Social Policy*, London, Routledge & Kegan Paul.

Madison, B. (1980), *The Meaning of Social Policy*, London, Croom Helm.

Mishra, R. (1981), *Society and Social Policy*, London, Macmillan.

Parry, N., *et al.* (1979), *Social Work, Welfare and the State*, London, Edward Arnold.

Pateman, T. (1972), *Counter Course: A Handbook for Course Criticism*, Harmondsworth, Penguin.

Pinker, R. (1979), *The Idea of Welfare*, London, Heinemann.

Pinker, R. (1981), 'The enterprise of social work', inaugural lecture, London School of Economics and Political Science.

Rodgers, B., *et al.* (1979), *The Study of Social Policy: A Comparative Approach*, London, Allen & Unwin.

Room, G. (1979), *The Sociology of Welfare*, Oxford, Basil Blackwell; London, Martin Robertson.

Younghusband, E. (1978), *Social Work in Britain 1975: A Follow-up Study*, vol. 2, London, Allen & Unwin.

Chapter 11
Crime and the welfare state
Terence Morris

There can be hardly anyone whose political consciousness goes back as far as 1945 who can have forgotten what the very mention of the words 'Welfare State' could do in the most civilised of social gatherings. Almost more than the word 'nationalisation' it could polarise the conversation at a dinner table throughout the six post-war years of Attlee's Labour administration. It excited the kinds of passions, stimulated the sorts of prejudices and produced the kinds of misinformed comment that characterise those issues that are the essential accompaniment of ideological conflict between the seemingly irreconcilable beliefs of those who glower at each other from the opposing camps of the two great political parties. Labour, with its massive majority of 196 in the Commons, was embarking upon the most extensive programme of social legislation since the Liberal government of 1906. The Liberals themselves had been all but annihilated in the election and the Conservatives, having taken a considerable battering, were dispirited that notwithstanding Churchill's leadership they had been spurned by the voters. Thus the exuberance of Labour and the gloomy bitterness of the Conservatives combined to produce a great acidity in the debates on the Bills that were to found the new 'Welfare State'.

It is important to get some of the history right before it is possible to disentangle some of the arguments. The Liberals, after their landslide victory in 1906, had begun to introduce measures to alleviate the worst excesses of the poverty that had become the inevitable consequence of the later stages of industrial capitalism. In the context of a nearly free market the wealth of late-Victorian and Edwardian England had been based in part upon an ample supply of cheap labour. The political consequences of this at a time when the right to vote was being gradually extended downwards did not escape the more astute political realists of the day. In Germany Bismarck had already seen fit to head off the growth of a socialist opposition by introducing various welfare packages that were dubbed 'state socialism'. By 1906 it had become clear in Britain, both from the independent surveys of Rowntree and Booth and the experience of the recruiting sergeants mustering men to fight the Boers, that the consequences of this poverty – disease, malnutrition, drink and criminality – had rendered a significant section of the lower orders of society of marginal utility for service in either the factory or the battlefield. It was a situation in which the moral demands of humanitarianism coincided with the instrumental requirements of an imperialist industrial society. It is perhaps no accident that the legislation that produced a school medical service and the first comprehensive Children's Act also gave us the borstal system, the juvenile court and the seeds of the probation service. It also provided the first Labour Exchanges (lineal ancestors of the modern Job Centres) and a limited form of state medicine in the institution of the 'Panel' doctor. Whereas the elderly had until then been dependent upon the Poor Law (established in 1601 and amended in 1834) they could now enjoy a five shilling pension from the state each week.

The objects of such legislation might be perceived in various ways. To the humanitarian eye they seemed proper ways of relieving the misery endured by the poor and those otherwise vulnerable through age or sickness. To the more narrowly instrumental they appeared as a way of improving the efficacy of the labour force while at the same time pulling the rug from under the socialist agitators who sought to deprive entrepreneurs and shareholders of the fruits of their industry and abstinence. To those more subtly concerned about the increasing domination of society by a philistine plutocracy, such as the *savant* and maverick Liberal MP Hilaire Belloc, these were the foundations of the Servile State. Behind it all, however, lay a deeper and in many ways more consistent social philosophy, its roots in Utilitarianism as purveyed by the younger Mill and given expression variously in the writings of Herbert Spencer and the teachings of Leonard Trelawney Hobhouse.

Social progress, it was widely believed, was a reality manifested in an inexorable forward movement of mankind. Like evolution it was a supra-human force that could not be arrested. Continually stimulated by technological advance, one of its consequences was that men would become morally better as their temporal existence improved. The positivist element in all this, which had cemented the foundations of nineteenth-century social science, was given expression in the kinds of social inquiry that provided the justification for these welfare measures. The Fabian Society was heavily involved. One cannot but speculate upon how Sidney Webb and his friends perceived the future for their infant London School of Economics and its role in the promotion of a later Welfare State by the writings of one of its subsequent Directors, William Beveridge; what is certain is that Mrs Webb, reigning supreme among the number crunchers of her day, had very clear ideas about What Had To Be Done.

The England of the Edwardian sunset that was swallowed up into the darkness of 1914 and the four years of carnage that followed provided hardly any opportunity to observe whether any of these social theories was viable. Would men become better morally as their health, their housing, their nutrition and their working conditions improved? There was really no way of knowing, save to observe events in the passage of time and the interlude of European peace that prevailed between 1919 and 1939. Unfortunately that period was characterised by the Great Depression which set in in 1929, and although it did not continue to anything like the extent of the present economic situation its effects were sufficient to push conditions of life for the poor and the marginal groups within the wage earning population back to where they had been before the temporary prosperity of the war economy of 1914–18 had lifted them up. In 1939 it was discovered that some children could not be evacuated from the poorer areas of cities because they had no footwear; had things changed so much then, since 1899 or 1909? Infant and child mortality still ran at an unacceptably high level. Among adults mortality and morbidity from the old diseases showed similar trends. Poverty was still omnipresent and if the Public Assistance had taken the place of The Guardians the spirit of Chadwick's Poor Law of 1834 remained active. And what of that time-honoured index of morality, crime? Both in terms of the number of crimes known to the police and the number of offenders before the courts it had continued to rise from 1920 onwards.

The problem of increased crime between the wars has to be viewed with caution. Many of the increased number of offenders before the courts were in fact a new class of criminals, the traffic offender, a species that multiplied at a great rate after 1930. Admittedly fewer people were going to prison, but that was largely on account of the greater use of probation. And if juveniles were less often seen in adult institutions it was because the borstal system established in 1908 and the Approved

Schools – as the old industrial and reformatory schools were renamed in 1933 – were incarcerating young offenders just as effectively.

Clearly, what benevolence had been extended by the state to the 'lower orders' of society, whether by improvements to their education, their health, their housing or their occupational prospects had achieved little by way of making them more persuaded of the attractiveness of such middle-class virtues as respect for property. It must be remembered that then, as now, the overwhelming proportion of those charged with the traditional crimes against property and of violence came from what had been known as the 'lower orders' or, in Mary Carpenter's phrase, 'the dangerous and perishing classes'. In Marxist terms it might be argued that the bulk of offenders came from a lumpenproletariat whose parasitic activities had personally irritated both Marx and Engels. Their particular expression of false consciousness had a vested interest in the maintenance of property relations as they were since their operations were largely predatory. It can be argued that it was this group, inhabiting the slum streets and tenement blocks of the great industrial cities, who profited least from that modest redistribution of income that the old Liberal legislation had stimulated. Even outside the slums proper, they became increasingly confined by deliberate housing strategy to the new 'council' estates where, despite significant improvements in housing in the form of sound if spartan construction, persistence in traditional ways resulted in these places becoming new delinquency areas.

Two problems emerge at this stage. One is the problem of deciding upon a general *theory* to explain deviant social behaviour, of which crime may be seen as the most troublesome manifestation; the other is the *strategy* by which deviance may be eliminated. Positivism in the social sciences had presented the progressive thinking Victorian with a basis for understanding every social institution and, at the same time, with a means of explaining nonconformity. Those very processes that were the manifestation of inexorable social laws had very largely eliminated individual choice from the list of available explanations. If the children of the poor stole it had to be understood in the context of their *poverty*; the have-nots stole from those who had and extremes of wealth and poverty merely accentuated the phenomenon. There was little awareness that there could be theft among those who already *had*. With the best will in the world, those humanitarian reformers who adopted such an approach to crime and delinquency never considered the possibility of their being such a thing as 'white-collar' crime. In understanding the relationship of property to the social order they were closer to Locke than to Marx.

Positivism, at least in the criminological field, has had distinctly feline qualities. No sooner was Lombroso's 'born criminal' discredited than there emerged the 'subnormally intelligent' criminal. After the improvement in intelligence testing had scotched that creature the 'disturbed' offender came on scene. And on all that great shimmering *rialto* of ideas where science and charlatanry rub shoulders the emergence of psychoanalysis was outstanding. The first child guidance *clinic* appeared somewhat improbably in Glasgow in the early 1930s. The foundation of the Institute for the Scientific Treatment of Delinquency occurred at about the same time. (The ISTD later substituted 'Study' for 'Scientific'.) The wilder excesses of forensic psychoanalysis made little impression upon those committed to traditional explanations of crime, not least in the legal profession. But if the judges were dismissive, the same was not true of the personnel of the juvenile court. In Parsonian terms the juvenile court became dominated in the 1930s by affective (female) role players. This domination was in no small part due to the dominance of the London juvenile courts where women were, and still are, quite unusually influential. The last and most pervasive strain of forensic positivism, psychoanalysis, was to leave its mark not only upon the juvenile bench, but upon the probation service for a whole generation. Those who attended the lectures of Hermann Mannheim at the LSE from 1936 onwards, even if he was not wholly committed to positivism, were nurtured in an atmosphere in which its primary assumptions were a kind of *quicunque vult*.

So much then, for the theory. Since the one striking element in the theory was the implicit irrelevance of individual *choice*, the strategy had to be based upon changes in those external constraints upon behaviour as would induce change. Of these the emphasis upon rationality in social planning was the most obvious choice. It was no coincidence that while the second war against Germany was at its height Abercrombie was beginning to shape town planning as we were to come to know it and Beveridge to produce the plan that was to become in a sense the blueprint for so much of the legislation of the Attlee government of 1945–50. Now it may of course be objected that the social positivism of Victorian and Edwardian England was vigorously countered by the traditional moralists, not least those of a religious persuasion, who not only considered that crime and vice were the result of moral choices that were deliberate, but who had serious doubts concerning the moral deserts of those in poverty. The activities of those who disbursed what was termed 'charity' no less than those who administered the system of public 'relief' provided by the local rates were exposed by writers from Dickens onwards. The attitudes which it was thought would be extinguished when the old Poor Law was finally laid to rest in 1948 persisted within the new structures. Public Assistance became National Assistance and then Social Security, yet the sorts of complaints that were once made of the way in which discretion was exercised by the old 'relieving officers' seem little different from those made about the operation of Supplementary Benefits from time to time.

But politicians, and the policy makers who stand back in the shadows behind them, are, for the most part, more frequently motivated and activated by instrumental concerns rather than high moral purposes. The Liberal legislation of 1906–11 was intended to improve the health and welfare of the nation in order that it could remain a strong influence in world politics and trade. The mood of optimism that began to grow in the wartime Britain of a generation later once it had become clear that the defeat of Germany was but a matter of time drew heavily upon the kinds of social positivism that had by now permeated the intellectual fabric of practical, and certainly radical, politics. The key word was 'planning'. The amazing success of Keynesian economics as embodied in Roosevelt's New Deal showed what could be done if indisciplined market forces could be brought under control. To the Liberal philosophy of the turn of the century and its unfinished agenda was brought the idea of rational planning, not merely in social policy, but throughout the economy. The books and especially the pamphlets of some Local Authorities produced in the period 1944–50 give some indication of the confident expectations of their authors. Harold Calvert, the Secondary Modern Headmaster in Angus Wilson's *Late Call* typifies this naïveté in his devotion to his New Town. (His wife had done a 'Social Science Certificate' – possibly at the LSE.)

Full employment, new housing, a National Health Service, the full implementation of the Butler Education Act of 1944, a new National Assistance scheme whereby poverty would be sympathetically, since objectively, overcome – these were the institutional features of the New Britain. Specifically, in the penological field, the Criminal Justice Act of 1948 would introduce legislation that would, equally, make the treatment of offenders at the same time more humane and more effective.

That 'Law 'n' Order' has today become a key political issue (though by no means as dominant as in the United States) is an interesting commentary on the failure of either social positivism or planned welfare to eliminate crime from the catalogue of social ills that continue to afflict society. But if we examine the content of political debate in the post-war period it is possible to identify common elements in the Conservative opposition to the new 'Welfare State' and the generalised conservatism that was deeply suspicious of penal reform.

The National Health Service perhaps excited the most hostility. Aneurin Bevan's frequently misplaced observation about some people being 'less than vermin' led to the foundation of the Vermin Club by the eager Young Conservatives who sported curly pipes and drove pretty girls about in their MG Midgets. The opposition was probably as much motivated by a fear within the medical profession of a limitation of its market power. But in more general terms there was opposition to the notion of 'welfare' on the ground that hard work, enterprise and effort, combined with financial prudence and sobriety, would ensure that no man, nor his family, need be in want – least of all in a society character-ised by full employment. 'Full employment' – a central pillar of Labour policy – was criticised as it was disliked as a limitation of the mobility of labour and seen as undermining industrial discipline. 'What strikers want is a good dose of unemployment' was a frequent expression of the period. The protestant ethic, far from being dead, seemed to enjoy its resurrection, not least in those aspects that confused morality with the constraints imposed by the essentially capitalist economy that economic and social planning was not merely keeping alive but preparing for its boom in the Macmillan years of Never Having It So Good.

If strikers and those dependent upon welfare were variously repre-sented as hostile and parasitic, the same was also true of offenders. Those who have argued that the cautious, almost schoolmasterish approach of Attlee and his senior ministers was essentially conservative can find supporting evidence in the way in which the government dealt with two important issues in law reform; capital punishment and divorce. The abolition of the death penalty had been omitted from the Criminal Justice Bill of 1948, though judicial corporal punishment was scheduled for repeal. Sydney Silverman tabled a private amendment and there is little doubt that if it had been accepted by the government the Commons would have readily gone along with it. But Chuter Ede, the Home Secretary, stalled even though he was an abolitionist. Attlee decided the issue was altogether too delicate and referred it to a Royal Commission under the Chairmanship of Sir Ernest Gowers, though first confining its terms of reference to limitation *short of abolition*!

Gowers produced a classic report in 1953, two years after the defeat of Labour at the polls. At about the same time Eirene White, then Member for Flint, attempted to introduce a Bill to reform divorce. It was in the tradition of the sensible proposals that A.P. Herbert had manfully striven for some years earlier. Again, Attlee drew back from so dangerous a step and established a Royal Commission under Lord Morton of Henryton. Its Report, not long after Gowers, is interesting only perhaps on account of its being quite exceptionally abysmal in its lack of understanding of what had happened and was happening in contemporary Britain. Contrary to the mythology disseminated by those on the political right – often among especially receptive suburban audiences – the Labour Government was not dismantling the fabric of society, undermining the family, law and order. Claud Mullins, a London Stipendiary magistrate, inveighed against the Legal Aid and Advice Act of 1949 in his little volume *Marriage Failures and the Children*, echoing the sentiments of the Morton Commission, and blaming the Act for the increasing break-up of family life by making divorce easier. In reality the new law was of very limited effect and did surprisingly little to give the less well off the ability to litigate that had always been possessed by the wealthy. Even today, the Legal Aid system has more in common with the Panel Doctor of 1911 than the Health Service of 1948.

In spite of everything comprised within a Welfare State that was supposed to care for the individual from the cradle to the grave the tide of crime rose higher every year until 1951. Juvenile delinquency, that great concern of moralists and psychoanalysts alike, positively burgeoned. If, in 1982, we were to return to the crime levels of 1951, any government would proclaim that it had won the war against crime, but in those days 750,000 indictable crimes known to the police were held as monumental. The Member for Wembley, Wing-Commander Bullus, with substantial support from suburban signatories, attempted by a Private Bill to reintroduce birching as a judicial punishment – but failed. Capital punishment, which had been in abeyance during the sitting of the Gowers Commission, became effective once more in 1953 and the hangman was to have another thirteen years of work before him.

The constant complaint was that if poverty and deprivation were the causes of crime and delinquency, as so many reformers had claimed, then how was it that notwithstanding the universal benefits of the Welfare State crime not only persisted but flourished like the green bay tree? To some extent the fowls of foolishness had come home to roost for the naïve social positivists. Clearly, there was more to the whole problem of deviance and its control. Yet before attacking the positivists of welfare too mercilessly, it is worth bearing in mind that whole areas of the penal system were as yet largely untouched by many of the changes that had occurred in society. The social composition of the judiciary was not at all changed from bygone days. Rayner Goddard, that Rhadamanthus of the Court of Criminal Appeal, who presided – some would say maintained a reign of terror – as Lord Chief Justice in this period would have been at home with Fitzjames Stephen (by curious chance uncle to Virginia Woolf) who argued that criminals should be positively hated. As for the Magistracy, things were little better. Various London Stipendiaries continued to send people down for three months for stealing bars of soap, and the lay magistracy was little better. Appointed by a system of covert political patronage 'JP' was a kind of poor man's OBE. Mayors of boroughs sat on the bench *ex officio*. Only in the London Juvenile Courts, where selection was made directly by the Lord Chancellor, was there anything approaching a system of rational appointment as distinct from vulgar political reward. Prisons in 1951 had changed little, if at all, from what they had been like in 1901. Some were still gas lit. All of them had Visiting Magistrates who could and often did order floggings for offences against prison discipline. The canvas suit and the strait jacket, like bread and water, were familiar parts of prison life. If things were better in the borstal system it was because the humane reforms that had characterised it in the 1930s had become part of its conventional fabric. Neither prisons nor borstals could be described with any truth as like 'holiday camps'; the ill-fitting clothing, the dreadful sanitation and the appalling food were sufficient testimony of that. When the inmate had done his time he was at the charitable mercy of the local Discharged Prisoners' Aid Society. To sit on one of their committees was to take a trip back in a time-machine to the days of the pre-1914 Poor Law. Men were questioned about whether they were going back to their wives or to the other woman, grudgingly given a voucher for the Salvation Army hostel, a second-hand jacket and half a crown and often sent on their way with a great deal of gratuitous and sickeningly patronising moral exhortation. Or so it seemed to those of us who were students in those days.

The legal establishment and many of those who staffed the various constituent parts of the criminal justice system often had only the simplest conceptions of the social significance of deviance. Their conceptions of welfare were often no less mono-dimensional. But they assumed, even when kindly disposed towards offenders, that crime was crime. The notion that the concept of crime is relative, that its definitions often depend upon the success of dominant groups within society in persuading others that certain things *are* criminal – in distinction to other acts that are not – and that in consequence whole areas of behaviour that might be held as socially unacceptable were conveniently outside the sphere of crime control, simply did not occur to them. The exception was homosexuality, a great *cause célèbre* throughout the 1950s on account of the public notoriety of certain trials. At worst it was a filthy, evil perversion that had accelerated the decay of the Roman Empire; at best it was a disease for which the sufferer deserved the chance of treatment.

Two important social facts about the post-war period, and certainly its latter part, remained unperceived by many of the protagonists in the debate about the relationship between crime and welfare. The first was that as Britain, in common with some other countries, had become especially prosperous in the late 1950s and early 1960s, relative deprivation came to take the place of absolute poverty as a critical social variable. The expansion of the economy and a consequent rise in living standards was not uniformly experienced. As has often been the case since 1832, the middle classes had done proportionately better than anyone else. At the same time the rapid expansion of advertising, especially through commercial TV, projected a new and strident image of material consumption as an index of social status. Not that there was anything new in this; it was after all known to Veblen who, when observing the America of the end of the nineteenth century, was prompted to write his *Theory of the Leisure Class*. But whereas those relatively poorly off were well aware that there were others more privileged than themselves their awareness took on a new egalitarian dimension. Ironically, it was an egalitarianism deriving less from an articulate political consciousness than from the growth of consumerism. In terms of the institutional fabric of society it is possible to argue that comparatively little social change was the result of structural change; after all, comprehensive schools and the new universities made little impact upon the recruitment patterns of the higher civil service, the legal profession or the judiciary. The medium through which the new egalitarianism was expressed was material consumption; in reality it expressed the underlying patterns of differential opportunity. In a 'talk' on the Third Programme entitled 'The Carrot out of Reach' I attempted in the late 1950s to adapt Merton's ideas about the relationship of anomie and differential opportunity to the growth of crime in the Never Had It So Good society. If status was derivative from infinitely increasing material consumption then there would be some who would recognise that, as in every fairground, some of the most glittering prizes will be for ever out of reach. And whatever the incentives that existed in the context of social and educational opportunity some goals were by definition unattainable. Even finding room at the top by laying the boss's daughter represented only limited mobility; no one could become a high court judge by that method.

Those affected by relative deprivation were concentrated among those sectors of the population who were still doing less well than the middle classes from the expansion of welfare in its various manifestations. They were still to be found in the ghetto estates where the 'unsatisfactory tenants' of a Ministry of Housing Circular of that name were located. But the second important social fact about change in post-war Britain was the rise of what was termed 'youth culture'. The child boom after 1945 had transformed the place of the young. No longer a minority group, their numbers were increasing and they were finding employment in an expanding economy based on cheap oil. Those who were not at work were in receipt of more ample parental *largesse*. Abrams' *Teen Age Consumer* indicated what they were doing with their money. Much of it was spent in the newly expanding world of pop music. Now the significance of this was that through the media of song and dance many, if not all, the formal barriers of class-bound culture that separated young people began to dissolve. Clothing and hair styles ceased to be accurate sources of social identification. But more important, the ethos of pop culture was suspended in a medium of essentially a-political, classless revolt against the established order of society. CND was but one manifestation of it; the 'protest' songs imported from the United States were another. In its upper reaches, the new 'pop' culture scaled high artistic and aesthetic peaks – Beatles music is a clear example. In its cloacal depths it came to represent nothing more than a nasty, brutish rejection of those features of the protestant ethic that had at least protected certain social decencies. In the pursuit of unbridled hedonism it rejected order for a negativistic, almost anarchic state. Somehow, as the prosperity of society declined, this level of activity degenerated into a kind of Clockwork Orange world of violence, gang rape, mugging, vandalistic squatting and petty theft.

The moral entrepreneurs of British society found the greatest difficulty in coming to terms with youth culture. They suspected its hedonism, but most of all they resented the way in which fashionable social liberalism, especially in the field of education, seemed to have sold the pass, and so cheaply. All the hard-won gains of the Board Schools, to say nothing of the institutions of more formal social control – workhouses, asylums, mental defective colonies, approved schools and prisons – were now lost. The decline of the economies of the industrial West (once the world of Islam had discovered the oil weapon in the struggle against Israel) has had the most lasting effects upon the young who have inherited not merely what is left of the youth culture of the years of affluence but the social expectations of consumerism.

The impact of youth culture was undoubtedly amplified by the fact that an increasing birth-rate had resulted in post-war Britain acquiring a new demographic profile. Children who had been in a minority in the 1930s – the age of the childless or one-child family – were now an increasing proportion of the population, as were the elderly whom new drugs and improved social services were preserving to a greater age than before. All the while affluence was characteristic of the economy, the social problems consequent upon these changes seemed often, if not irrelevant, then certainly not the most pressing among social issues. But the decline of the industrial prosperity of the country since 1972 has sharpened the focus to an astonishing degree. Where it was said that the delinquent young 'had too much money' or 'more than was good for them', there are few who fail to recognise that youth unemployment is now a major problem of our time. For the elderly living on welfare benefits that shrink in real terms, poverty is their problem. Some of them now shop-lift food from supermarkets; others die of hypothermia because they are terrified of the price of 'the electric' (its cost increased not so much by market forces as the directive of government intent on reducing the PSBR; Beveridge, thou should'st be living at this hour!). But for the young unemployed it is not simply a question of poverty but rather that blow to self-esteem that confirms the suspicion that the adult world adjudges them probably worthless and certainly expendable. Since work and the money it brings is a primary source of the income whereby the symbols of status in consumerist society may be acquired, living on 'Social' is a stimulus to both anomie and outright hostility to the world about them.

Perhaps more than any other single social change in the last decade youth unemployment has contributed towards the amplification of crime and deviance. Quite apart from the fact that in the north of Ireland it has been a recruiting sergeant for the IRA and its 'loyalist' counterparts who have taken to violence, it has in this country produced a rootless mass of youngsters who have for the most part absolutely nothing to do except mischief. Now this is not, of course, true of every youngster without work. But it is at the heart of the social disorders of the decaying inner cities where yet another excursion into the provision of welfare – public housing – has been crowned with disastrous results. The torn down slums, replaced by the tower blocks set in wastelands that are the home of abandoned cars and feral dogs are the delinquency areas of our time. The reformers of a century ago looked aghast at the East End of London and its counterparts in Liverpool and Glasgow; what would they say if they could see those pinnacles of loneliness and prefabricated squalor with which the skyline of every major city is now ringed. It is among the lumpenproletariat who inhabited the Victorian slum, the inter-war housing estate for 'unsatisfactory tenants' and who are now to be found in the decaying inner city because they lack the industrial skills that would give them even a marginal chance to compete in the labour market, that crime and delinquency are again a major part of life. Crime is not merely a mode of subsistence in that its gains augment the welfare payments that come from a welfare state that is increasingly dependent upon North Sea oil; it is the one kind of activity that supplies some of the psychological satisfactions that would otherwise come from work. Add to the economic verities the facts of race and social discrimination and there is to be found in certain inner cities a recipe not merely for social disasters on the scale of Brixton, St Paul's and Toxteth, but for the objectives of a civilised, 'caring' or simply benevolent society to become permanently discredited.

Although to some extent obscured, the wreck of an important vessel of positivist penology has come about during this period of economic decline. It used to be part of the received doctrine that a steady, regular job was a good index of the delinquent's rehabilitation. Now any job may be very hard to come by. Given that much of the so-called 'training' that takes place in penal institutions is directed towards the acquisition of habits of industry there is a serious problem. If there is no work, what can be the objects of 'training'?

To a considerable degree the most successful agencies of welfare have, over the last 150 years, been among the most effective informal agencies of social control. Informal, that is, in that their expressed purposes were perhaps different from their controlling functions. But whereas those who were inmates of the workhouse *were* controlled under the rigorous eye of the workhouse master himself as they picked their oakum, the inhabitants of the welfare ghetto who take down their Giro cheques to the post office are not controlled in the same way. The iron discipline of the Board School has given way to the anarchic Hobbesian world of the blackboard jungle. The tower-block estate is as difficult to police as the Old Nichol – possibly more so. But perhaps even more striking is that we live in a society which has in large measure lost much of its resolution. The cataract of gloom and despondency that constitutes the average week of news bulletins, magnified by an all-embracing system of mass communication, has created widespread belief that the world is getting daily worse and there is no cure for any of it. Admittedly, there are political ideologues who would have us believe otherwise. But the management of 'socialist' economies throughout the Soviet Empire suggests that people can come close to starving even when there is not a world war in progress. At home the high priests of monetarism have succeeded, through their insistence on reducing public expenditure, in undermining many of the solid achievements of the welfare state that owed debts to post-war governments of both the old parties.

Having lost its resolution it is prey to the danger of turning inwards upon itself. There is anger against the welfare 'scrounger' no less than against the offender. The only additional civil servants taken on seem to be those to root out social security frauds; the only part of the public sector to get pay rises in double percentage figures is the police. At 15 per cent they seem set to be identified as the Praetorian Guard of monetarist society, for when the cities burn they should at least stay loyal.

There is no evidence which suggests that the provision of 'welfare', whether in the form of goods, services or cash payments, by itself offers any respite from those forms of behaviour that are predatory. Neither theft nor burglary, nor shoplifting nor the taking of cars, nor violent assaults at football matches nor the vandalistic treatment of buses has been shown to respond to a penny more of child benefit or any other benefit for that matter. It is impossible to legislate for virtue and the best that the law can achieve is to limit the extent and consequences of vice. For a great deal of what now troubles our society is in fact vicious and selfish, be it the beating up of old folk to betray the secret hiding-places of their pensions or the gang banging of young women cornered in the stairways of flats. Not that this is the total extent of vice and selfishness, for the fraudsmen, the con-men and the white-collar criminals who operate from smart offices are no less selfish or uncaring about their victims.

What the evidence of industrial decline seems to suggest is that there has been a return to a degree of subsistence crime such as we have not had since the last century. Where unemployment is permanent and the cash benefits of welfare limited there is an incentive to indulge in a kind of forcible redistribution of property – theft – and to convert stolen goods into cash. The world of the thief and the fence is the mirror image of the world of legitimate consumerism. The same is true of the white-collar criminal; as times get harder he must of necessity become sharper. Increasingly, the political mood shapes up towards social policies for dealing with social problems that are essentially based on *control* theories rather than theories of therapy or prophylaxis. Investment in police loyalty and riot gear is at one end of the spectrum; reliance on the 'short sharp shock' as part of institutional regimes is its penological equivalent. But interestingly enough, the objects of control theories are identified not across the spectrum of deviance, but are concentrated towards one end. There are really no prizes for guessing that those who make greatest use of public space, whose deviance is most visible and whose behaviour may be most readily related to the symbolic stereotypes of the deviant are likely to be those who experience the consequences of such identification. Increasingly, crime is defined as a problem of public order. Thus we are more concerned about football hooligans than crooks in the double glazing business, more troubled about single parents who make false statements to Social Security than corrupt councillors and officials who take backhanders from businessmen.

Control policies have their limitations, not least in often doing little more than push back the problem a little further. Even wholesale capital punishment and transportation did not prevent the late eighteenth and early nineteenth centuries from experiencing high levels of urban crime. Some impact might be made upon subsistence crime by any raising of living standards among those most vulnerable to the effects of relative poverty. But there is more to human life than eating and being housed, important though these considerations may be. Without that moral improvement that the early theorists of social progress believed was the inevitable consequence of rising living standards there is unlikely to be any reduction in those crimes which are characterised by a selfish or aggressive disregard for the rights and comforts of others. Juveniles will only cease to beat up the elderly when they come to respect the elderly as people; packs of youths will only cease to gang bang their victims when they come to accept some idea of the dignity of women.

What the Welfare State has signally failed to do is to provide some kind of inoculation against crime by redistributing both wealth and social opportunity in some degree. Thanks to infant welfare and school dinners our juvenile delinquents are probably better physical specimens than those eighty years ago. But they are not necessarily more civilised nor more aware of the rights of others who are vulnerable to their depredations. In one sense they are more deprived than ever in that the consumer society has confused so many of the moral verities. Needs, wants and rights are all terribly confused. The school system has not merely failed them in many cases as a means of learning to become literate and numerate; it has failed to provide them with the consistent structure that makes some sense of the world. For whatever the short-comings of the authoritarian Board School it possessed none of the uncertainties that stem from the hedonistic thrust of some modern educational theories.

The theorists of social progress were terribly wrong. Perhaps because they reacted against institutionalised religion they omitted to consider that the 'imagination of man's heart is evil from his youth'. If those criminological theorists at the turn of the century who sought to improve housing and nutrition and all the rest had been able to consider that the better off, although they did not commit the subsistence crimes of the poor, nor the public order offences, were still capable of behaviour that possessed similar moral ingredients, hopes might never have been raised so high nor been so cruelly disappointed in the long run. What made a factory owner insist on the use of dangerous machinery? Was the fate of those workers who died after a lifetime of working with toxic substances less frightful than that of those who died of wounds inflicted by violent crimes?

Ironically, the contemporary advocates of control theories and policies are as blind to the idea of justice as were the theorists of progress to the moral dimensions of deviance. At its most benevolent the state can distribute 'welfare' in the context of bread and circuses – royal weddings watched on television by one-parent families on the 'Social' – and at its least alluring can contain the potentially riotous lower orders by heavy investment in police manpower and hardware. At its most intelligent it can redefine the location of many of the arenas of conflict in society; some it can neutralise, others it can eliminate. The choices are, in the last analysis, political. But the judgments need to be informed and therein lies the rub. When the life of governments is but five years or less most politicians are in too great a hurry to be delayed by facts.

Chapter 12
Prevention in the neighbourhood: community social work on a council estate
Robert Holman

Last evening I was back at the university. Not to lecture but to play with the cricket team from the council estate where I work in a match against the social science staff. A burly dad, scorning the wearing of pads as soft, hit out like a village blacksmith. He has had a stormy relationship with his delinquent son. So I was pleased at dad's obvious pleasure when the teenager took some wickets. A skinhead, previously in a detention centre, tried to bowl too fast and gave away byes. I watched him struggling to control his explosive temper. Our team won and returned home claiming – falsely – that we had defeated 'the university'.

The match somehow brought together two parts of my life. For a decade I taught students and studied social problems. My research methods included statistical surveys, interviews and literature searches. From the results I drew out recommendations for practice and policy. These proposals, I must add, were usually met with a deafening silence. The last six years have been spent running a community project on a council estate which can be called Edgetown. The influences on my thinking are now not so much books and statistics: instead, my ideas are shaped by people, by neighbours, friends, fellow cricketers. In this essay I will give a short account of three such people and then deduce some implications for running a community social work project. All very unscientific and lacking in research methodology. None the less, the lessons learned by experience may come over with more force than those derived from academic study.

Initially, it is necessary to say something about the project. As an academic, I concluded that the efforts of local authority social workers to prevent children from coming into public care or from becoming delinquent suffered a twofold handicap. The social workers rarely lived in the localities where they worked. Consequently they could not gain an intimate knowledge of or use the resources in the local neighbourhood. Further, they tended to carry extensive statutory caseloads and so had little opportunity to try anything except individualised casework. In response, I founded a project on a council estate marked by a high number of referrals to the Social Services Department.

Funded by two trusts and administered by the Church of England Children's Society, I became the project worker and moved into a house alongside Edgetown in 1976. The aims were to prevent the reception of children into public care; to work with delinquents; and to provide youth facilities on a neglected estate. The method was simply that a worker, freed of statutory obligations, would be available and could use any approaches which seemed appropriate. This was termed community social work. The story of the first three years has been written up elsewhere (Holman, Wiles and Lewis, 1981). Here I intend to pinpoint some of the approaches which were employed with three people. I shall then be in a position to discuss the main ingredients of the project. Finally, I shall consider its applicability to local authorities.

In 1977, a local resident, Dave Wiles, joined the project and two years later a social worker, Jane Thomas, also became part of the team. They are identified with the project and hence in this essay I shall sometimes use 'we' and sometimes 'I'. Not very tidy English but then community social work is a very untidy practice.

Drew

The film ended. The audience rose to leave. A fourteen-year-old skinhead suddenly jumped on the stage, dropped his trousers, bent over and gave the filmgoers an extra showing. He then dashed outside, leaving the youth club leaders to face the irate manager.

I've known this boy, Drew, for over five years. His mum has struggled to provide material comforts but has been unable to control him. His provocative aggressiveness makes him feared in some quarters. Recently he entered a field where some lads were playing cricket: immediately an older boy turned and fled. When I asked why he didn't stand up to Drew, he explained (as if I didn't know) that Drew's steel-capped boots were lethal. Some youngsters avoid the youth clubs because of him, parents complain to us about him.

Drew is drawn to the National Front side of the punk scene like a moth to a flame. This attention-seeking bravado, along with his nicking, landed him in court. He attended the local authority IT group until he dropped out following some aggro. He has been banned from several shops and the cinema. A usually amiable policeman has declared his intent 'to get him'. He has been suspended from school. Drew is well along the route that leads to custody and removal from home.

We are determined to keep Drew out of public care. Why? Because sending him away is unlikely to improve him. His older brother was sent to a community school where his persistent absconding and association with other delinquents actually made him worse. Drew might well glory in being sent away and would certainly identify with the most reckless and violent boys. Improvement seemed possible only by keeping him at home.

But how could his removal be prevented? Our approach was simply to divert him away from situations which provoked his delinquency and aggression. This meant that he spent much time with us. The project was suited to this ploy for it had initiated a number of clubs, and our home was near to Drew's. Thus, while suspended from school, he would join us at about noon when a few boys habitually come to the house for lunch. He would then accompany us on whatever we were doing and, after tea, return either to attend a club or to mix with other kids who usually gathered in the back garden.

Diversion was not an easy option. Drew got on particularly well with Dave Wiles, but even so for much of the time he was loud-mouthed, suggestive and obscene. He seemed to resent others coming to the home. When a mothers' group assembled, he stuck his head through the door and called them a 'f— load of whores'. We always reprimanded him even if the effect was only temporary. In response he would sometimes turn on us saying we were 'queers', 'a bunch of layabouts', and that we never did anything for him.

So what did diversion achieve? It gave Drew something to do in the many hours he spent outside his home. It was an alternative to the boredom that led him to seek illegal excitement, to the mixing with and attempts to score off other difficult teenagers in the city centre, to the scenes where clashes with authority were provoked.

In addition, the diversion activities enabled us to see other sides of Drew's personality. Suddenly he would be calm, offer to wash up the plates and sweep up the fag ends in the garden. Best of all, when mums brought their babies or when we had combined activities with handicapped children from a nearby home, he sometimes displayed a caring, more gentle side. We caught a glimpse of what he might become. There was hope.

Not least, the long hours spent with him occasionally allowed him to drop his hostile and suspicious attitudes so as to take us into his confidence. For years he refused even to consider that he had any problems. No, 'people picked on him'. Then he reached the stage of admitting that something was wrong. Once I observed that he seemed so full of hate towards other kids. In reply he recounted how he had overheard his dad saying about him, 'I hate that little bastard out there'. We proceeded to discuss whether Drew's own venom was somehow a reaction to his dad's feelings towards him. The revelation did not become a cure-all therapy for him. It did give us a bit more understanding about him and increased our readiness to tolerate his nastiness and to divert him away from trouble.

Kes

Kes was a well-known skinhead, proud of his reputation as a hard man. Not long out of detention centre, he committed another burglary. His long record of fighting, drunkenness and thieving indicated that he would go to borstal. Kes lived on the outskirts of our patch so his probation officer introduced him to the project. He communicated well with Dave Wiles who came from a similar background. At court both the probation officer and Dave put in pleas for Kes with the result that the magistrates gave him a last chance – a heavy fine and a community service order. Much of the latter was to be spent with our project.

What had we to offer Kes? We did not want to treat him as different from everyone else so we encouraged him to attend the clubs and to drop into the house as did other youngsters. Being local and unemployed, he was able to call often. He also began dating a girl who was a member of the senior youth club. He came to the lunch group for a bowl of soup and a bit of company. He played in our cricket team. In short, he became part of the group of youngsters who identified closely with the project. Mixing with this group meant that he now had other demands on his time and loyalties. These demands could counter some of the pressures put on him in other directions. For instance, his habit had been to drink heavily on a Friday evening and end up in fights or other forms of excitement. Now he felt a pull – particularly from his girl-friend – to change his behaviour.

Our other approach was to place certain responsibilities on his shoulders. Long before Kes arrived we were convinced that residents of the neighbourhood must be involved in running the project. One reason was that – like Dave – they were often the best equipped people to do so. Further, we realised the dangers of casting people into the role of clients. Human beings need to give as well as to receive. Those who are always treated as recipients are almost forced to produce behaviour which proves that they are clients. I can look back with regret at people whom I have overwhelmed with my helpfulness and whose own potential I stifled. Kes, therefore, was made an assistant leader at two of the clubs. In time he also took on responsibilities at the lunch group. Recently he accompanied the senior youth club on their annual holiday in the role of leader.

How has Kes fared in the face of all this mixing and taking on of responsibilities? Initially he was unsure of himself. At the junior boys' club he found it difficult to tolerate the demands of the young pests and tended to over-react. A couple of parents complained about his roughness towards their sons. Again, he wanted to dominate and took delight in slogging the youngsters' bowling all over the cricket field. But gradually he settled down and accepted the role of helping youngsters to enjoy themselves.

With some of the older teenagers, Kes would frequently boast about his past exploits. Looking at a shapely girl, as we drove by in the minibus, he would explain how he used 'to get his leg over her'. Or, seeing an old enemy, he would describe how he booted his ribs in. To his credit, Kes showed no resentment when Dave asked him to modify his boasting and language, explaining that Kes could be an example for good or bad on youngsters who tended to hold him in some awe.

Once these problems were sorted out, Kes made steady progress. He was often placed in the position of having to control boys who were fighting, spitting at pedestrians from the minibus, shouting sexual obscenities or attempting to nick goods from shops. Interestingly, he perceived that he was restraining them from doing the very things which were a temptation to him. He thus saw his own behaviour from another standpoint. Further, amongst the younger lads, he found that he was popular because of his skills at football, swimming and fishing. He was able to gain satisfactions from behaviour that was not only legitimate but which was also beneficial to others.

Of course the improvement was not without its disasters. At times Kes thought his old mates were regarding him as 'soft' and he wanted to chuck in his new activities. A crisis came when, after securing a job for a short period, he was sacked. At this point he decided that he would get money by going back to burglary. But he expressed these feelings to Dave Wiles, who managed to persuade him otherwise. It cannot be claimed that Kes will always go straight. However, it does seem certain that he will now complete his Community Service Order without committing a further offence.

The Bunters

'Bob, Bob, wait a minute, don't go'. We had just squeezed the last teenager into the minibus prior to a visit to the skating rink. 'Please come up, they're fighting like mad'. The speaker was twelve-year-old Glen. His young eyes displayed anguish and pleading. Dave continued with the skating party while I accompanied Glen Bunter back to his home. Even before we reached the door I could hear the row. A panel in the front door was smashed. As I entered, Ralph and Dolly Bunter both tried to enlist my support, accusing each other of unfaithfulness, extravagance and greed. At least they stopped fighting. I explained that I had to go to help Dave control some of our tearaways and suggested that Glen accompany me. They agreed. I hate roller skating and spent most of the evening crawling on the floor or thinking of excuses to stay in the cafe. Glen enjoyed it although he was obviously on edge. When we returned, a tearful Dolly was waiting on my doorstep – 'He's kicked us out', she sobbed.

I had known the Bunters for over three years. Initially they kept their distance. Glen joined one of our clubs and I occasionally talked to his parents about his interest. Once they sought my advice over a financial matter. Then they both began to call on me concerning their matrimonial problems. It took three years before they had the confidence to do this. The project was not only a local one but its workers were committed to staying. It therefore had the advantage of time. Often it took time before people would voice their need for help. Sometimes help was possible only over a long time-span.

Dolly's presence on the doorstep was not entirely unexpected. She was a tall, slim, strong-willed redhead. Frustrated with being a housewife, she wanted a job outside the home. She craved for excitement and tended to over-dramatise events. Ralph was a strapping bearded chef. More introverted than his wife, his ideas on the woman's role were definitely Victorian. He wanted Dolly at home, his meals on time, and to know all her movements. Dolly and Ralph wanted freedom for themselves yet were extremely jealous of each other. Not surprisingly, opportunities for rows were legion and increasingly they were exploding into fights between them. In the middle was their only child, Glen. He tended to side with mum and so also became the object of Ralph's anger. Then Ralph got the sack and money became another point of friction. Ralph lost the satisfaction he had possessed from holding a good job while Dolly argued more vehemently that she should take employment.

At the time Glen came to my house, I was already worried that the Bunters' family life was disintegrating. Dolly and Ralph were acting so extremely that I feared that either or both were on the verge of a breakdown. Just as serious was the effect upon Glen who was becoming increasingly morose and nervous. I had already had long talks with Dolly and Ralph. I had tried to identify the different expectations they had of marriage and the pain and distress they were causing their son. At their request I had also explained the procedures for and the implications of divorce. In Dolly's case, I had advised her how to obtain legal protection from attack.

So Dolly stood on the doorstep that night and told me that Ralph had beaten her. She bared her flesh to prove her point. 'I can't go back. It's over. What can I do?' There was only one thing to do – I took Dolly and Glen into our home for a few days. The project had few resources but we workers had freedom to use them as we saw fit. In short, we possessed flexibility. Thus without any red tape, shelter was found for them. No application had to be made to the local authority to take Glen into care. Simultaneously, I was near enough to Ralph to pop round in order to explain what was happening. Dolly stayed a few days and gradually recovered some stability.

The Bunters' problems were not resolved. They did get together again but further rows flared up. Subsequently Dolly and Glen again stayed at our house. Then Ralph stayed with us for a couple of days as we attempted to find a solution. Unfortunately, we did not possess sufficient skills in marital casework and we failed to be of much help in the sense of enabling them to have a happier marriage. All we did was to offer shelter and friendship in the hope that a respite might contribute to a lessening of family conflict and lead to a safe and stable home for Glen.

Ingredients of the project

Writing about the project gives rise to the temptation of rosy exaggeration. So the limitations of this tinpot outfit must be acknowledged. It has all the impact of a fleabite on the structural problems of low income and unemployment which afflict many people on the estate. Even judged by social work standards, the failings are evident. The workers do not possess the therapeutic skills which might aid some disturbed individuals. A few youngsters have proved too much for us. We have not reached some families.

These failings apart, the project can make some claims. A host of services have been provided on an estate which previously possessed hardly any. The number of receptions into care, the extent of delinquency and vandalism do appear to have dropped. Most important, local parents and children seem to back the project and want it to continue.

If the project has had some limited success, the question is posed: can it be repeated elsewhere? Further, if this is to happen then it is necessary to identify the components of the project. The case examples have been presented in order to illustrate these ingredients. First, the main strength rests in the project's relationship with the local community, in other words its degree of *local involvement and local responsibility*. The story of Kes stressed that his participation enabled him to break down the expectation that he was always a client. But there is more to it than that. Dave Wiles was a local delinquent. He joined as a full-time worker in 1976. In 1981 he took over as project leader. Jim Davis, a teenager born and bred on the estate, also joined as a full-time member in 1981. In addition, an outside grant meant that eight teenagers have been designated as assistant youth leaders and given £3 a week to work evenings in the clubs. They had to attend regularly, have tutorials with a full-timer and attend two residential training weekends. Involvement is not confined to youngsters. Three mums are also paid small sums to help. At the 1981 play scheme twenty-five parents helped in some capacity.

The vast number of activities would not be possible unless residents did accept responsibility. But their involvement is also considered a vital ingredient for other reasons. It provides the project with neighbourhood backing and approval without which it would surely flounder or become irrelevant. Further, such involvement means that the helpers are frequently people who themselves have experienced various problems. Thus Dave Wiles has been able to communicate effectively with 'at risk'

youngsters because he was once a truant, a drug-taker and a proba-
tioner.

The second ingredient is simply *time*. Local authority social workers
are often short on time. Short in the sense of not staying for long in the
same job. Rapid promotion or disillusionment has meant a high staff
turnover (although the signs are now of greater stability). The result is
that many statutory social workers have not 'grown up' with their clients.
And short in the sense that high and varied caseloads have meant that
little time can be given to each individual. Frequently assessments are
made only when a crisis occurs while subsequent contact may be as little
as an hour a month. By contrast, living in the area, seeing people daily,
committed to staying, the project workers found that time brought
distinct advantages. As with the Bunters, only after a length of time can
some people reveal their worries. Recently a teenager was washing up in
our house. Normally reserved and reticent, he began to talk about his
dad, about his alcoholism, his apparent cure, his return to boozing and
the effects on the family. Five years had passed before be felt able to
share this anxiety. Further, over time both the strengths and weaknesses
of people are revealed. When the SSD has investigated child abuse
reports, we have been able to provide a balanced view of the parents,
having seen them in periods when they were coping and not just at the
point of crisis. Not least, time brings forth encouragements. A woman in
severe financial troubles, under constant medication, ever complaining,
has received much support from Jane Thomas. Today she is a cheerful
mainstay of one of the clubs. The project does not claim the credit for
this change. But we do draw hope from the evidence that people can and
do overcome problems over time.

The project has stressed using local residents over a long period.
Given these foundations, its third ingredient has been *mixing*. Intermediate treatment is now an established part of social work (DHSS,
1976). One school of thought within intermediate treatment argues that
its resources and expertise should be directed solely towards the
minority of 'hard' cases. Our outlook was and is the complete opposite.
Although we were prepared to devote much time to youngsters like
Drew and Kes, our aim was to place them within the ordinary life of the
community. Setting delinquents or 'at risk' youngsters apart from other
people emphasises and reinforces their differences. By mixing them
with more 'ordinary' youngsters, we hoped that the values and behaviour
patterns of the latter would predominate. Compared with most youth
clubs, our senior club had a high proportion of youngsters who had

committed offences, were truants or displayed behavioural problems. But they were never a majority and hopefully they began to draw satisfaction from being regarded as acceptable members rather than as deviants within the neighbourhood.

Mixing also strengthened our efforts not to cast adults in the role of perpetual clients. As indicated, our summer play activities were manned by local parents. Some were long-standing residents who never needed a social worker. Others included a middle-aged man with a young family who was shattered when his wife suddenly left; an elderly man just made redundant; a lone mum finding it difficult to manage her kids. The chance to mix with and be treated the same as others lessened the social work danger of always regarding clients as being 'cases', a tendency which can actually intensify rather than lessen their problems.

The fourth ingredient was the simple ploy of *diversion*. If asked to explain delinquency and vandalism a large number of local youngsters would answer 'boredom', 'there's nothing to do', 'I had to do something'. Obviously, boredom is not *the* explanation, for many bored kids do not get into trouble. But it is a part of the problem. Consequently the project tended to revolve around clubs, groups, and sporting activities. At the time of writing the project has just completed six weeks of almost non-stop summer activities – play schemes, outings, camps, cricket matches, swimming, games and so on. Over 300 different children were involved. The experts might argue that such a superficial approach does not reach the root of either individual or social pathology. True – but the summer was marked by an absence of crime and vandalism in the area. Diversion by our recreational activities has certain advantages. It does not require highly trained professionals. Local people can be involved. It is appreciated by the community and youngsters seem to enjoy and do spend time on the activities.

The fifth ingredient was *flexibility*. The Bunters' needs were met at various stages by individual counselling, by financial assistance, and by residential shelter. Similarly, the project's workers might run small groups or larger clubs. The workers' activities ranged from climbing mountains to doing the shopping. Despite being such a modest outfit, the project was able to respond quickly and in a variety of ways to local needs and demands. This flexibility sprang from the way the CECS handled the project. While providing administrative backing and moral support, the Society gave the team freedom to make its own decisions (as long as they did not exceed the objectives of the project); it allowed the workers to decide how to spend the financial resources; it allowed them to determine the methods of work; not least it freed them from excessive form filling.

Community social work and local authorities

The ingredients of the project have now been identified as the use of local residents over a considerable time span with an emphasis on providing activities which allowed mixing and diversion combined with a flexibility which could draw upon other approaches. Of course, the personalities and skills of workers were also important but these attributes were allowed to develop because of the above features.

The next question is, can this community social work be run by local authority Social Service Departments? The query might be dismissed with the retort that they already do so. Thus in the late 1960s and early 1970s some SSDs (and previously the Children's Departments) began to experiment with Family Advice Centres. More recently they have devised 'patch systems'. A brief mention must be made of their nature.

Seven Family Advice Centres (FACs) have been studied in minute detail by Leissner, Herdman and Davies (1971). Their functions were to provide advice, guidance and assistance, usually in areas of high social need. The authors strongly advocate that local authorities should run the centres but admit that certain difficulties were encountered. For instance, some FACs appeared little different from traditional social work offices. The workers found it almost impossible to rid themselves of the roles they had executed as statutory officials. They were not adept at running playgroups, youth clubs or other community services. Further, the departments' administrators could not free them from the rules and regulations which other social workers had to observe. On the other hand, those centres which were detached from the main offices were successful in making services more accessible, in improving the image of social workers, and in stimulating some collective action in the neighbourhood.

Whatever their pros and cons, FACs have not multiplied. Indeed, even some of the seven have folded up. I regret this for any initiatives which break down the barriers between social workers and communities is to be welcomed. However, FACs are not the same as the neighbourhood project described in this essay. The former tended to be based on buildings, not homes, they were not usually available during evenings and weekends and they did not, to the same degree, revolve around clubs.

The 'patch system' is defined as teams 'functioning . . . from a small geographical base and with community orientated methods of working'. Hadley and McGrath (1979) go on to say that the teams are characterised by a readiness to use volunteers, informal methods, an emphasis on teamwork rather than administrative rigidity and an identification with localities with populations usually between 5,000 and 10,000, but occasionally up to 20,000.

Despite the similarities, considerable differences exist between SSD patch systems and the neighbourhood project which I have described. First, to state the obvious, the former are obliged to maintain certain statutory obligations. Second, the local authority team is responsible for the elderly, the chronically sick, the disabled and the mentally disordered in the community and are not confined to work with families. Third, the patch system does not necessarily entail workers living in and being a part of the neighbourhood. Fourth, the volunteer help may be drawn from outside the patch and hence there may not be the same emphasis on residents assuming responsibilities. The patch system, in my estimation, is a valuable attempt to make social services more accessible and more responsive to localities. But this cannot be equated with neighbourhood community social work as recounted in this essay.

So there is little evidence that SSDs are already running such preventive projects on any scale. Even if convinced of their value, I now recognise some of the disadvantages SSDs would face if attempting to incorporate them into their set-ups. For instance, SSDs are obliged to concentrate on those children most 'at risk' and so might find it difficult to justify expenditure on clubs and activities which serve a whole neighbourhood. Of course, a local authority as a whole (in particular its Youth Department) can provide such clubs but in our project the focus is on a social work strategy whereby a minority of youngsters are mixed into activities which embrace a whole locality. Next, SSDs – because of their size and complex procedures – do find it difficult to free social workers from the constraints of bureaucracy (see Twelvetrees, 1981). I am convinced that the creativity, the liveliness and the commitment to initiate and maintain neighbourhood projects are more likely to occur where workers possess the minimum of statutory and administrative duties and the maximum freedom and flexibility. Perhaps these advantages are not unknown within SSDs but certainly they are rare. Not least, SSDs appear stretched to their limits and it is doubtful if many would tolerate their social workers confining themselves to very small localities. Moreover, there is no guarantee that the latter would want to live there. It follows that SSDs might be ill-placed to provide the facilities which promote diversion and mixing, the local concentration which stimulates resident involvement and the organisational freedom which allows flexibility.

If preventive projects of this nature are to be expanded, the most sensible form of progress is not for SSDs to run them but for local authorities to back voluntary bodies. Only statutory agencies have the resources to fund a large number of projects spread over the country in areas where children are most likely to be taken into care or to appear before courts. Yet voluntary organisations are the ones most likely to promote the ingredients which make for effective community social work. However, local authorities as a whole, not just their SSDs, would need to take the initiative. SSDs are not empowered to run clubs for the whole locality but councils are. Youth Departments are not empowered to engage in preventive work but councils are. Needless to say, the 1980s is hardly the moment to urge statutory bodies to increase their expenditure on new outlets. But the backing of community social work would be an investment. For a start, the local authority contribution would draw forth a contribution – in terms of finance and expertise – from the voluntary societies. In turn, they would then utilise the often neglected abilities of local residents. But, in the end, the question turns on how much local authorities are prepared to devote to projects which can prevent youngsters having to leave their families in order to enter public care. And the outcome should be measured not just in cash spent but in how much distress and unhappiness has been averted.

In 1962 I commenced my social work career as a child care officer in a local authority Children's Department (as they were then called). The following year, the Children and Young Persons' Act seemed to signify the development of statutory preventive work. Looking back, I realise that I – and others – made several arrogant assumptions, namely that

local authorities would achieve effective preventive work and that the contribution from voluntary sources was marginal;
within the local authorities, one department (the Children's Department) was the natural leader in this operation;
the main method of intervention was casework combined with a little practical relief;
the service would be dominated by trained social work professionals.

Twenty years later I find myself challenging all these assumptions.

Without relieving statutory bodies of their obligations, I now look to voluntary societies being treated as partners. I advocate services which serve neighbourhoods rather than those which offer casework to a few selected deviants. Above all, I put my faith in projects which not only involve residents but which also give them responsibilities and powers.

References

DHSS (1976), *Social Work Service*, no. 11 (October).

Hadley, R., and McGrath, M. (1979), 'Patch based social services', *Community Care* (11 October).

Holman, R., Wiles, D., and Lewis, S. (1981), *Kids at the door*, Oxford, Blackwell.

Leissner, A., Herdman, K., and Davies, E. (1971), *Advice, Guidance and Assistance*, London, Longmans.

Twelvetrees, A. (1981), 'Partners in time', *Social Work Today* (July 28).

Chapter 13
The gestation of reform: the Children Act 1948
R. A. Parker

Four major pieces of legislation were implemented on 5 July 1948. They were the National Insurance and the National Health Service Acts of 1946 and the National Assistance and the Children Acts of 1948. At the time the Children Act attracted almost no public attention. Yet it came to be regarded as a landmark in the development of services for children deprived of a normal home life. It is curious, therefore, that accounts of its origins have been so cursory. Typically, they mention the letter which Lady Allen of Hurtwood wrote to *The Times* in July 1944; the tragedy of Dennis O'Neill who died in a foster home early in the following year, and then the Curtis committee[1] upon whose recommendations, published towards the end of 1946, the government duly acted. None of these events was unconnected with the eventual Children Act, but its antecedents were rather more complicated and other factors were also important. In particular, an unresolved conflict between the Home Office and the Ministry of Health about the disposition of central responsibility for children's services influenced matters considerably between 1943 and 1947. This was partly a continuation of differences that had been evident since at least the 1920s[2] but which were reactivated by the prospect of problems with the end of evacuation. Thereafter, they were further aggravated by the implications of impending legislation in the fields of social security and health, but especially by the need to decide how to distribute the functions of a Poor Law system destined for replacement.

I

In 1943 an informal committee was formed within the Ministry of

Health to consider the problems which would arise when the government evacuation scheme came to an end. The committee's principal task was to suggest how evacuation could be put into reverse in order to return to their homes a population which might number as many as 750,000 people. However, the committee was concerned that there would be some who, for one reason or another, could not go back to the cities from which they had come. In particular, it was expected that that group would contain a large number of unaccompanied children. Estimates varied, but 10,000 was frequently mentioned at the time. In fact, when, in 1948, the new local children's departments assumed responsibility for the children who had been left behind their number had dwindled to 1,500.[3] However, that was not what was expected in 1943; a start had to be made on plans to deal with the problem.

Matters could not be left in the hands of the reception authorities, for they were mainly district councils with no experience of the Poor Law or other welfare functions. Furthermore they, together with the householders in their areas, would want to be relieved as soon as possible of the burden of caring for evacuees. As things stood the only way this could be achieved was by transferring responsibility for those who did not return to their families to the Poor Law. This, however, was assumed to 'be objectionable to public opinion because of the stigma traditionally attached to the Poor Law'. Moreover, it was felt to be indefensible to pass legislation 'to keep these evacuated children and old people out of the care of the Poor Law and not do the same for others of the same classes who are now under such care'.[4]

In response to its committee's report the Ministry of Health prepared a paper entitled 'The Break-up of the Poor Law and the Care of Children and Old People' and circulated it early in 1944.[5] Amongst other things it proposed that *all* homeless children should be the responsibility of a children's committee in each county and county borough, jointly appointed by local health and education departments. The report did not stop there, however. It went on to propose that the inspection of children in voluntary homes should be kept separate 'from any association, however slight, with the authorities responsible for the police and the punishment of crime'.[6] When the report was received at the Home Office this caused a flurry of apprehension. It was clear that the Ministry of Health thought that, in future, *it* should be the single central authority responsible for separated children – as it already was for those who came within the jurisdiction of the Poor Law. The Home Office thereupon began to marshal its arguments against the Ministry of

Health scheme. There was the fact that it had carried out important work for children over the years; it already *had* a children's branch and a longstanding and effective inspectorate. Moreover, the Ministry of Health's proposal would lead to 'the substitution of one stigma for another by the isolation of the juvenile delinquent'.[7]

Thus, by the summer of 1944 clear and opposing positions on the question of children's services had been occupied by the Ministry of Health and the Home Office. The Board of Education had so far been little involved. What began as a discussion about provision for the evacuees who remained in the reception areas after the war grew into the issue which was to dog the course of child care reform for at least the next four years: namely, in which single central department should responsibility for children's services be vested?

II

A compromise which permitted some continuing measure of joint responsibility was made increasingly unlikely by other events of 1944. An important conference was held in London in February. It was sponsored by the Women's Group on Public Welfare and the National Council for Maternity and Child Welfare. Its theme was the care and education of children up to seven years of age, and its object was to influence the policies which were being shaped in readiness for the post-war period. Many of the most influential women in the fields of education and child welfare attended. The Home Office sent one of its inspectors as an observer and she reported her impressions. There had been strong pleas, she wrote, for a move away from large institutions and for more account to be taken of the mental health aspects of child care provision. Services for the deprived child should more closely resemble life in an ordinary family and community. Lucy Fildes, the chief psychologist at the child guidance training centre (later to become a member of the Curtis committee), made a particularly telling contribution. She had spoken, it was reported,

> with great feeling and the Conference was greatly stirred by her speech. Only the chairman's ruling that resolutions were not in order prevented Lady Allen of Hurtwood putting forward a resolution calling for the Government to take steps to assess the situation of children in institutions and the possible future provision for them.[8]

It is well known that Lady Allen wrote to *The Times* in July 1944, calling for a committee of inquiry into the poor standards and lack of integration in the services for deprived children. However, that was a relatively late manoeuvre in the lobbying which she and others began almost immediately after the London conference. In March 1944, for instance, Mary Stocks wrote to the *Manchester Guardian* expressing her grave disquiet about what she called 'the legion of lost children', and ended by advocating an inter-departmental committee of inquiry to consider a range of issues connected with the care of deprived children.[9] The following day Lady Allen wrote to the Home Secretary and to the Minister of Education drawing especial attention to the lack of co-ordination as well as the low standards of residential care for separated children.[10]

At the Home Office Herbert Morrison thought that her letter would be newsworthy[11] but did not reply (except by way of acknowledgment) until several months later at the beginning of July. Advised by the children's branch, he then explained that the problem she raised had 'already been considered by the Home Office and must be reviewed in relation to social reconstruction schemes . . . but I am not at present convinced that an Enquiry . . . is essential'.[12]

Doubtless frustrated by the delay and the inconsequential nature of Morrison's reply Lady Allen despatched her letter to *The Times*, where it was published on Saturday, 15 July 1944. When Morrison read it he scribbled to Sir Alexander Maxwell (his permanent under secretary): 'Now we're off! We shall get PQs about this and there will probably be more letters.' He was right on both counts; but he also asked for representatives of the relevant departments to be brought together in order to draw up a report on the matter for Cabinet.[13] Maxwell counselled caution for, amongst other things, he did not feel that the Board of Education should be approached until it had been discovered whether there was any possibility of a 'concordat' with the Ministry of Health.[14] Morrison reluctantly agreed but was concerned that 'time passes. I may yet have to institute an Enquiry. The Times correspondence is impressive. I want HO to lead.'[15]

As he had expected, matters were not allowed to rest. Two other pressures were brought swiftly to bear. First, further letters did appear in *The Times*. By the end of the month twenty-one had been published. Significant support came from people like Susan Isaacs; John Watson (the chairman of the Tower Bridge magistrates); John Moss (the public assistance officer from Kent); Otto Neimeyer (president of the Child

Guidance Council); John Litten (secretary of the Associated Council of Children's Homes, which represented the main voluntary children's organisations from the principal denominations); Denis Brogan; Lord Lytton; Cicely Craven (secretary of the Howard League), and Noel Buxton (president of the Save the Children Fund).

By the end of July the editor of *The Times* obviously felt that such a heavy correspondence deserved some comment. The leader which appeared on the 31st began by deploring the fact that the government had rejected an amendment to the Education Bill which would have made local education authorities responsible for all separated children. Then, tactfully acknowledging that the various strictures did not apply to *all* institutions, the editorial went on to conclude that the support for an inquiry was 'too impressive to be ignored'; because of the problem of divided responsibilities it suggested that the inquiry might be sponsored by the Ministry of Reconstruction.

Lady Allen had evidently been thinking along the same lines. A week after the publication of her first letter to *The Times* she wrote to Lord Woolton, the Minister of Reconstruction, asking him to take action in a bid to cut through the delays that she foresaw because of the involvement of several departments of state.[16] This was the second initiative. Copies of the letter were sent to Butler at Education, Willink at the Ministry of Health, and to Morrison at the Home Office. Sir Norman Brook, Woolton's senior civil servant, met with his counterparts in these departments to decide what kind of reply should be given. They agreed that the matter was an appropriate subject for the Reconstruction Committee of the Cabinet since there were no precise departmental boundary lines. Furthermore, were Woolton to refuse to take up the question it 'would give Lady Allen of Hurtwood further grounds for representing (fallaciously) that progress and reform are blocked because several Government departments are concerned'.[17] Nonetheless, it was also agreed that Lord Woolton should not take the initiative in preparing the matter for the Reconstruction Committee: it would be best dealt with by a joint presentation on the part of the departments principally concerned.

Woolton duly wrote a holding letter to Lady Allen, saying that he was going into the matter with his colleagues. The details of the 'joint approach', however, still had to be settled, and this called for the preparation of papers, further meetings and negotiations between representatives of the departments initially involved, as well as the Scottish Office and the Ministry of Pensions (which was responsible for the war ophans of service families).

Whilst these deliberations proceeded a third initiative was launched; this time in parliament. To begin with, a series of parliamentary questions were asked from August onwards about different aspects of the subject. Most of them sought to elicit factual information which Lady Allen required in preparing a pamphlet detailing the case for an inquiry.[18] However, they also had the effect of keeping the issue alive within the Home Office where most of the answers had to be provided. A further parliamentary initiative followed on 3 November 1944, when a motion was tabled in the House of Commons calling upon the government to appoint a committee to inquire into conditions in institutional homes for children. The motion received considerable backing, being signed by 158 MPs of all parties.

Knowing that this was likely, Brook at the Ministry of Reconstruction expressed his concern to the Home Office about the slow progress in bringing the issue of the care of deprived children to the Reconstruction Committee. He summarised his anxieties as follows:

> The public interest, which Lady Allen aroused in this subject, seems for the time being to have subsided: but it is clear from her correspondence with Lord Woolton that she is holding off temporarily only because of his assurance that he is going into the matter with his colleagues in the Government. It is already more than a month since he told her this, and promised to let her know the result of his enquiries. I fear that before very long she will return to the charge.[19]

He urged that a joint memorandum should be brought to the Reconstruction Committee of the War Cabinet as soon as possible. Sir Frank Newsam at the Home Office was inclined not to rush ahead with an inquiry, although recommending that an immediate announcement be made of the intention to set it up; for 'that might prevent an attack on the address'.[20] Sir John Maude, at Health, took a different view. He agreed, he wrote to Maxwell, that there was a lot to be said on practical grounds for postponing the inquiry for a few months, but he doubted

> whether it would be wise to put this ground for postponement to the House, and secondly, whether we can afford the time. The position is as you know that the Poor Law ought to be brought to an end at least concurrently with the institution of the main social insurance scheme and preferably with the institution of the Health Service. . . . That being so, it seems to me that there is not much time to spare. . . we

ought to aim at getting this body [a committee of inquiry] to work, say, by the middle of January.[21]

The Scottish Office struck a similar note, concluding that in view of the degree of public feeling on the subject, and the parliamentary pressure for an inquiry, 'it was impossible not to take some action'. It had earlier been agreed that if there were to be an inquiry in England and Wales it would be 'difficult to avoid taking action in Scotland' but that, as regards the question of central responsibility, Scotland was in a more fortunate position because one minister was responsible for the three departments.[22]

Prompted by the obvious political need to avoid further delay, a joint memorandum on provision for homeless children was drawn up by the Home Office, Education, Health and the Scottish Office and submitted for consideration to the Reconstruction Committee of the Cabinet at the beginning of December 1944. It expressed support for an inter-departmental committee of inquiry but made it clear that

questions of administrative responsibility should be examined forthwith so that when the decision to appoint the Committee is announced the Government may be in a position to say that they have already under consideration the question of central administrative machinery.[23]

Although it was agreed that there would be an inquiry into children's services the Reconstruction Committee was concerned lest an inquiry made under wartime conditions should be 'unfair' but, more significantly, it decided that the question of adjusting existing departmental responsibilities should be referred to the Machinery of Government Committee.[24] This was another Cabinet committee under the chairmanship of Sir Alan Barlow (Treasury) charged with advising on the various issues of departmental boundaries which the spate of new legislation created.

The decision to set up a committee of inquiry was announced in parliament on 7 December 1944 but its terms of reference specifically precluded any consideration of the sensitive issue of the allocation of central responsibility. The government would let the committee know its views on that question as soon as possible after its appointment.[25] What came to be known as the Curtis committee was eventually established in March 1945. The campaign, in this respect at least, had achieved its goal.

III

Two events occurred at the end of 1944 and early in the new year which drew further attention to the inadequate quality of the care provided for children who were separated from their families. On 15 November 1944 several newspapers carried reports of a statement by John Watson, chairman of the magistrates at Tower Bridge juvenile court, to the effect that a child of seven had been removed from her home pending the trial of her parents and was placed by the London County Council in a remand home in which she shared lessons and toilets with girls aged 14–17, some of whom had been convicted of crime and some of whom were prostitutes suffering from venereal disease. Watson called it 'a crying scandal'. Basil Henriques, chairman of the Toynbee Hall juvenile court, reinforced Watson's criticism in a statement to the press on the same day.

A committee was duly appointed just over a week later to inquire into Watson's charges. Godfrey Vick, KC, and Myra Curtis – the two members of the team – speedily produced a report which was published in February 1945. It was a carefully measured document. In making their attack on the LCC Watson and Henriques had sought to draw public attention to the deficiencies which they considered to exist. None the less, the report maintained that

> in representing the London County Council to the public as guilty of a grave dereliction of duty . . . the Magistrates . . . showed a lack of that moderation of statement and steadiness of judgement which might have been expected in persons of their position.[26]

No scandal was proved, therefore, but further attention was drawn to serious shortcomings in collaboration at all levels; and, of course, at the outset the Home Office could not be sure whether or not the issue *would* develop into a full-scale scandal.

Even whilst the Vick committee sat, however, the death of Dennis O'Neill was to cause a public outcry of much greater magnitude. Thirteen-year-old Dennis died on 9 January 1945 as a result of starvation and beatings at the hands of Reginald Gough. Gough and his wife were the childless foster parents with whom Dennis and his older brother Terence had been placed in Shropshire by the Newport Education Committee.

The coroner's court heard that Dennis was undernourished, thin and wasted, and had septic ulcers on his feet. His death was due to acute cardiac failure, following violence applied to his chest and back. The jury took the unusual step of adding a rider recording their grave concern about the serious lack of supervision of the foster home. Newspapers, from the *Mirror* to *The Times*,[27] carried extensive reports, pictures and, in some cases, interviews with Dennis's mother, from whom he had been removed on a fit person order in December 1939.[28]

Faced with such press criticism and the rider to the coroner's verdict the deputy town clerk of Newport wrote to Herbert Morrison pressing for a public inquiry to protect the position of the local authority.[29] This he agreed to, but not until the criminal proceedings had been completed. Gough and his wife were sentenced at Stafford Assizes on 20 March. The trial completed, the Home Office's own inquiry, conducted by Sir Walter Monckton, was able to go ahead. He submitted his findings in the first week of May and, a week later, they were presented to parliament.[30]

His report recounted a catalogue of accidents, delays and slipshod supervision, much of which seemed to spring from the fact that the authority with responsibility (Newport) had acted through agents of another local authority (Shropshire) because the child had been placed outside their area. The failure to detect, and later to follow up, suspicions of ill-treatment had allowed the most horrifying perpetuation of the violence and cruelty which eventually led to Dennis's sad death. It was somewhat ironic that hitherto most of the discussion of the deficiencies in the child care services had concentrated upon the lack of integration at the central level and on the poor standards of care provided in residential institutions. This tragedy, and the extremely widespread coverage which it obtained in the press, emphasised, as nothing else had so far done, that there were also other issues to be considered.

However, it is important to make two points. First, the decision to set up the Curtis committee was taken *before* the O'Neill tragedy – not in response to it; nor were its terms of reference altered in any way as a result. Second, the reforms which followed upon the Curtis committee's report were likely to have occurred even without that unnecessary and untimely death. Indeed, what is surprising is how little additional pressure it seemed to exert upon the government. This was partly because the Curtis committee *had* been announced and assurances could be given that it would take account of what had happened. There was also the fact that that committee was not formally appointed until 8 March 1945 – midway through the Goughs' trial. Furthermore, because the foster parents stood trial, accompanied by extensive press coverage, attention was readily diverted to *their* guilt. Pressure upon the government was also diffused because, almost for the first time (the Vick report excepted), the local authorities were brought into the picture and deficiencies at that level revealed – especially by the Monckton inquiry.

It is understandable – and perhaps comforting – to maintain, as many accounts of the evolution of child care legislation do, that Dennis O'Neill's death led to the Curtis committee and thereby to major reforms. The imperatives for change, however, were by then already in existence and had been building up since at least 1943. What still remained was for the Curtis committee to finish its work and for the issue of central responsibility to be settled once and for all.

IV

It will be recalled that the sensitive matter of the disposition of central responsibility for children's services had been referred to the Barlow committee on the Machinery of Government during the autumn of 1944. Each of the interested departments duly supplied it with memoranda setting out their views. The Home Office document was largely a restatement of earlier arguments but it now included a straight bid to assume overall responsibility. The Ministry of Health submission was in direct opposition. They contended that the police functions of the Home Office made it an inappropriate setting for children's services whilst, in response, the Home Office dismissed the Health document as 'an ingenious piece of special pleading'.[31]

Faced with increasingly entrenched and opposing positions on the part of these two departments, Sir Alan Barlow and his committee were clearly at something of a loss to know how best to proceed. Barlow saw Maxwell and Maude and suggested that some outside people concerned with the care of children might be consulted on the question.[32] The names put forward however did not recommend themselves to either one department or the other and, in any case, their support for the idea was only lukewarm. Eventually, therefore, the Barlow committee drew up its own recommendations. They took the view that on grounds of general principle the main central department for the purpose of overseeing children's services should be the Home Office. Explaining their decision they wrote that they had taken account of the argument that it is contrary to the public interest for the Home Office to be shorn of too many functions not purely repressive in character. As we pointed out in our Report on Industrial Safety, Health and Welfare [another contentious area] this argument is not at all decisive in any single case but acquires considerable force on an accumulation of cases; we therefore recommended that notwithstanding that argument the administration of the Factory Acts should be transferred to the Ministry of Labour but added that acceptance of this recommendation would make it the more necessary to examine very carefully any other proposal for removing functions from the Home Office: in saying this we had in mind the functions now under discussion.[33]

The Machinery of Government committee's recommendations were accepted by the Cabinet on 26 April 1945. By now it was becoming increasingly urgent to tell Myra Curtis – whose committee had now started its work – what the decision was. For reasons which are not clear she was not actually informed until towards the end of June – at which time Maxwell also impressed upon her the urgency of a training scheme. She agreed to have her committee prepare an interim report on the matter.[34]

The question of central responsibility seemed to be settled. However, the local authorities still had not been consulted or much considered. The problem of determining the shape of the reformed children's services had only begun to be set within the context of the reforms in the health and social security services which themselves increasingly raised the issue of just *how* the demolition of the Poor Law was to be achieved and synchronised. The Ministry of Education had played no significant part in the controversy about the central (or indeed local) responsibility for children's services. In addition, a new Labour government was soon to replace the wartime National Coalition under whose administration all the proceedings had so far been conducted. Each of these factors, in their different ways, was to conspire to reopen the issue of central responsibility.

V

There was a growing concern with the problem of synchronising plans for national health, national insurance, national assistance and children's services. In August 1945 the recently elected Labour government therefore established a social services committee of the Cabinet under the chairmanship of the Lord Privy Seal (Arthur Greenwood). The Ministry of Health thereupon took the opportunity which the new committee offered to reopen the question of central responsibility for children. They did not regard the matter as finally disposed of by the report of the Barlow committee and, in any case, it was by no means certain that the Labour administration was bound by that earlier decision.[35] The Education interests were not content with the settlement either. Competition for central responsibility was to become a three-cornered contest as the Ministry of Education, the new Education Act now launched, devoted increasing attention to the issue. Their membership of the Cabinet social services committee gave them a better sense of what was going on and, furthermore, outside bodies were voicing support for Education to become the cornerstone of future children's services. Early in March 1946, for instance, the Standing Joint Committee of Working Women's Organisations argued for Education to be responsible, both centrally and locally, and introduced the proposal at the National Executive Committee of the Labour party. They also wrote to Herbert Morrison – now Lord President of the Council and chairman of the Cabinet social services committee – pressing the desirability of such a solution.[36] By this time it was clear that any arrangement which did not assign the children's services to Education would be controversial and that the LCC, in particular, would spearhead a considerable opposition.

In the meantime an inter-departmental committee on the break-up of the Poor Law had been established as a result of a meeting of ministers held under Morrison's chairmanship in March 1946. Sir Arthur Rucker (deputy secretary at the Ministry of Health) was chairman, and his task was to prepare proposals for legislation to end the Poor Law. When ready, his suggestions were to be submitted to the Cabinet social services committee and, if approved, taken up with local authorities.[37]

Various papers were prepared by the departments for Rucker's group and his report was duly considered by the social services committee in July 1946. Its main parts dealt with the general pattern of the new national assistance service; the arrangements to be made for institutional care; the welfare services to be provided by the local authorities for the handicapped and, finally, the problem of the deprived child. It was contended that recommendations on this last matter could not be made until the reports of the Curtis and Clyde committees had been received. Nevertheless, Rucker's report did include a detailed appendix on the subject which had been drawn up by a sub-committee comprising representatives of the Home Office, the Ministry of Health, the Ministry of Education and the Scottish Office.[38]

There had, of course, been contact with Curtis and by then it was known which way her committee's recommendations were likely to go. Despite this, however, the sub-committee did not settle very much. One thing they did agree upon, however, was that at the local level the service should be the responsibility of only one local authority committee – and in this respect they saw three possibilities. First, that there should be a new and separate children's committee with its own chief officer (which by now – July 1946 – they knew that Curtis intended to advocate). The Ministry of Education, however, was opposed to such special committees and a second option was therefore included: that all these functions should be assigned to the local education committees. This, indeed, was the view expressed by such powerful bodies as the Association of Education Committees; the Association of Municipal Corporations and the LCC to the Curtis committee in evidence. The third suggestion was for a general welfare committee which would also be responsible for such things as old people's homes and services for the disabled. The Rucker sub-committee, however, did not favour this because such a local committee would have to deal with 'a large and undifferentiated section of the classes of persons now dealt with under the Poor Law' and therefore 'would savour of the old Public Assistance Committee under a new name. The proposal would probably not be welcomed by public opinion' it felt, for this wished 'to see the treatment of homeless children dealt with as a special problem'.[39]

However, the problem of *local* responsibility was as nothing alongside the continuing saga of just how a settlement of the question of *central* administration was to be achieved. Curtis, it was known, would recommend a single department but would refrain from nominating any one in particular – as she had been warned against doing from the outset. Of course, everyone agreed that a single department was needed but now the decision about the local level was more specifically linked with that to be made about the centre. If the services went to education locally then the Ministry of Education would naturally be the appropriate central department; if there were to be general welfare committees then the Ministry of Health should be in charge. The most *likely* local solution – the creation of special children's committees – posed the greatest problem for a central settlement. Three possibilities were suggested by Rucker's sub-committee:

1 that the Home Office should be responsible, although the main objection to that was that 'in the public mind' it might appear to be primarily concerned with delinquency;

2 that a statutory board should be created to deal exclusively with the separated child, albeit that the Home Secretary would be the minister responsible to parliament;

3 that an executive board might be set up, along the lines of the Assistance Board, with its *own* staff of local officers.[40]

The sub-committee's report on children, together with the rest of the recommendations of the Rucker committee, went to the Cabinet social services committee in July 1946. Most of that meeting was occupied with the details of the main report and nothing was decided about the children's services.[41]

VI

Myra Curtis delivered her report on 13 September 1946. Almost at once senior civil servants at the Home Office, the Ministry of Health and the Ministry of Education suggested that a special Cabinet committee should be established to consider it. This was done, and the group of ministers chosen to take forward the work held their first meeting in December 1946 under the chairmanship of Herbert Morrison. Still nothing was resolved, largely because of the continuing dispute about which department of state should exercise overall responsibility. Probably as a means of breaking the impasse, and at Attlee's instigation, the Lord Privy Seal (Arthur Greenwood) together with the Lord President of the Council (Herbert Morrison) and the Chancellor of the Exchequer (Hugh Dalton), prepared a memorandum in which they said what they thought should happen.[42] They voted for the Home Office and for children's committees at the local level. The Lord Privy Seal's document, together with other papers setting out the objections of the Ministries of Health and Education to its conclusions, went to the full Cabinet in March 1947. Bevan's memorandum from the Ministry of Health stressed several points in opposing the conclusions drawn by the Lord Privy Seal. If responsibility were to be entrusted to the Home Office there would be, he contended,

widespread indignation throughout the country generally and among Government supporters in particular . . . it would be represented that the Government had handed over the care of those unfortunate children to the Department which looked after delinquent children and that they would come under the police.[43]

Three main arguments were then adduced for assigning responsibility to the Ministry of Health. First, under the National Health Service Act and the National Assistance Bill the Ministry of Health was in any case about to preside over a welfare scheme which was to cater for all those who were 'unable adequately to look after themselves, through misfortune, infirmity or age'. Why should children be an exception? Second, given the wish to keep down the numbers of national and local government staff it was sensible to develop a specialised child care staff from the existing core of health visitors. No other service had 'such an intimate knowledge of British homes, or such opportunities of effective, educative and preventive work' – or was so well placed to recruit foster parents. Third, the Ministry of Health was at pains to stress its 'old traditions of friendly association with local government' which, by implication, the Home Office did not have.

George Tomlinson, who had succeeded Ellen Wilkinson at Education, reiterated his department's position in the memorandum which he, in his turn, submitted to the Cabinet: central responsibility should be vested in the Ministry acting through local education authorities.[44] Two main points were made by way of elaboration. First, that the Ministry of Education was concerned with *many* aspects of childhood and children's services – from child guidance clinics to youth clubs. By contrast, only one of the activities of the Home Office made it seem suitable: 'most of its other activities make it, at any rate in appearance, unsuitable'. Second, Tomlinson's memorandum maintained that there was no evidence that the administrative difficulties of transferring responsibility for deprived children to any department other than the Home Office would be as great as the Lord Privy Seal's paper had made out. 'In any case, they should not be allowed to count by comparison with the welfare of the children.' It seemed to him, Tomlinson added, 'fundamentally wrong deliberately to subordinate the interests of the children so as to use them as guinea pigs for experiments which may be hoped to result in penal reform'.[45] This was the first time that the relationship between the question of Home Office responsibility for children and its 'softening' effect on that department's *other* responsibilities for policing and penal provision had been elucidated explicitly.

Despite these rearguard actions by the Ministries of Health and

Education the Cabinet agreed to accept the Lord Privy Seal's recommendations at its meeting of 18 March 1947 and this decision was announced by the prime minister a week later. The protracted dispute about the allocation of administrative responsibility for the reformed children's services was finally resolved – at least until the Seebohm committee of the late 1960s.[46] Now came the detailed work of formulating a Bill based upon the Curtis and Clyde reports.

VII

From this point four things needed to be done. First, the local authority organisations had to be brought into the planning and sufficient time allowed for individual local authorities to make their preparations. Second, the child care functions of the Ministry of Health which were scheduled for reallocation had to be transferred formally to the Home Office by Order in Council as soon as possible. Third, a Bill had to be prepared. Finally, all this had to be fitted into an already tightly-packed legislative programme. However, matters were now becoming urgent since all the other major legislative changes with which a Children Act had to be harmonised had either already received the Royal Assent or were at fairly advanced stages of the legislative process.

The Home Office and the Scottish Office began the task of preparing the Bill. Fortunately, most of the recommendations made by the Curtis and Clyde committees were similar and most were incorporated as the Bill began to take shape. There were only a few cases where their recommendations differed; for instance, Clyde proposed an upper age for care of 18 – whereas Curtis suggested 16. Clyde was preferred.

Despite the growing urgency several things conspired to defer the Bill's introduction until the session 1947–48, rather than 1946–47 as had been intended. The Clyde committee's report had not been delivered until the end of July 1946 and that from Curtis did not follow until September. This left little time for including a reform provision in the King's Speech to be made in October. More important, however, it will be recalled that at that time the reopened issue of central responsibility still remained to be settled, and no discussion had yet been held with the local authorities, who only received copies of the Curtis report in September. In any case the legislative programme for the session 1946–47 was already crowded. It was decided, therefore, not to include reference to any children legislation in the 1946 Address. Its omission provoked an extensively debated amendment. Nevertheless, Arthur Greenwood, the Lord Privy Seal, successfully rode out much hostile criticism for not giving higher priority to such a 'humanitarian' measure.[47]

However, by early 1947 the road was clear at last of all such obstacles and legislation could be timetabled for the next session. A Children Bill made its first parliamentary appearance in the early part of 1948. It passed through its various stages relatively smoothly just in time to come into operation on the day in July 1948 appointed for the commencement of so much other important social legislation with which, over the years, its fortunes had been closely linked.

VIII

Was the Children Act the significant piece of social legislation that many believed it to have been? In several respects it failed to promote important changes. For example, it did not deal with the question of prevention; so that it was not until 1963 that local authorities were permitted to devote any resources to reducing the number of children coming into care. Nor was there any modification of the longstanding provision whereby local authorities could assume parental rights without recourse to a court of law. Moreover, despite outward appearances, the 1948 legislation was not comprehensive: the 1933 Children and Young Persons Act remained as a separate enactment.

In other respects, however, the Act heralded changes which were to have wider repercussions than were foreseen at the time. For instance, child care training was inaugurated under a central council and in collaboration with several universities. That laid a foundation for a child care profession which, in time, was to make an important contribution to a social work profession. Unlike the local welfare departments, which dealt with the elderly and the handicapped after 1948, the new children's departments recruited university-trained women, many of whom introduced fresh impetus for change. This was nowhere more apparent than in the appointment of children's officers. For the first time in local government a large group of extremely able and committed women became chief officers. There was an infusion of new blood and new ideas at the top. In addition, the expansion of the Home Office children's inspectorate provided a mixture of experience, determination and freshness which also played its part in the generation and dissemination of new ideas and new expectations.

Of course, none of this happened overnight; large children's homes remained; untrained staff were still numerous and mistakes were made. Nevertheless, seeds of change were sown. This did not happen in the welfare services which took over the Poor Law functions with respect to the old and the handicapped. For them there was no Old People's Act; their field staff included many of the former Poor Law relieving officers (male); there was no requirement for a statutory chief officer or committee; no special inspectorate existed at the Ministry of Health, and there was very little training. As a result, it took much longer to raise standards and extend services in these departments than it did in neighbouring children's departments.

IX

Inevitably, there are omissions in this brief history of the events which led to the Children Act. The evidence I have looked at, for example, does not suggest that official concern about a declining population extended to the child care field or that questions of social control played much part; nor (with the exception of one or two notable pieces of evidence to Curtis) did the views of the children and parents who were directly involved. On the other hand, there is some evidence of a general kind – which I have not dealt with – that changing ideas about the nature and needs of childhood increased the sense of urgency for reform. Such ideas stemmed from the work of a growing child guidance movement; from a few charismatic practitioners, and from the research of a small band of psychologists and educationalists.[48] In addition, a wider acquaintance with the trauma of child separation must not be discounted. In the debates, for instance, some MPs referred quite explicitly to their interest in the problems of children deprived of a normal home life having been aroused by their contact with evacuees.

Are there any comparable trends which might constitute the backcloth against which the politics of child care would be conducted today? Ideas about the problems of adolescence might well be significant now in a way in which they were not in the 1940s. Not only are there considerably more older children in care but widespread juvenile unemployment must, sooner or later, leave its imprint on the development of many of the social services. Important changes are also occurring in assumptions about marriage and the family; changes with which the women's movement is closely involved. The campaign for child care reform in the 1940s was mounted by leading women of the day; the children's departments of the 1950s and 1960s were staffed by a preponderance of women and led by others of considerable energy and ability. Indeed, the 1948 Children Act might well rank as an important instance of the successful exercise of political influence by women. One wonders what part today's women's movement can or will play in shaping policies for children in the 1980s and 1990s.

Looking back at the evolution of the 1948 Children Act it might be asked whether such a reform could be achieved today. Would the pattern of events be different? Several things are immediately apparent: to begin with the country is not at war and we do not have a coalition government. Beyond that, however, it is certain that the local authorities would play – or seek to play – a much more influential part. More *organised* pressure groups would also be active. As a result the network of partisan interests would be more complicated, although not necessarily more successful. In addition, there are now more and better organised professional bodies and trade unions to be taken into account. It is unlikely that proceedings would be able to be kept quite so firmly contained within the 'inner circle'; although, of course, government has become more skilful and experienced in dealing with the proliferation of interests – not least because it is better informed. It should be noted, for example, that the first comprehensive collection of statistics for children in care was not undertaken until 1951.

One should also pause to consider the changing role of the media between the 1940s and now. 'Correspondence in the Times' begins to seem a somewhat out-moded vehicle for conveying pressure. Would today's *Times* (or any other paper for that matter) devote so much space to correspondence on one subject in so concentrated a period? There are other channels nowadays – notably television, but also the popular but more specialised journals like *New Society*.

Alongside these changes perceptions within government of what amounts to 'pressure that cannot be ignored' seem to have altered significantly – especially during the life of the present government. The consequences of ignoring certain pressures have been put to the test and the outcome found not seriously to erode support. The matters which demand a *political* response are changing, partly because of the dominance of an economic policy which is preoccupied with reducing public expenditure. There appears to be both a redefinition and a recalculation of the nature and force of 'public outrage'. In any event, more of the case scandals have to be dealt with by local government as a result of the growth of locally administered personal social services.

Some things seem to have been less subject to change over the years. In particular, the internal politics of the civil service; their accepted procedures; their forms of negotiation with each other, and their concern to protect the interests of their departments as they see them – often in the sincere belief that that will ensure the best administration in the interests of the public. Many ministers also remain fiercely partisan in their commitment to the protection of their domains. The 'Whitehall politics' of the 1940s seem to be remarkably similar to those described by Heclo and Wildavsky[49] in the 1970s and by others since.

Despite such continuities in the civil service – and indeed in parliamentary procedures – it is obvious that the political climate has altered. To expect the process of change to conform any longer with comfortable assumptions about liberal reform is unrealistic. Increased pressure group activity is matched by an increased readiness and ability on the part of governments to deal with it. Governments are now more wary of the costs that may be associated with changes which appear to call for no more than the replacement of one administrative system by another. Furthermore, in the present political climate, an interrelationship between several major social policy initiatives is likely to hamper rather than facilitate the progress of a particular drive for reform. For reasons such as these, legislation like the 1948 Children Act would only be achieved today after a much harder fight.

Notes

1 *Report of the Care of Children Committee*, Cmd. 6922, London, HMSO, 1946. The parallel report in Scotland was: Scottish Home Department, *Report of the Committee on Homeless Children*, (Clyde), Cmd. 6911, Edinburgh, HMSO, 1946.

2 See, for example, the dilemma set out in Ministry of Reconstruction, *Report of the Machinery of Government Committee*, Cd. 9230, London, HMSO, 1918, p. 76.

3 See R. M. Titmuss, *Problems of Social Policy*, London, HMSO, 1950, p. 436.

4 *Public Record Office*, MH 102, 1157/11.

5 PRO, MH 102, 1378; Sir John Maude (secretary at the Ministry of Health) to Sir Alexander Maxwell, 9.5.44, enclosing the report.

6 Ibid; pp. 9–10 of the report.

7 PRO, MH 102, 1378; notes on the Ministry of Health's memorandum prepared by S. W. Harris (assistant under secretary, Home Office), 13.6.44.

8 PRO, MH 102, 1158/13A; Mrs Cuffe's report, 1.3.44.

9 *Manchester Guardian*, 23.3.44.

10 PRO, MH 102, 1293/20; Lady Allen of Hurtwood to Herbert Morrison, 24.3.44.

11 Ibid.; Morrison's notes written on Lady Allen's letter.

12 PRO, MH 102, 1293/20; Herbert Morrison to Lady Allen of Hurtwood, 4.7.44.

13 PRO, MH 102, 1378; Morrison's note, 16.7.44.

14 PRO, MH 102, 1378; Maxwell to Morrison, 26.7.44.

15 PRO, MH 102, 1378; Morrison to Maxwell, 26.7.44.

16 PRO, MH 102, 1161/17; Lady Allen to Lord Woolton, 28.7.44.

17 PRO, MH 102, 1161/17; Maxwell's minute of a meeting with Sir Norman Brook, 4.8.44.

18 Later to be published as *Whose Children?*, London, Simpkin Marshall, n.d.

19 PRO, MH 102, 1161/17; Brook to Sir Frank Newsam (deputy under secretary at the Home Office), 28.10.44.

20 PRO, MH 102, 1161/17; Newsam's minute, 14.11.44.

21 PRO, MH 102, 1161/17; Maude to Sir Alexander Maxwell, 15.11.44.

22 PRO, MH 102, 1161/17; Hamilton to Maxwell, 23.11.44.

23 PRO, MH 102, 1161/17; War Cabinet Reconstruction Committee, Joint Memorandum, *Enquiry into Methods of Providing for Homeless Children*, 30.11.44.

24 PRO, MH 102, 1161/17; extract from the minutes of the War Cabinet Reconstruction Committee, 4.12.44.

25 *HC debates*, 7.12.44; reply to question no. 84 (Mr Keeling).

26 Home Office, *London County Council Remand Homes: Report of Committee of Inquiry*, Cmd. 6594, London, HMSO, 1945, para. 37, p. 20.

27 For example, the *Mirror*, 7.2.45, and *The Times*, 6.2.45.

28 See Tom O'Neill, *A Place Called Hope*, Oxford, Blackwell, 1981. Tom was Dennis's elder brother. Hope was the name of the place where Dennis was placed on an isolated farm.

29 PRO, MH 102, 1329; deputy town clerk, Newport, to Morrison, 10.2.45.

30 *Report on the Circumstances which led to the Boarding-out of Dennis and Terence O'Neill at Bank Farm, Minsterley, and the Steps taken to supervise their Welfare*, Cmd. 6636, London, HMSO, 1945.

31 PRO, MH 102, 1380.

32 PRO, MH 102, 1379; see for example, Maxwell to Sir Alan Barlow, 26.1.45.

33 PRO, MH 102, 1382; the Barlow committee's report, 8.3.45.

34 Later published as the *Interim Report of the Care of Children Committee*, Cmd. 6760, London, HMSO, 1946.

35 PRO, MH 102, 1385; see for example, Maxwell's minute, 26.10.45.

36 PRO, MH 102, 1386.
37 PRO, MH 102, 1390; memorandum by the Minister of Health, the
    Secretary of State for Scotland and the Minister of National Insurance on
    the *Report of the Committee on the Break-up of the Poor Law*, SS(46)13,
    12.7.46.
38 Ibid.
39 Ibid.; appendix 1, 'Children', pp. 38–9.
40 Ibid.; pp. 39–40.
41 PRO, MH 102, 1390; minutes of Cabinet social services committee,
    18.7.46. It was noted that Ellen Wilkinson, the Minister of Education, took
    'strong exception to certain of the proposals with regard to children . . .
    these proposals seemed to take no account of the new conception of the
    responsibilities of the Ministry of Education and the local education
    authorities' (p. 4).
42 PRO, MH 102, 1393; memorandum by the Lord Privy Seal, *Responsibility for
    the Care of Deprived Children*, CP(47)80, 12.3.47.
43 PRO, MH 102, 1393; memorandum by the Ministry of Health, CP(47)85,
    12.3.47, para. 2.
44 PRO, MH 102, 1393; memorandum by the Ministry of Education,
    CP(47)88, 13.3.47.
45 PRO, MH 102, 1393; CP (47) 88, op. cit., para. 2(e).
46 See Phoebe Hall, *Reforming the Welfare*, London, Heinemann, 1976.
47 *HC debates*, 19.11.46.
48 For example, Susan Isaacs, *The Cambridge Evacuation Survey*, London,
    Methuen, 1941, and her earlier publications, such as *The Nursery Years*,
    London, Routledge, 1929; Dorothy Burlingham and Anna Freud, *Young
    Children in War-Time in a Residential Nursery*, London, Allen & Unwin,
    1942.
49 H. Heclo and A. Wildavsky, *The Private Government of Public Money*, London,
    Macmillan, 1976.

Chapter 14
Services for the mentally ill: the death of a concept
Kathleen Jones

In order to make comparisons, whether in space or in time, it is advisable to have three pieces of intellectual equipment: a frame of reference sufficiently wide to include the subjects to be compared, but sufficiently tightly drawn to exclude extraneous concerns; a taxonomy, or relatively value-free set of criteria on which comparisons can be based; and an agreed vocabulary, so that the same factors can be discussed in different circumstances. A comparison of 'services for the mentally ill' in the 1940s and the early 1980s involves difficulties on all three scores.

It is easy enough to describe the services of the 1940s, which were largely hospital-based, because the hospitals were labelled 'mental hospitals', and the patients were labelled 'mental patients'. The record of change over the years is largely one of how the labels were removed, the services were diversified, and how the care and treatment of the mentally ill became so merged in general medicine and generic social work that only a fraction of it can now be separately identified. A taxonomy presents similar problems: if we take the items which were thought appropriate in the 1940s (hospital admissions and discharges, resident populations, staff/patient ratios, length of stay) they rapidly become meaningless as we venture into the statistical quicksands of community care; and the work of a whole generation of sociologists and anti-psychiatrists, by questioning the basic concept of 'mental illness' and raising issues of medical dominance and social control, has robbed us even of the terms in which the issues might be discussed.

To deal with the last issue first: in the following discussion, the term 'mental illness' will be used without quotation marks, to connote the condition of people who are suffering from lasting and disabling stress for no ascertainable and sufficient social or physical cause, or whose behaviour is so bizarre or so unacceptable that it is causing considerable stress to those around them. The use of the term is not intended to imply either acceptance or rejection of the medical model, or any particular ideological stance. It is used simply because it is more precise than 'deviance', which includes many people whose behaviour may be anti-social, but is explicable in other terms, and it is less pejorative than 'madness'. The medical labels – 'schizophrenia', 'clinical depression', 'personality disorder' and the rest – may be rejected as judgmental and imprecise, but the human predicaments remain, and we must call them something. How large a section of the population suffers from mental illness, and how far any definition ought to include people who get categorised in other ways, such as 'inadequate offenders' or 'long-term problem clients', is a matter for debate. We may draw the line in different places, or refuse to draw it at all on the grounds that 'normality' is a fiction; but at least we need a starting-point.

The second step is to find a date for the first part of the comparison. No decade has a unitary character, and the 1940s saw considerable fluctuations in the fortunes of mental hospitals. At the beginning of the period the 'phoney war' had only just begun. Mental hospitals were highly organised and fully staffed, and there had been nine years of improvement under the guidance of the Board of Control, following the Mental Treatment Act of 1930. The real war led to a very rapid deterioration of conditions – about half the available mental hospital beds were taken over for the special Emergency Medical Services set up for Forces personnel and air-raid casualties, and those patients who could not be sent home were crowded together on under-staffed wards with minimal care. The effects of these poor conditions were seen most clearly in a rapidly rising tuberculosis rate. By the end of the decade most of the neglect which the hospitals had suffered in the war years had been repaired, and they faced an apparently bright future as part of the new National Health Service. We will take a stand on the Appointed Day for the NHS Act – 5 July 1948 – and make an imaginary visit to a typical large mental hospital. (The account which follows is based on personal experience of a number of mental hospitals between 1947 and 1952).

Services for the mentally ill in 1948

The first thing to note is that the hospital has a high wall round it.

Nobody has yet recognised its symbolism, or proposed knocking it down. On the way through the grounds we see the male and female admission units, built with great hopes in the 1930s for the new category of 'voluntary' patients. Both are still fully utilised as tuberculosis units, and the patients have the unnaturally bright eyes and the hectic flush which suggests that many of them will die before the use of antibiotics and the new surgical techniques developed in the past few years can save them.

On to the imposing front entrance: the doormat bears the initials 'CMH' (for County Mental Hospital). That refers to yesterday – today this is a National Health Service hospital, but it will be some years before those initials, which are inscribed throughout the hospital on any article remotely likely to be portable, finally disappear. There is a door labelled 'Medical Superintendent': we tiptoe past. Another, much humbler, door labelled 'Clerk and Steward' is open to reveal office staff busy with the paper work consequent on reorganisation.

Once past the main offices, the hospital bifurcates. There is a male side, under the control of a Chief Male Nurse, and a female side, under the control of a Matron. Patients and nursing staff are strictly segregated according to sex. Only doctors, social workers and the chaplains cross the barrier.

There is a good deal of movement on the corridors. Queues of patients can be seen walking (or shuffling) from place to place, or waiting at ward doors while the staff unlock them with much jangling of keys. Keys are important: anyone possessing them has power and status, anyone losing them is liable to be 'sent down the drive' or dismissed. Patients are carefully counted in or out, to make sure that they do not wander off or escape. Sometimes a member of staff gets counted by mistake, and this gives rise to general amusement, though nobody yet appreciates the significance of the identity joke.

The patients may have been to occupational therapy, to the remedial gymnast's class, to the education centre, to the twice-weekly cinema, or to a show. There are many shows, ranging from the local concert party where the chief comic will make jokes about the Medical Superintendent and the Matron, who are sitting in the front row, to Shakespeare plays, or musical quartets who play Mozart in full evening dress. The patients are mustered to them all, and go without question. There are also sporting activities – gymnastics and Keep Fit for the women, cricket and football for the men. The first teams will have blazers with the hospital crest on the pocket ('CMH' will survive here too for some years) and will go off in coaches to play teams in other mental hospitals perhaps twenty or thirty miles away.

About half the patients have 'voluntary' status, which means that they have signed a form requesting treatment (sometimes under considerable pressure) and that they can discharge themselves at 72 hours' notice (though they may be met at the gate and certified if they try). The rest are certified as 'patients of unsound mind', a procedure which involves a magistrate's order. Whether voluntary or certified, those patients who can do so are expected to work, receiving sweets, cigarettes or small amounts of pocket-money in return. Some 'work out' – men in the grounds or on the farm, women in the kitchens or laundries or in staff houses. Most patients left school at thirteen or fourteen. Those with a better education may be found a job in the education centre or the library. Patients who are not working out clean the wards or serve the food.

There is a complicated 'parole' system for some patients. Nobody thinks twice about the use of the prison term, and medical and nursing staff decide what degree of parole individual patients should have. Patients on hospital parole can walk about the hospital unaccompanied; those on ground parole have the freedom, in their spare time, of what is virtually a country estate, and are trusted not to go beyond the gates; those few with 'outside parole' can go into town on special occasions, such as Saturday afternoon. Parole is a privilege, and can very easily be withdrawn. Nobody talks about patients' rights.

On the wards the decoration is dingy. The walls are peeling, the linoleum scuffed, and the furniture elaborate late Victorian. There is a huge day-room, with a coal fire at each end. Above the fires are large mirrors, specked and flawed, in which the confused movements of the ward are distortedly reflected, and on which (probably to prevent the disorientating effects) people write messages in toothpaste. The ward is overcrowded. In the dormitory, beds are jammed close together, and run head to foot down the centre of the room. One or two patients can be seen lethargically pushing a heavy 'jumbo' or polishing pad up and down the length of the room.

There are still refractory wards, where visitors are few, and need to be escorted by staff for their own protection. It is a familiar sight to see a patient erupt into violence on the male wards: burly male staff will twist him round expertly, pulling his coat back over his shoulders to pinion his arms to his sides. Female patients are more likely to have hysterics, and to succumb to reproaches (this is before Women's Lib). There are still padded cells, and staff will point out that it is much kinder to put a patient in the 'pads' for a while than to leave him to bang his head against a wall. Refractory patients rarely leave the wards, except to take exercise in the airing courts – small gardens surrounded by high wire, where they walk in circles or occasionally hang on the wire, cat-calling at passers-by.

Most of the nursing staff are decent and kindly. They have to be, for misbehaviour towards patients is strictly forbidden, every bruise has to be accounted for to the Board of Control, and striking or roughly handling a patient, like losing keys, can lead to instant dismissal. The female wards are immaculately clean, with curtains and flowers, and the nurses attentive. Matron, who is doubly qualified, prides herself on good nursing standards. The Chief Male Nurse runs a different sort of empire, the culture being closer to that of a barracks or a prison than that of a general hospital. Male nurses do not take kindly to the Nightingale ethos. Most of them came into mental hospital work in the slump of the early 1930s, when there were few alternatives to this lowly-paid and socially-stigmatised form of employment. The chief qualifications asked for were prowess at cricket or football and ability to play a musical instrument.

The administration is taut and hierarchical. At the head is the Medical Superintendent, who has considerable power, and lives in considerable state. Four or five patients work in his house. Doctors, Matron, Chief Male Nurse, Clerk and Steward all defer to him as the first officer of the hospital, with a command not unlike that of the captain of a ship.

Patients who come into the hospital know that they are coming in for several months, and that they have to learn a new way of life. Their relatives will probably be asked not to visit them for the first month, to give them 'time to settle down'. They grumble about the food, which is unimaginatively prepared in antiquated kitchens, and brought to the ward through long draughty corridors in unheated trolleys; but nobody listens. The staff, after all, know what is best.

It is a tightly-closed world, cheerful and busy, determinedly low-key. Staff try to keep up an air of normality, but violence is often fairly close to the surface. Some patients exhibit gross symptoms of a kind now rarely seen except in some Third World countries, where modern chemo-therapy is still not available. Manic patients erupt into frenzy, depressed patients are red-eyed or weeping, obsessional patients have raw hands from too-frequent washing or cling to a chair or table in terror, hallucin-ating patients talk to Hitler or Napoleon or the thirteen little Irishmen under the table. This does not happen all the time or in every case, but it is sufficiently frequent to make the atmosphere, except on the convalescent wards, somewhat surrealist, and sharply different from that of the outside world. Nobody doubts the existence of mental illness – they know what it looks like.

Outside the hospital, there is very little in the way of care. Duly Authorised Officers from the Public Assistance Department are in the process of moving over to the Medical Officer of Health's Department, where they will go on calling themselves DAOs and thinking that their main job is to take certified patients into mental hospitals, though the MoH tells them that there is a possibility of doing what section 28 of the NHS Act calls 'after-care'. Nobody knows what this is, or how to do it. There is some out-patient clinic work, carried out by the hospital psychiatrists either in the mental hospital or the nearby general hospital. Some of them would like to have a psychiatric social worker. There are very few of these about outside Child Guidance Clinics, and their psychoanalytic skills are highly respected. Psychoanalysis proper is also highly respected, but it exists only in Harley Street and a few university clinics. Most psychiatrists would like to know more about it. Their armoury of medical treatment is limited, insulin therapy and leucotomy are very drastic, and the understanding of individual and group behaviour seems to offer the best way forward.

A projection in time

One of the most basic traps in the study of social policy is the fallacy of linear progress: the assumption that we can 'trace the development' of this service or that from one point in time to another as a smoothly-unfolding and somehow inevitable story. History seldom works out in that way – there are sharp bends, unexpected discontinuities and new developments which could not possibly have been foreseen. If an enlightened, progressive, intelligent observer working in a mental hospital in 1948 had been asked to predict what the services for the mentally ill would look like in the early 1980s, the reply might have looked something like this:

1 The interrelationship between mental and physical illness will increasingly be recognised, to the point where most illness is treated as psychosomatic.

2 Psychiatry, based on a combination of medical and social science, will play a major part in this process as an equal partner with physical medicine.

3 As money becomes available, new, modern mental hospitals will be built in place of the old ones. They will take the patients for whom social therapy and rehabilitation is prescribed, while cases in which physical symptoms predominate will be treated in general hospitals.

4 More psychiatric social workers will be trained and employed in mental hospitals.

5 The stigma attached to mental illness will gradually be conquered, until people seek treatment as readily as they do for a stomach ulcer or a broken leg.

All these predictions would have involved the building up of an active and specialised Mental Health Service based on mental hospitals, and its invasion of the world of general medicine; and all of them would have been wrong. If they now seem somewhat far-fetched, it should be added that the first three are derived from the recommendations of the Macmillan Report of 1926, the fourth from the Mackintosh Report of 1951, and the last from the Feversham Report of 1939.

From where we stand in the early 1980s, it is clear that what has happened is not a projection from a 1948 base. The move has been to different concepts, and to services of a different order. Whether they are 'better' or 'worse' must await the telling of the second half of the story.

What really happened

The main development of services for the mentally ill from 1948 to the present day (Jones, 1972) can be briefly summarised:

1948 Establishment of the National Health Service. Mental hospitals were upgraded, but in most Regions separately administered.

1952 Publication of Maxwell Jones's *Social Psychiatry*, the first full account of the therapeutic community movement, which attacked hierarchical power structures and used group dynamics as a means of therapy.

1953 Development of the psychotropic drugs, which were to revolutionise (and medicalise) psychiatric treatment.

1955 New training for hospital (later health service) administrators. Their status rapidly improved.

1957 General Nursing Council took over training for psychiatric nurses.

1959 Mental Health Act. Existing law was codified and modernised. Informal treatment became possible for well over 90 per cent of patients. Powers of local authority social workers (then known as mental welfare officers) were extended. Powers of local authorities to provide residential accommodation, training and social work services were specified.

1960 Abolition of the status of Medical Superintendent.

1961 Announcement by the Minister of Health (Enoch Powell) of the Government's intention to reduce beds for mental illness by half, and place most of them in general hospitals. The Community Care Blue Book of the same year described the intended development of care for four groups: the mentally ill, the chronic sick, maternity cases and geriatric patients.

1962 Publication in England of Erving Goffman's *Asylums*, the beginning of an anti-institutional movement in the social sciences.

1964 Publication of R. D. Laing and A. Esterson's *Sanity, Madness and the Family* denying the reality of schizophrenia.

1966 Salmon Report on Senior Nurse Staffing Structure.

1967 Cogwheel Report on The Organisation of Medical Work in Hospitals.

1968 Report of the Seebohm Committee, recommending the setting up of local authority Social Services Departments.

1970 Foundation of the British Association of Social Workers. End of the separate Association of Psychiatric Social Workers.

1971 Royal College of Psychiatrists set up. Local Authority Social Services Act.

1972 Report of the Committee of Inquiry into Whittingham Hospital – the first of a series of public inquiries bringing to light abuses in mental hospitals.

1974 Reorganisation of the National Health Service.

1975 White Paper, *Better Services for the Mentally Ill* (DHSS). Psychiatry was thought to have 'come in from the cold'. Community services were acknowledged to be inadequate, and social services facilities 'minimal'. Plan for an 'ideal service' based on the concept of the primary care team – general practitioner, health visitor, district nurse and social worker.

1977 Publication of Larry Gostin's *A Human Condition*. Development of a campaign on American lines to secure the legal rights of mental hospital patients backed by MIND.

1978 The Nodder Report on *The Organisation and Management Problems of Mental Illness Hospitals*.

1981 Mental Health (Amendment) Bill.

1982 Second reorganisation of the National Health Service to eliminate Area Health Authorities.

The combined impact of all these measures, ideas and policy statements has been to pull services for the mentally ill in a direction (or a number of directions) very different from those which must have seemed possible or probable in 1948. Probably the most important single factor was the development of the psychotropic drugs which made possible the control of mood-swings and hence the suppression of symptoms. *Better Services for the Mentally Ill* devotes some consideration to their effects, which are only partially understood, and may be principally palliative. Many doctors (and many patients) are concerned at the side-effects experienced, the implications for new possibilities of social control, and the effect of masking severe social and psychological problems without working through them.

Further research may refine the effect of these drugs, and perhaps induce a greater caution in those doctors who have tended to over-prescribe. However, the consequences of the new pharmacotherapy go far beyond individual prescriptions. It has made possible a massive reduction in mental hospital beds by enabling many patients to be treated by their general practitioners, or in out-patient clinics, and others to stay for much shorter periods. It has enabled mental hospitals to open the doors for most wards, and to give patients a much greater freedom of movement. It has 'normalised' the behaviour of most mentally ill people to the point where R. D. Laing, most sociologists and some social workers doubt whether there is an entity called mental illness at all. It has pulled psychiatrists into general medicine, since most of their work consists in prescribing, and away from the human sciences. Psychiatry has not influenced general medicine in the direction of human relations; it has become a minor specialism of general medicine. The psychiatrist is no longer a father figure, counsellor and elder of the tribe: his practice is increasingly standardised. Psychiatrists are still hospital-based, organised through a Medical Committee, with a Chairman who may change from time to time, and their responsibilities include out-patient clinics, day hospitals and a variety of consultancies to other agencies.

Most general practitioners still do not get much training in the human sciences. They do not need to, for they also have access to modern pharmacotherapy, and they can always send a patient to an out-patient clinic to have new and stronger drugs prescribed, or the dosage regulated. They do not have time, for they are as busy as ever, and if they stopped to enquire into the human problems of every patient for whom Valium or Librium offered a relief, they would never get any other work done; and some do not want to know about the human sciences, for Sociology has been remarkably destructive for the past twenty years, and much of its attack has been directed at the medical profession.

As the old medical power-structure has crumbled, other empires have been built up. Health service administrators take the major responsibility for district planning and financial control, and the hospital is merely one of their responsibilities. Nurses, under the aegis of the General Nursing Council, have developed their own administrative skills, and the nursing structure, like the planning and finance structure, is district-based, not hospital-based, and includes Community Nurses. Nursing has also become strongly unionised, and the Confederation of Health Service Employees is a power to be reckoned with.

Beyond the Health Service are the Personal Social Services, which are the responsibility of the local authority Social Services Departments. They are responsible for field social work, for homes and hostels, for training centres and day centres. When the Area Health Authorities existed, there was at least one administrative tier at which Health Services and Personal Social Services had common boundaries. The 1982 reorganisation has removed this, and weakened the links between the two sets of authorities, who have never found co-operation very easy.

Social workers, like other professionals, are generally much better trained than they were in the 1940s. But training (and unionisation) have made it more difficult to work with other professionals rather than less. The psychiatric component in social workers' training is often very limited and they are not trained to work with (or under the control of) doctors – a fact which many doctors deplore. Recent developments in social work theory have led away from psychoanalytic schools of thought. Freud, Adler, Jung, even Fromm and Karen Horney, are out; contract theory and behavioural therapy, which deal with surface events and require no understanding of the mainsprings of human behaviour, are in. These methods protect the social worker (by enabling him or her to demonstrate 'success' in definable terms to the employing authority) but they may act to suppress problems, much as chemotherapy does.

The 1975 White Paper struck a note of despair, estimating that it would be at least twenty-five years before an adequate network of community services would be available. The Nodder Report of 1978 (written in the light of the public inquiries into abuses in some hospitals, and never published) repeats it. We are told that there are repeated complaints of a lack of clear lines of responsibility; of a lack of contact between the different disciplines involved in the care of patients; of a 'very worrying lack of contact' between the hospitals and the health service authorities; and of lack of co-ordination between health and social services. The magnitude of the task of replacing a hospital-based service with a community-based service has been underestimated, and repeated economic setbacks have compounded difficulties. While the 'more attractive' elements of the replacement services have taken short-stay patients with mild conditions, mental hospitals are left with the 'more intractable problems'. Many of their medical staff now come from overseas – 'relatively few graduates of British universities are making their careers in psychiatry'.

> The mental health services remain services which do not in practice get high priority for resources. The emphasis on community care has not been matched by resources going into such care. Unless resources are spent much faster than in recent years . . . mental illness services cannot be made satisfactory simply by changes in organisation and management. (para. 2.12).

These factors are depressingly familiar. Are there any new solutions?

Apparently not: the Report goes on to consider the problems of mental hospitals in isolation, and in terms reminiscent of the DHSS 'Grey Book' on *Management Arrangements for the Reorganised Health Service* of 1973. None of the disillusion which many Health Service staff feel concerning that limited philosophy comes through: the discussion is framed in terms of 'objectives, standards and targets', 'evaluation and monitoring', tripartite management and two-dimensional diagrams of responsibility and control. The basic problems – lack of money, poor staff morale, antiquated buildings, lack of communication, lack of integration with community services, lack of public prestige – are touched upon and, as ever, ignored. The 'management' philosophy might be seen as another suppressive technique, enabling administrators and planners to keep busy while the nature of the problems goes unexamined.

The Mental Health Amendment Bill 1981 is concerned primarily with legal issues relating to the small proportion of patients now legally detained. While it goes some way towards meeting the contention of MIND that some provisions of the existing law contravene human rights, it does not involve any fundamental restructuring of the services as such.

Statistical checks

The new network of community services is inadequate, and officially acknowledged to be so – less a network than a maze, with many important parts missing or barely functioning; but how inadequate?

It would be satisfying to make a statistical comparison between provision in 1948 and provision in the early 1980s, which would at least demonstrate where the major gaps occur. Unfortunately the material is simply not available. The basis on which mental health statistics were collected was subject to major changes in 1959, the year of the Mental Health Act, which means that figures before and after that year are not comparable. While figures for mental hospital admissions, discharges and resident populations are still collected, these become less and less meaningful. Statistics for local authority, voluntary and private Homes and hostels refer to 'places and persons', but give no indication of turnover. Day hospital statistics are given in terms of places (with no indication of whether they are used by the same patients on different days of the week) and 'new patients'. Out-patient statistics refer to 'new patients' and the total number of attendances. We have no information on whether individual patients use several services at once or in succession, no information on whether the new patients have come from another service, no information on the mental health component in the work of general practitioners and social workers. To compound the problems still further, tables are aggregated and disaggregated in succeeding years: Wales is included, then excluded. The term 'psychiatric services' sometimes includes services for the mentally handicapped. People over the age of sixty-five and children are sometimes included and sometimes excluded. And even this kind of information virtually comes to an end in the mid 1970s. The last detailed *Mental Health Inquiry for England and Wales* was published in 1977. The figures are those for 1976. The Nodder report gives 1976 statistics for mental hospitals, day hospitals, day centres and residential Homes on the limited basis described above, drawn from the DHSS *Health and Personal Social Services Statistics* of the same year. *Health and Personal Social Services Statistics*, formerly an annual publication, was last published in 1978. The figures are those for 1977. The Royal Commission on the National Health Service (1979) gives no mental health statistics at all, and devotes no separate consideration to the problems of mental illness. MIND's pamphlet on Mental Health statistics, published in 1979 and still on sale in 1982, is based on the 1976 figures. *Social Trends* and the *Annual Abstract of Statistics* for 1981 give no information on services for the mentally ill, being predictably concerned with such matters as unemployment and law and order. The latest comparable published figures are as follows:

Hospital psychiatric services, England (mental illness)

	(thousands)			
	1959	*1969*	*1973*	*1977*
Mental hospitals:				
average daily occupied beds	135.2	110.1	94.2	80.8
Day cases:				
attendances	—	—	22.6	12.9
Out-patients:				
new cases	151.0*	218.6	208.6	191.7
attendances	1,108.2†	1,479.9	1,602.6	1,639.7

* Includes a proportion of mentally handicapped – probably about 2,000.
† Includes a proportion of mentally handicapped – probably about 6,000.
Source: Health and Personal Social Services Statistics, HMSO, 1978, Table 9.2

These figures illustrate the paucity of published information now available, and the difficulty of bringing information for one setting into relation with that for another. If mental hospital beds have fallen in numbers by some 55,000 since 1959, though the population at risk has risen, where have all the patients gone? One probability is faster through-put, for admission rates have continued to rise – indeed the rate of admission per hundred thousand population, which was 374 in 1970, was 385 by 1977 (HPSS, Table 9.4). Length of stay figures (Table 9.7) tell us only how many patients have been in hospital less than a year, 1–5 years and over 5 years. Table 9.8 gives a more detailed breakdown, but treats 'leaving or dying' as a single category, which is not informative.

There are other factors which require explanation: why have 'day cases' fallen off, and what is the relationship between the figures given here and some remarkably uninformative figures for 'regular day patients', also in Table 9.2, which cover both mental illness and mental handicap? Why are new out-patient cases now decreasing, but total out-patient attendances going up?

It is not possible from the available information to obtain any reliable picture of what is happening to patients. There are no figures for mental health work covered by general practitioners. Local authority statistics refer only to residential homes, and tend to be meaningless, since some authorities mix the physically handicapped and the mentally ill, others mix the mentally handicapped and the mentally ill, some mix lucid but frail old people with psychogeriatric patients. It is seldom clear when this is done as a matter of conviction about 'integration', or when it is done as a measure of economy. For one cause or another, the general mixed workhouse is being reinvented in some areas.

The foreword to *Better Services for the Mentally Ill* in 1975 stated that 'about five million people a year' then consulted their general practitioners for mental health problems, and that 'some 600,000' were referred annually to a psychiatrist for consultation. No source is given, and these figures may only be educated official guesses. Mental illness is described as 'a major health problem – perhaps the major health problem of our time' but there is no statistical backing for the statement.

Since 1977 there have been no detailed figures. Government statistical services have shrunk with the cuts in public expenditure: and the problems of collecting meaningful information in a quantifiable form, even given the possibilities offered by computer linkage, are severe. Computer linkage might be held to be an invasion of privacy – people who seek advice usually wish to do so without being traced from one agency to another; and it would be very difficult to say how much of the work of GPs and social workers could be categorised as mental health advice in 1948 terms.

Better or worse?

Have the services for the mentally ill improved or deteriorated? The answer must be that we do not know: all we know is that they are different. A whole world of social control and compulsion has gone, and with it has gone some of the stigma, but more of the social dynamic. Authoritarianism has been replaced, not with democracy but with *laissez-faire*. If we go back to the imaginary hospital of our 1948 visit in the 1980s, it is much less easy to generalise, for while all mental hospitals then had a strong 'family likeness', they have diversified. But it is likely that the wall has gone, though the Victorian buildings still stand. In the grounds, an industrial therapy unit, a day hospital and perhaps a hostel replace the old tuberculosis units. The administrators are still busy with paper work, because there is another reorganisation to be dealt with, but they are attached to the district – the hospital is merely where they have their offices. The consultants, many of them Indian or Pakistani, hurry along the corridors – much of their work is in out-patient clinics or day hospitals or as consultants to outside agencies. Senior nursing staff are part of the district nursing structure, and responsible for community nursing as well as hospital nursing. There are no queues of patients, and no jangling keys. Most ward doors are open, and there are no identity jokes.

Patients no longer do the menial work of the hospital, or work in staff houses. If they are able to work, they go to the industrial therapy unit and earn a wage, banking the money in the hospital bank and spending it as they please. There is no parole system. Most patients can go out, and their visitors can come in, at most times. The length of stay is usually short, and the separation from the outside world less marked.

The wards are well heated, with modern decorations and furnishings. The work of the Hospital Advisory Service has led to impressive upgrading. Most of the patients sit quietly around watching colour television. The padded rooms have been turned into single bedrooms or offices, and the airing courts into gardens or car parks.

For most patients, life is much less regimented than in a general hospital. The highly-organised activity programmes have lapsed, and if they are not working, they can please themselves how they occupy their time. Nursing staff may not be very interested.

The most striking facts are that the wards are half-empty, and most of the patients over forty. Comparatively few young people come in, though some go to the Drug Addiction Unit in town. The hospital has become elderly, and quieter. Most of the patients are women. The barrack-like culture of the male wards has disappeared. There are nurses of both sexes, and the male nurses are seldom of the burly type formerly required. This is true even on the few locked wards, where security has to be maintained. Male and female patients are on adjacent wards, and may share day-rooms. ·

A visit to a general hospital psychiatric unit, the day hospital, or to a local authority Home or day centre, will probably reveal the same kind of diffuse activity, the same *laissez-faire* attitudes, the same privatisation. It is not only that the focus has moved outside the hospital – there is no focus, unless it lies in the office of the district planners, who dream of pulling the hospital down in the year 2000.

One can only guess at the total effect of change: people suffering from comparatively mild degrees of stress or neurosis, as most of us do at some time or other, can clearly seek help far more easily from a general practitioner or a social worker than they could in the 1940s. Whether that help is really effective, or whether it merely suppresses symptoms, leaving some to live chaotic and tangled lives, depends largely on their own capacity to solve their basic problems. People suffering from severe conditions probably fare less well, or remain a considerable burden to their families. Some do not reach or stay in the mental health maze: they swell the ranks of the single homeless, sleeping rough and surfacing only in night shelters, or they go to prison, categorised as 'bad' rather than 'mad'.

John Leach and John Wing (1980) found a high prevalence of mental illness and personality disorders in their sample of homeless men, though this was difficult to quantify. A Glasgow survey (*Homeless Men Speak for Themselves,* Glasgow Council for the Single Homeless, 1980) rated only one per cent of that sample as 'mentally ill', but well over half as having 'family problems' or 'marital problems'. Nigel Walker and Sarah McCabe, in a study of 908 male 'offender-patients' made subject to a hospital order by the Courts, found that two-thirds had prior hospital admissions, three-quarters had prior convictions, and nearly half had both. There are repeated references to a 'stage army' which can appear from either the prison or the mental hospital (Walker and McCabe, 1973, pp. 116, 151–4, 240). The American evidence, documented by Andrew Scull (1977), suggests the failure of 'decarceration' or reducing institutional populations. The writer comments: 'Much of the time, it appears as if the policy makers simply do not know what will happen when their schemes are put into effect. Nor do they seem very concerned to find out' (p. 1).

Perhaps that is the major change since 1948.

References

Department of Health and Social Security (DHSS) (1973), *Management Arrangements for the Reorganised NHS* (The 'Grey Book').

DHSS (1975), *Better Services for the Mentally Ill*, White Paper, Cmnd. 6233.

DHSS (1978), *Health and Personal Social Services Statistics*.

DHSS (1978), *The Organisation and Management Problems of Mental Illness Hospitals* (The Nodder Report, unpublished, circulated in typescript).

Glasgow Council for the Single Homeless, (1980) *Homeless Men Speak for Themselves*.

Goffman, E. (1961), *Asylums; essays on the social situation of mental patients and other inmates*, New York, Anchor Books.

Gostin, L. (1977), *A Human Condition*, 2 vols, MIND, 22 Harley Street, London W1.

Jones, K. (1972), *A History of the Mental Health Services*, London, Routledge & Kegan Paul.

Jones, M. (1952), *Social Psychiatry*, London, Tavistock.

Laing, R. D., and Esterson, A. (1964), *Sanity, Madness and the Family*, London, Tavistock.

Leach, J., and Wing, J. (1980), *Helping Destitute Men*, London, Tavistock.

Ministry of Health (1926), *Lunacy and Mental Disorder*, Report of Royal Commission (MacMillan Report).

Ministry of Health (1939), *Voluntary Mental Health Services*, Report of Committee (Feversham Report).

Ministry of Health (1951), *Social Workers in the Mental Health Services*, Report of Committee (Mackintosh Report).

Scull, A. (1973), *Decarceration: Community treatment and the radical view*, New York, Prentice Hall.

Walker, N., and McCabe, S. (1973), *Crime and Insanity in England*, Edinburgh University Press.

Chapter 15
Idealism and realism in education: 1940 and 1980
Roger Cox

Idealism

In the preface to his book *Education and Social Change* Clarke (1940, p. 1) wrote:

> We do not need to be told today that not all our destiny is under our control. But in so far as we may be able to direct the course of events we can do so only on condition that we submit ourselves and the working presuppositions of our English society to a rigorous and radical process of self-examination. Then the negative task of clearing away irrelevancies, obsolete survivals, and pseudo-principles that are no more than the disguise of material interest, will make all the easier the positive task of formulating more relevant and defensible standards of action.

A familiar enough refrain and eminently suitable for an essay about to chronicle the fall from grace of yet another of those sons of war-time hope. Perhaps less familiar in tone and striking even by the standards of the 1940s is Clarke's conclusion (1940, p. 70): 'It may be, then, that the most essentially religious thing in us is that by virtue of which we cohere as a society, and that here is the heart of education's business.'

It is perhaps too tempting to embalm such phrases in their own piety, preserving them as quaint aberrations produced by the shock of war, worthy reminders of the search for a possible but highly improbable state of virtue. The temptation is to be resisted, however, for several reasons. In the first place these are calls to action, not mere statements of piety. As Vidler says in his general preface,

> We live in a changing society; it is still an open question what the outcome of change will be. It is the duty of Christians to be aware of what is happening and, while the situation is still fluid, to exercise their utmost influence upon the course of events. In politics the old party lines are vanishing and new groups are being formed. Christians ought to play a decided part both by thought and action in these developments (Clarke, 1940, p. ii).

Author and editor both are committed to action based upon vigorous radical thought; a politics of fearless analysis leading to necessary action. There is a sense too in which both Clarke and Vidler believe they are doing something new, something foreign to the English tradition. They are demanding intellectual effort, not indeed of the flighty continental variety, but a rethinking and reinterpreting radically based upon a profound conservatism: 'the course taken by English development over long centuries makes the paradox profoundly true that if we are conservative enough we can afford to be thoroughly radical, not only without loss, but with much gain'. The aim is thus 'Honest and sustained intellectual effort. . . a vital part of Home Defence, unless, indeed, we are prepared to see much that we claim to be fighting for dissipated before our eyes' (Clarke, 1940, p. vi).

In these few pages of preface and introduction Vidler and Clarke map out an approach to policy making which in some ways is very characteristic of the 1940s. The 'Dad's Army' intellectuals with Beveridge in their kitbags, the clear Christian motivation and the radical conservatism in pursuit of the impossible make for a curious combination, perhaps, but it is by no means trivial and far from being simply pious. José Harris illuminates something more than a great man's private dream when she concludes her biography of Beveridge by quoting his own favourite line from Sophocles' *Antigone*: 'When I have ceased to hanker after the impossible I shall have ceased to breathe' (Harris, 1977, p. 476).

Indulgence in *fin de siècle* cynicism at the expense of the 1940s is, therefore, to be resisted, not only because the vision embodied such a strong commitment to action, but also for the much simpler reason that it excuses the subsequent fall from grace by appealing to nothing better than increased realism. No doubt Adam and Eve lived with greater realism in the knowledge of both good and evil, but it was scarcely a higher state of virtue. Whilst in some other areas of social policy it may be possible to refer to better material conditions as justifying the means, in education it is virtue alone which must be means and ends. The tragedy of the 1980s lies in the fact that whilst this truth is forcing itself to the surface of political debate, there is nowhere any discernibly coherent discourse about what virtue is or how it can be taught. The crass instrumentality of the debate on the relationship between education and industry and the extreme tenuousness of its validity even in its own instrumental terms is opposed by a sociological debate, which even in its more recent creative attempts (Willis, 1977; CCCS, 1981) is held within the determinist stance of much contemporary social theory.

But what was the state of virtue which the reformers of the 1940s thought they saw? The answer has already been alluded to in that 'essentially religious' sense of commonality which it is the business of education to enhance. If social insurance, conceived in essentially bureaucratic terms, was for Beveridge the 'structural embodiment of the social and economic interdependence of modern man' (Harris, 1977, p. 476), then education was to provide the spiritual thrust and make conscious the implicit social integration. It was to be the act of communion in the ritual of the mass. The resonances, however, are not only religious, but refer also to a powerful secular belief that the nature of English society would, after the war, be fundamentally changed. Clarke himself bore witness to this faith when he wrote: 'let us remember that the bonds which will hold a regenerate England together are greater than England itself, as man is greater than his own social institutions' (1940, p. 70).

Orwell in *The Lion and the Unicorn* expressed it more colourfully:

> This war. . . will wipe out most of the existing class privileges. . . . Nor need we fear that as the pattern changes life in England will lose its peculiar flavour. . . . The gentleness, the hypocrisy, the thoughtlessness, the reverence for law and the hatred of uniforms will remain along with suet pudding and the misty skies. . . . The Stock Exchange will be pulled down, the horse plough will give way to the tractor, the country houses will be turned into children's holiday camps, the Eton and Harrow match will be forgotten, but England will still be England, an everlasting animal stretching into the future and the past, and, like all living things, having the power to change out of recognition and yet remain the same (quoted in van der Eyken, 1973).

Clarke's own position in the 1940s is significant enough to merit further comment. An educationalist who spent much of his working life in the Dominions, mostly in South Africa, he returned home as Principal of the Institute of Education of London University. His subsequent appointment by Butler as the first Chairman of the Central Advisory Council for England was, say Curtis and Boultwood, 'received with great satisfaction' (1960, p. 198). Whilst Principal of the Institute, Clarke persuaded Mannheim to come and lecture there, thus introducing sociology into the curriculum for student teachers. Of the books and pamphlets published during the war which are discussed by Dent (1944), Clarke's *Education and Social Change* is the one that has endured the longest in the bibliographies of educational historians. Referred to by Lawson and Silver as 'a powerful book' (1973, p. 417) and by Simon as 'a seminal little book' which 'did much to stimulate an awakening' of interest in education at the start of the war (1974, p. 271, 295), it clearly had a considerable impact upon the educational debate of the early war years. As Barnard puts it, its small size was 'out of all proportion to its importance' (1961, p. 315). That it had such an impact is due to several factors. First, it reflected the resurgence of Christian feeling and the belief that education rather than the family or even the church was the best place for the propagation of Christian values (Lawson and Silver, 1973, p. 417). The 'Christian News-Letter' (under the auspices of which Clarke published his own book) was clearly influential, especially in 1940, and was the medium through which T. S. Eliot chose to deliver himself of the opinion that the aim of education had less to do with equality of opportunity and more to do with Wisdom and Holiness (Dent, 1944, p. 174).

More significantly, Eliot saw education as a defence against the atomisation of society. The scope of education, he claimed, 'is no longer the task of merely training individuals in and for society, but also the much larger task of training a society itself – without', he added ominously, 'our having any fundamental accepted principles on which to train it' (quoted in Dent, 1944, p. 174).

Whilst Eliot was perhaps not over keen on any system of mass education, the belief that education should serve more than individual purposes was very strong. The point had been taken and thoroughly understood that in fascist Germany and Italy education had been used to shape a powerful national consciousness which the individualism of English educational theory seemed not to foster. It was Clarke who gave the most adequate expression to this feeling (Armytage, 1964, p. 238; Barnard, 1961, p. 315). In summarising a later work of Clarke's,

Freedom in an Educative Society, published in 1947, Curtis and Boultwood say:

> A new culture would emerge from the common life and experiences of a healthy society. A common purpose of that society would define itself, and this should be heeded both in school and outside. The whole content of education should be relevant to it, and the teachers chosen should be its especially sensitive representatives. That is, education cannot create a new society, it can only reflect the one in which it exists (1960, p. 266).

This belief that education must grow out of society and not be used to change it, except on the basis of profound conservatism, is the major theme of *Education and Social Change*. It can be understood first of all as a defence against fascism. If it was necessary for education to have some collective purpose, then that purpose must be found in the nature of the society itself and not in abstract principles, or worse in foreign ideologies. But for Clarke particularly (and clearly under the influence of Mannheim), finding this purpose specifically involved the use of sociology in order to explore the nature of the society which education was to reflect. *Education and Social Change*, he says, adopts 'unreservedly what may well be called the sociological standpoint', its aim being 'to exhibit as well as we can its concrete application to the field of English education' (1940, p. 1). As Curtis and Boultwood say (1960, p. 267), the main impact of Clarke's work was 'to stimulate and reinforce the claims of sociology to a place in the field of studies covered by education'.

Finding precise intellectual ancestors or progeny for Clarke is rather more difficult. The most obvious parallel is, of course, Durkheim whose *The Evolution of Educational Thought* is a much more extended and rigorous working out of Clarke's theme. It may well be that Clarke knew something of Durkheim's work, but there is no specific acknowledgment and it is improbable that he was aware how appropriate a model Durkheim had provided in his education lectures at the Sorbonne. Clarke's own references are not entirely but mostly English and consist of a number of references to literary figures, from Milton and his *Tractate* to Keats and his view of the world as a 'vale of soul-makers'. Added to this are appeals to a number of standard nineteenth-century worthies from Thomas Arnold to Robert Morant. Apart from a reference to Weber, via Mannheim, there is no use of social theory and the sociology is, in fact, no more than the homespun history characteristic of many educational commentators of the period, and later. Matthew Arnold might stand as one possible ancestor but progeny are equally difficult to find. Raymond Williams is one possibility but, of course, from a much sharper intellectual tradition. In the Eliot-Bantock-C. B. Cox line, there is a kind of connection, but they rail against the idea of mass education and against the notion of a common culture which Clarke so warmly embraced. For the most part then Clarke's book is a curiously isolated phenomenon, having many superficial connections with the more general debates of the 1940s, but particularly in its Durkheimian implications, having in its deeper aims little connection with the English educational tradition which was, and is, intensely individualistic.

Perhaps the frailty of Clarke's vision lies in the very intimacy of the educational process and its stress, especially in England and America, upon social relationships. Whilst Beveridge could keep Sophocles to himself and get on with the business of constructing vast bureaucratic organisations whose material consequences could withstand political storms, the substance of education, once it breaks out of a restricted elite context and begins to offer something more than basic literacy to the masses, becomes highly problematic and heavily dependent upon its instrumental functions of selection, sorting and social control for its legitimation. What Durkheim sought to establish on the basis of a sociological theory which made education a functional *necessity* of social integration, Clarke tried to establish on the basis of Christian feeling and a few scattered references to a humanistic, literary tradition.

Realism

'Thought and practice', wrote Clarke, 'are much more closely conditioned by social realities which are themselves the result of historical and economic forces, than by the highly generalised principles which figure so prominently in the textbooks' (1940, p. 1).

That the sociological project that Clarke wanted did not produce the ends that he envisaged is hardly surprising. Whilst it is true that the search for social reality was mounted with great vigour and enterprise, it was carried out in a spirit of antagonism to the reality it disclosed. With a series of well-planned explosions educational sociology sought to lay bare the complex reality of the relationship of education to the economy and the social structure. The attacks upon intelligence testing; upon the persistent inequalities of access to the higher stages of education (by class particularly but also by sex and race); the assault upon the curriculum and upon the internal workings of the school; all these have blasted holes in the legitimacy of the orthodoxy that developed around the 1944 Act. And whilst the coming of the comprehensive school and the expansion of higher education allowed temporary repairs to be carried out, by 1980 they were exposed in their frailty and ruthlessly attacked in their turn by the so-called 'new educational right' in what became the 'age of the educational "common man"'' (Fowler in Bernbaum, 1979, p. 75).

It is not a question of sociology having failed to deliver in terms of explanation, so much as the fact that the distance between explanation and normative theories of education which provide its legitimacy has increased at an accelerating rate. Of course, from one point of view this is necessary in that, if radical change is sought, the confrontation of reality and orthodox legitimation is a continuing prerequisite to change, however deep the analysis must delve into the bowels of education, society and, indeed, sociology itself. One or two examples must suffice to illustrate the nature of the educational discourse at the beginning of the 1980s.

Perhaps the most interesting recent account of post-war educational policy is that provided by the Education Group of the Centre for Contemporary Cultural Studies (CCCS, 1981). Their book, *Unpopular Education*, charts the rise and fall, or rather 'the making', 'the limits' and 'the breaking' of social democracy. They note, for example, the importance of the concept of 'citizenship' in the 1940s in displacing the overt class-related politics of the inter-war period (p. 64), and point out, quite correctly, how 'huge divergencies of experience by class and by sex especially, were hidden away in the key terms of an uncomplicated populism: "the people", "the common people", "everyman", "the citizen"'' (p. 69).

Whilst one may quibble about whether Clarke, in particular, represents an 'uncomplicated populism', their general strictures on wartime and early post-war debates are just. But what is equally interesting is their comment: 'What was missing here was an adequate political economy, any knowledge of the actual nature of labour processes and therefore a more concrete account of the education-production relation' (p. 69).

Granted its Marxist orientation, it still seems to contain the seeds of self-destruction which they themselves attribute to the old sociology of Glass and Halsey (CCCS, 1981, p. 130). The assumption that an 'adequate political economy' can produce, *by itself*, the foundation of knowledge upon which to build a mass education system is as fragile a belief as that which spurred on the 'old' sociologists in their investigations of class differentials in access to secondary and higher education. The claim that through the old sociology 'all sense of education as a lived process was lost' (p. 72) may well be true, but one should be clear about what they, in their turn, are offering. Their insistence upon the distinction between education and schooling and their search for an organic Gramscian unity between intellectuals and 'the simple' (p. 261), is itself still an essentially instrumental view of education. Education is only the *means* of transformation, the medium through which the struggle is undertaken. Certainly education for struggle may be, indeed for some has been, a 'lived process' (p. 34), but without a theory of continuous revolution – and the CCCS do not seem to be suggesting that – the transformation must eventually give way to a less antagonistic role for education. If it cannot do so then the hoped-for unity between theory and praxis remains illusory. Of course, one could argue that a theory of transformation should be quite sufficient to satisfy the appetite of any radical group faced with the Britain of the 1980s, but there is a sense in which even they have missed the force of the 'new right' incursions into the educational debate, even though they analyse it so well, (CCCS, 1981, ch. 9). It is not merely that the new educational right is able to represent its views as 'a valuable recall to common sense against the aloof expertise of theorists and bureaucrats' (p. 201), remarkable though that achievement, and that of Rhodes Boyson in particular, is. It is also that 'common sense', itself, is represented as a short sharp transformation back to a foundation of eternal verities which will then endure. Here is a unity of theory and praxis that transcends any strategy of mere transformation, and by its crude simplicity provides a vision of the state of virtue, however vulgar.

The mainstream political discourse of the 1980s will almost certainly focus on the relationship of industry (and by implication hopes for renewed economic growth) and education. Whilst the needs of industry is an oft recurring theme of educational history (see Salter and Tapper, 1981, p. 32), it has in the 1980s reappeared in a particularly virulent form. Whilst the human investment theories of the 1950s may, as the CCCS group suggest, have 'permitted the collapse of human needs into economic imperatives' (1981, p. 77), yet given the breadth and generality of their expression, they were theories which supported rather than contradicted the expansion of high level education. The debate of the 1980s is of an altogether different order. The CCCS group see the Green Paper *Education in Schools* (HMSO, 1977) as formally setting 'the seal on the school-work bond as the rationale for schooling' (CCCS, 1981, p. 225). The Green Paper is explicit enough:

> Young people need to reach maturity with a basic understanding of the economy and the activities, especially manufacturing industry, which are necessary for the creation of Britain's wealth. It is an important task of secondary schools to develop this understanding and opportunities for its development should be offered to pupils of all abilities. These opportunities are needed not only by young people who may have careers in industry later but perhaps even more by those who may work elsewhere so that the role of industry becomes soundly appreciated by society in general (HMSO, 1977, p. 35).

The Great Debate and its aftermath, and the rise of the Manpower Services Commission, are all adequately dealt with elsewhere (e.g. David, 1980; CCCS, 1981; Salter and Tapper, 1981): suffice it to note that behind the affability of the Green Paper lies a restricted, highly instrumental conception of the function of education. The rhetoric of human investment is still there as, for example, in *Educating Our Children*: 'In examining the extent to which education is fulfilling its function to prepare pupils for working life we must not forget the importance of developing children's all-round personalities, talents and sensitivities' (DES, 1977, p. 12).

But the talents and sensitivities are tacked on as a pleasing afterthought: no longer does talent *create* economic growth, it has become an optional extra, an embellishment, a bourgeois accomplishment to be exhibited in the drawing-room after a hard day of wealth creation. Teachers are now to learn about industry, but not industry about education (DES, 1977, p. 14; CCCS, 1981, p. 146). The subtle differences of language and tone between *Educating Our Children* and *Education in Schools* on the one hand, and the official reports and papers of the early 1940s would be well worth further comment, but perhaps one further rather trivial example from *Educating our Children* is permissible. After acknowledging very graciously that some jobs are unattractive, it goes on to make the utterly cynical suggestion that employers should 'make the job (*or at least its image*) attractive' (DES, 1977, p. 14, author's italics). Trivial though it is, the fact that such a comment could pass through the hands of senior civil servants and probably a Secretary of State without censure, is itself an indication of the paucity of contemporary educational debate. Perhaps one should welcome the recognition that not all work is a joy and a delight, but note that the honesty is not to be granted to careers teachers, children or their parents, but only to the advertising men whose job it becomes to deceive everybody else.

But behind this debate lurks another issue which threatens to produce an explosion greater than any seen before and possibly fatal to any conception of a national education system, however instrumentally conveyed. By the 1980s the legitimation for the collective provision of education has been reduced to the crude assertion of the schoolwork bond. Now whilst credentialism (Salter and Tapper, 1981, p. 33) and the need to socialise the labour force, both productive and reproductive, (CCCS, 1981, ch. 7) clearly support this conception, the substantive core of the legitimation hangs upon the belief that school teaches skills which industry needs. If even this residual assertion fails, then education for the mass of children in the terms in which it was conceived in 1944 is essentially dead. The challenge comes, of course, most specifically from Braverman who in the final chapter of *Labour and Monopoly Capital*, like a pathologist over a decomposing corpse, describes the characteristics of his subject. Political control, socialisation for urban living, the growth of high-level technology (irrelevant to the mass of pupils), the self-sustaining nature of the education 'industry': all these sustain the physical form of education, but none give it life. Thus, he argues,

> the schools have developed into immense teen-sitting organisations,
> their function having less and less to do with imparting to the young
> those things that society thinks they must learn. In this situation the
> content of education deteriorated as its duration lengthened. The
> knowledge imparted in the course of an elementary education was
> more or less expanded to fill the prevalent twelve-year educational
> sojourn, and in a great many cases school systems have difficulty in
> instilling in twelve years the basic skills of literacy and numbers that,
> several generations ago, occupied eight. This in turn gave a greater
> impetus to employers to demand of job applicants a high school
> diploma, as a guarantee – not always valid – of getting workers who
> can read (Braverman, 1974, p. 439).

Here, indeed, is a worthy prophet of doom:

> Just as in the labour process, where the more there is to know the less
> the worker need know, in the schools the mass of future workers

attend the more there is to learn, the less reason there is for teachers to teach and students to learn. In this more than in any other single factor – the purposelessness, futility, and empty forms of the education system – we have the source of the growing antagonism between the young and their schools which threatens to tear the schools apart (Braverman, 1974, p. 440).

The realism is here complete; shorn of its last vestiges of liberal ideology the education system stands condemned in terms of its own final defence – the imparting of skills. Entwistle elaborates upon this divorce of ideology from economic function,

> From the point of view of education it is evident that even the most rudimentary of skills (even minimal literacy and numeracy as well as craft skills) make far greater intellectual demands of the pupil than those he is likely to be called upon to meet in industry for the remainder of his working life (in Simon and Taylor, 1981, p. 39).

And like Braverman, Entwistle locates this dislocation within the economic organisation of capitalist societies,

> one of the contradictions of capitalism [is] that its educational ideology commits us to the complete and harmonious development of every individual's human potential, whilst its economic arrangements are incapable of generating work opportunities for the majority which even begin to honour this educational axiom (in Simon and Taylor, 1981, p. 44).

Given this assessment, an educational debate tied to the narrowly productive capacity of the educational system is frail indeed, but this is precisely the orthodoxy of the 1980s.

Idealism in realism

In short, what the educational discourse of the 1980s seems to offer is, at one end of an increasingly polarised debate, acute pessimism or strategies for the radical use of education (possibly outside the state system) as a means of transformation. At the other end is a crude reassertion of a more subtle nineteenth-century belief in the self-evident virtue of obedience of both children and their parents to the authority of the state (for what else is the ideology of the new educational right?). And this is coupled with a perilously fragile belief that education and industry can be linked in such a way as to provide concrete, observable benefits in terms of economic growth.

Of course, it is the educational *discourse* that is in a far greater state of crisis than the system itself as a bureaucratic structure. And even the discourse has a range of residual clichés, some limp conception of social functioning or of realising individual potential, with which to bolster its failing ego. But if the quality of education, rather than as during most of the post-war period its quantity, is at issue, then the quality of the discourse at all its levels is critical. In education, as in perhaps no other area of social policy, the discourse *is the thing itself*. If there is no valid, sustainable debate about education, then that lack will filter through to teachers and to pupils and their parents. Indeed, it may well be the pupils who are the first to sense the loss and give expression, as Braverman suggested, to their alienation. For most of the period following the Second World War education has been able to sustain itself upon its instrumental value to the individual. Prospects of individual upward mobility were given credence by relatively sustained economic growth and by the movements in the occupational structure towards higher status non-manual jobs. But there is no guarantee of this continuing, and indeed for many the illusion has already been cruelly shattered. Not only do the prospects for social mobility now appear more restricted, but the subjective experience of education itself, even at the highest levels, has become for too many a profoundly alienating experience.

To mimic a famous remark of Halsey's, the essential fact of post-war educational debate is that the sociological project has failed. In its current form (the possibility of radical transformation aside), it points directly to a return to the dualism of the nineteenth century, but without the hope that much nineteenth-century debate embodied. On the one hand the demands of capital are for a highly educated elite of scientists and technologists, with a more or less liberal supply of 'feminine' accomplishments provided by the arts and social sciences; on the other hand the demands of the *state* within capitalism are for minimal skills and meek aquiescence to its authority. The determinism involved in that scenario can only be overcome by a richer, more universal discourse that deals with education *as education*, itself a discourse about its own nature.

Clarke stood at a watershed in the history of educational thought. Behind him was a largely philosophical tradition of liberal humanism conceived without the context of a mass educational system, where social reality was understood only in terms of a ruling elite. Ahead of him was a powerful, critical, antagonistic sociological tradition through which the grasp of social reality was sharply increased, but at the expense of a strong, if restricted, normative tradition of educational philosophy. The strength of Clarke's approach was that he saw the necessity of holding the two together. Now, whilst there can be no return to Clarke because his sense of social reality, caricatured so splendidly if unintentionally by Orwell, was so hopelessly inadequate, this is no reason to abandon the project he conceived. Social democrats need it if they are to get beyond managerialism; egalitarians need it to escape the mechanistic metaphor that so frequently traps them; socialists need it if they are to offer more than a strategy of transformation; even the 'new right' may soon feel the need for it, as those poor downtrodden exponents of the one nation theory are already so painfully aware. If one grants the education system and those who work in it any degree of autonomy and creative imagination, it matters little from where the impetus comes so long as it does come.

If there is one contemporary exponent of Clarke's project, it is probably Harold Entwistle in his *Class, Culture and Education*. Whilst his discussion of class may not be adequate, and his belief that class cultures and sub-cultures overlap to produce both a common culture and a 'high culture' ignores the element of conflict inherent in opposing cultures (see Willis, 1977), yet his insistence that the philosophical and the sociological traditions must be merged and that some conception of *man* must be set alongside the inquiry into the nature of *men* is at the heart of Clarke's project. Entwistle's criticism (1978, p. 180) of Durkheim (from whom contemporary social theory has still much to learn, if it could but overcome its prejudices) is perhaps overstressed since, at least in *The Evolution of Educational Thought*, Durkheim concludes on an essentially rationalist, rather than a determinist, note – Cartesian man lives yet, at least in France (Durkheim, 1977, p. 348). But where Entwistle may well be right, and the more appropriate man for the moment, is in identifying the need for a sharper, stronger reassertion of the claims of the philosophical and the moral (as well as the purely intellectual), to turn the sociological from its missionary pessimism to a modest affirmation of the legitimacy of mass education.

For many in the 1980s, and not for de-schoolers alone, it will seem preferable to abandon secondary education as an education of the intellect and the senses, rather than to allow teachers and pupils to struggle on bound by an exchange relationship (see Willis, 1977, p. 67) that dehumanises and alienates both parties. But it was precisely the ideal of a national system of *secondary* education that was debated in the 1940s, and for all its naïveté and its restricted terms of reference, it is not an ideal that the realism of the 1980s should be allowed to destroy after a mere forty years.

References

Armytage, W. H. G. (1964), *Four Hundred Years of English Education*, Cambridge University Press.

Barnard, H. C. (1961, 2nd ed.), *A History of English Education*, London, University of London Press.

Bernbaum, G. (1979), *Schooling in Decline*, London, Macmillan.

Braverman, H. (1974), *Labour and Monopoly Capital*, New York, Monthly Review Press.

Centre for Contemporary Cultural Studies, University of Birmingham (1981), *Unpopular Education*, London, Hutchinson.

Clarke, F. (1940), *Education and Social Change*, London, Sheldon Press.

Curtis, S. J., and Boultwood, M. E. A. (1960), *An Introductory History of English Education since 1800*, London, University Tutorial Press.

David, M. (1980), *The Family, State and Education*, London, Routledge & Kegan Paul.

Dent, H. C. (1944), *Education in Transition*, London, Kegan Paul, Trench, Trubner.

DES (1977), *Educating Our Children*, London.

Durkheim, E. (1977), *The Evolution of Educational Thought*, London, Routledge & Kegan Paul.

Entwistle, H. (1978), *Class, Culture and Education*, London, Methuen.

Harris, J. (1977), *William Beveridge*, Oxford, Clarendon Press.

HMSO (1977), *Education in Schools*, Cmnd. 6869, London.

Lawson, J., and Silver, H. (1973), *A Social History of Education in England*, London, Methuen.

Salter, B., and Tapper, T. (1981), *Education, Politics and the State*, London, Grant McIntyre.

Simon, B. (1974), *The Politics of Educational Reform*, London, Lawrence & Wishart.

Simon, B., and Taylor, W. (1981), *Education in the Eighties*, London, Batsford.

van der Eyken, W. (1973), *Education, the Child and Society*, Harmondsworth, Penguin.

Willis, P. (1977), *Learning to Labour*, Farnborough, Saxon House.

Chapter 16
After the Rainbow Sign
Nicholas Deakin

God gave Noah the rainbow sign
No more water, the fire next time.
(Afro-American slave song, as quoted by James Baldwin – 1963)

Introduction

In this essay I will be reviewing the evolution of policy in an area where most of the concerns that have dominated the post-war debate on the evolution of the Welfare State have generally had little or no application. Race relations as a field for research and analysis is booby-trapped: excluded for long periods from the mainstream of debate by neglect (benign or malevolent), it erupts at intervals with the utmost ferocity into the centre of the political arena. When it does so, the normal rules are held to be suspended. Then academics and government agencies alike are called upon in peremptory style to embark without delay on crash programmes, regardless of expense or prospects of success. Small wonder, perhaps, that one distinguished academic specialist in social policy once categorised all those working in the field, practitioners and researchers alike, as being slightly deranged.

The period I propose to review runs approximately from the Conservative Government's return to power in October 1951 (that year conveniently also being a census year) to the publication of the Scarman Report at the end of 1981. By taking the past three decades as a period for examination I run the risk of distorting the picture in several important respects. The British obsession with decades as units of time for the analysis of social policy (and everything else from political

249

ideologies to hairstyles) tends to impose a spurious neatness on any account; any tendency in that direction in what follows should be discounted in advance. Perhaps more important, such an approach cuts off some important areas where explanations are likely to be found.

For a start, there is the pre-history of race relations in Britain, which has lately become the subject of intensive activity (Lunn, 1980). Some of this work, it must be said, is mere antiquarianism; it helps to add to the already ample substratum of quaint and curious information about minorities but not to our understanding about the role they have played. But an indication of the real change in perspective that has taken place is that any reputable social historian would now accept that British society has been for a considerable time significantly heterogeneous in ethnic terms. This has important implications. We are no longer prone – or should not be – to the illusion of homogeneity: the idea that these islands have for centuries been inhabited by a static population with unchanging culture and language. The great Jewish migrations of the last century remain probably the best known of the accretions of population, not least for their contribution to the 'fountains of new talent' from which our society has benefited. Every now and again a public event: the Pope's helicopter descending at Coventry, or less happily the resumption of the IRA's 'mainland' campaign, will remind true-born Englishmen of the presence among them of millions of fellow citizens of Irish descent. But because past migrations have generally affected limited geographical areas, their effect on the national consciousness has also been limited. Our hostility to new arrivals has at times in the past been intense: and there have been several clear-cut cases of continuity in the location and form of that hostility. In East London, the caterwauling of the British Brothers' League at the turn of the century leads on naturally to the post-war campaigns of the British Union of Fascists. There are continuities too, and well worth tracing, in the response to these campaigns against new minorities (I have tried this exercise myself – Deakin, 1978). But here again those who took part in these campaigns on both sides were – and indeed always have been – a minority. The general assumption has always been that the newcomers must be left to their own devices to make the adjustment required in order to become fully accepted. Such adjustments involve the obliteration of any cultural or linguistic differences that may be offensive to the tastes of the majority. George Mikes (*How to be an Alien*) has made a lifetime's living out of jokes about the ways in which foreigners may unwittingly offend: the folklore is full of quips about newcomers striving to become more English than the English (but being infallibly detected in the process).

Second, a cut-off at the beginning of the 1950s begs the huge question of the influence of the British Imperial experience. The precise economic consequences of imperialism are still hotly debated: whether Bristol and Liverpool really owe their past prosperity to the slave trade or whether it is merely rhetorically convenient to assume so is still an open question. The wealth of the Indies certainly furnished the wherewithal for the nabob's country houses and seats in Parliament: but does it necessarily follow that Orwell was right in supposing that what passed for the prosperity of the working class in Britain in the 1930s was due chiefly to exploitation of their fellow subjects in the Empire? What is beyond doubt, though, is the way in which the Imperial past affected attitudes among the British. The automatic assumption of the cultural and social inferiority of the native, reinforced (once again) by jokes passed from generation to generation, is one face of this automatic categorisation. The other is the benevolent (though highly unfashionable) visage of paternalism. The sense of responsibility for the 'lesser breeds' was still powerfully influential among the older generation of politicians and civil servants responsible for taking the decisions over British policy. Many of them had family connections – common enough in the upper middle class of the day – with the Indian empire (Beveridge, Butler, Gaitskell, Gordon Walker: to name only a few).

One essential point about the Empire was that, to put it crudely, they were there and we were here. A great gulf, not only social but geographical, was fixed between the two, even if the anxious architects of imperial migration policies did not anticipate the age of air travel. In E. J. B. Rose's telling phrase, we had taken care to keep our deep south three thousand miles away in the Caribbean. Which being so, it was ironic that it should have been American legislation (the McCarran-Walter Act of 1952) which provided the crucial impetus that set moving the migration in the West Indies that eventually assured, to quote a Labour Lord Chancellor, that 'neither our children nor their children will ever see the England which we have been used to seeing, because for good or ill England has become a multi-racial society' (Rose *et al.*, 1969).

The 1950s: the age of the gatekeepers

The decade of the 1950s is often portrayed as a period when the policy makers slept – the first and crucial example of indifference to the growth of a significant social policy issue (in the more heated conspiracy theory this is elevated to a species of treason). Sad though it is to spoil a good phrase (it is Dipak Nandy's), it is not the case that we acquired the migration 'in a fit of absence of mind'. Anxiety in Whitehall and Westminster about the progress of the migration was considerable, as the Public Record Office's decorous series of annual revelations from official sources has demonstrated. But action upon the anxiety was inhibited by three factors: first, the locus of administrative responsibility for the migration; second, the function that the migration was serving, and finally the focus of those internal and external debates that did occur. The migrants from the Caribbean and West Africa (the major source of new arrivals throughout the first half of the decade) were colonial subjects and hence the responsibility of the Colonial Office, which provided rather sketchy special welfare services quite outside the mainstream of welfare state provision. As the decade advanced, the migrants' countries of origin began to move towards independence; and the content of the migration itself also began to change, with an increasing element coming from the two independent Commonwealth countries in the Indian sub-continent. The balance of responsibility accordingly shifted to the Commonwealth Relations Office, at that stage committed to the maintenance of a close and harmonious association between the countries of a self-consciously multi-racial Commonwealth. Since this was the Office's principal *raison d'être* it is hardly surprising that it should argue for less significant policy goals to take second place. All this might have been – in fact nearly was – swept aside had it not been for the second key factor, the economic role played by the migration in making good labour shortages in the British economy. The availability of a source of skilled and semi-skilled labour from the Caribbean (many of them familiar with working conditions here from experience in wartime in Britain) was too useful not to be exploited. Hence the hearty approval of the Treasury for the open door. Hence, also, the deep suspicion of the Trade Unions whose members, fearful of the impact of cheap labour on their hard-won full employment, pressed continuously for migration to be stopped or, if not stopped, at least hedged about with permits and quotas.

Against the powerful Whitehall combination opposed to it, the Home Office struggled with limited success. For decades since the passage of emergency legislation at the beginning of the First World War that department had operated an immigration policy of immense severity, breached only with great reluctance for refugees (German Jews before the War, Poles during and after it) (Roche, 1969, describes the Home Office tradition as viewed from the inside). Now the Home Office faced the mortifying sight of a new migration of British passport-holders over which they could exercise no control. However, their officials did have one crucial success in imposing the form that the debate about their arrival would take. Should immigration prove too difficult to digest (the gastronomic metaphor was much in favour) then it should be dealt with by imposing controls over entry. Any suggestion of a welfare policy died with the end of Colonial Office responsibility. If the immigrants were equal citizens, they had by definition an equal entitlement to the whole range of Welfare State benefits (and, it should be remembered, this was the period at which the assumption that such benefits provided an adequate safeguard against the longer-term problems of deprivation was still prevalent). Local authorities in areas affected by immigration told different stories to anyone who was prepared to listen, with special emphasis on problems in housing, but there was no one willing to take responsibility for action. In the vacuum, the first stirrings of a spontaneous growth of small organisations bitterly hostile to the immigrants and their interests took place almost unnoticed.

The Notting Hill disturbances of 1958 administered the first of a series of salutary shocks to this complacency: but their main long-term effect was to push the issue of immigration control firmly on to the policy agenda. The full story of the internal struggle within the Conservative Party, in Whitehall and eventually in the Cabinet awaits the release of the official records: but the contours are already clearly evident. The Treasury, and public sector employers (especially in the health and transport services), and for quite separate reasons the Commonwealth Relations Office all had vested interests in sustaining the open door: in deference to their objections the expedient of negotiating self-limitation by the sending countries was tried but failed. The Conservative Party in Opposition had argued passionately in favour of keeping the door open; many of the older generation felt that entry to the metropolitan centre of the Commonwealth was an issue of lasting symbolic significance. Against them was ranged the Home Office, its hand strengthened after Notting Hill by the public order card, and the Tory populists, especially in the West Midlands, drawing on local government experience to press a case crudely compounded of basic racial prejudice, half remembered eugenic principles and a grain or two of truth about strain upon the local social services. Eventually the advocates of restriction won the day and control was legislated. The process of the passage of that legislation, however, has had lasting political consequences. The late Hugh Gaitskell, in a brilliant debating performance, destroyed the Home Secretary's case by demonstrating how feeble the argument for restriction was if placed in the broader context of economic and social policy. In doing so, he very nearly succeeded in preventing the Act from passing at all (how close is not yet evident, but see Butler, 1971): but he also left his Party permanently associated with opposition to control. The Conservatives had wholeheartedly advocated the principles of free entry in Opposition and held the door open for a decade in Government. Yet the public identified the Labour Party, which (with honourable individual exceptions) had taken no interest in race relations policy at all, and many of whose supporters strenuously opposed the entry of immigrants, as the political advocates of their arrival. No matter that the Labour Government coming into office in 1964 quietly buried its pledge to repeal the Act of 1962 and proceeded to operate it with considerably greater stringency: the political damage was done.

The 1962 legislation closes a chapter. After a decade of free entry Britain had a substantial visible minority population. The newcomers were no longer as they had been in the early and middle 1950s predominantly skilled workers from the Caribbean, but were swollen (in a large measure by the panic engendered by impending control), by a large contingent of unskilled and semi-skilled workers from the Indian sub-continent and Jamaica. As for coping with their problems on and after arrival, control of their entry and that of their families was virtually the sum total of policy. The residual welfare function had fallen away: advice (the long forgotten Commonwealth Immigrants Advisory Council) and 'liaison' were the only expedient that the Government had to offer. The Welfare State's founding concept of the provision of a universal range of services to citizens provided a basic range of benefits on the assumption of a homogeneous population in which the distribution of need would be broadly uniform. The principle of variation of individuals' circumstances at different stages in their life cycle had been understood since Rowntree; but that principle was not extended to include arrival in a new and demanding environment as an event of equal significance to childbirth, loss of job or retirement. The Parliamentary Secretary responsible for national insurance observed in 1958 that the immigrants arrived from the Indian sub-continent and 'immediately begin to draw national assistance' (quoted Rose, 1969) and their willingness to do so was widely cited against them. But in default of other arrangements it is difficult to see what else they could do. Sending governments worked hard to fill the gap (the Government of Barbados was exemplary in this respect). But except in the limited case of those who had recruited direct in the sending countries, like London Transport, the responsibility for coping with the stresses of new arrival rested in the communities themselves. The contrast with the arrival of the Poles in Britain after the Second World War is striking: official provision up to and including higher education was made available to this group – the difference no doubt lying in the definition of the problem in terms of refugee status. The economic refugees from the New Commonwealth could not expect the same treatment as the political refugees from Eastern Europe.

One further issue did raise its head during this period. It was persistently argued by a handful of Labour backbenchers that the rights of citizenship of the newcomers should be underwritten by protection in law. Equally persistently, successive Ministers argued that to make a special case of the immigrants was undesirable: their advocates had to rest content with the ringing but ultimately empty phrases of Mr Justice Salmon, sentencing the Notting Hill rioters: 'everyone, irrespective of the colour of their skin, is entitled to walk through our streets with their heads erect and free from fear' (Rose, 1969).

The 1960s: doing little by doing good?

After 1964 events on the political stage rapidly eroded the attempts of civil servants and politicians to treat race relations issues as ones of more – or less – effective gatekeeping. The 1964 General Election brought a narrow Labour victory, but with it the pay-off for the persistent campaign of West Midland Conservatives to tar their opponents with the brush of being pro-immigrant. The defeat of Patrick Gordon Walker at Smethwick stimulated that quintessential politician, the new Prime Minister (Harold Wilson) into an essentially political response. The rhetoric continued to assert that newcomers would be treated equally; but some clarification of the means by which this end was to be achieved had now become inescapable. A race relations policy had to be cobbled together: the field therefore rapidly acquired a Minister (rather strikingly based at the new Department of Economic Affairs) and a White Paper. This document (Home Office, 1965) displays all the faults of the period in a high relief. The constant refrain of the central government Social Service Departments is unchanged: the newcomers will benefit not from special measures but from the general improvements that will benefit the whole population. When special measures are grudgingly conceded, they are transitional in character and limited in scope. The novelty is the expansion of the voluntary liaison committee principle, originally an improvisation for improving race relations at local level, to the national scene, with the creation of the first of a series of bodies of confusingly similar names and functions, charged with the impossible task of standing between government and newcomers as advocates of each to the other (Hill and Issacheroff, 1971, still the best account). The only significant exception lay in the field of law. The Race Relations Act of 1965 represents the culmination of the struggle by Labour backbenchers with no significant support from their party. But the form it took derived from an initiative taken by a group of young lawyers and academics anxious to apply recent experience in the United States (which several of them had observed at first-hand) to the British situation. The Act was declaratory; it eliminated the petty discrimination of public notices (easy to ridicule if not experienced at first hand): more controversially, it placed a check on the use of racial insults. Its passage was keenly contested, not least by those who argued (in the teeth of ample evidence to the contrary) that attempts to alter attitudes by law were foredoomed to failure. The lobby that had secured its passage, emboldened by success, pressed on with attempts to secure a framework for positive interventions with the sanction of law. In this they enjoyed only lukewarm support from the Labour Party and had to contend with dogged opposition from within the Trade Union movement.

The 1965 White Paper represented a low point; but a change in attitude was not far off. Some form of official admission that special programmes were necessary became inevitable as soon as it was clear that the Welfare State provision was simply not proving adequate. The local authorities were encountering difficulties on a scale that could no longer be catered for by a simple formula of equal access regardless of special needs. In housing, the private rented sector was demonstrably failing to meet the demand as the Milner Holland Report (1965) made clear in London, and Elizabeth Burney (*Housing on Trial*, 1967) outside. In education, the immediate pressure of the practical problems of educating a substantial group of new arrivals with experiences and expectations radically different from their fellow pupils overthrew the conventional wisdom. The 1966 Local Government Act represented (largely symbolic) acceptance of the principle that resources would have to be diverted specifically to meet these needs, though the quantities were limited and the form in which they were made available was much too restricted.

During the latter part of the 1960s the apparatus of the Welfare State began to come to terms with the fact of ethnic diversity and the different needs generated by that fact. The debate on the best means of achieving this objective flowed alongside the debate on poverty, which had re-established itself on the national agenda as unmistakable evidence of its persistence began to appear over the same period. The form in which needs were to be met remained the subject of urgent discussion: the American parallel was invoked to reinforce the case for the role of law as the essential underpinning of any campaign for racial equality. The Race Relations Board, butt of a thousand saloon bar jokes, none the less succeeded in establishing itself as one means of ensuring remedies for discrimination, although hobbled in the key area of employment by clumsy procedures imposed by an alliance between both sides of industry. (So deep a mark did the Board make that five years after its absorption into the Commission for Racial Equality Conservative Party conferences still regularly propose it for abolition.) By this period the Home Office had acquired a Secretary of State (Roy Jenkins) with a commitment to positive policies for promoting equality and a senior civil servant (Derek Morell) capable of setting policy initiatives in a broader context. The first stirrings of an attempt at planning a systematic policy – which would be based on the principle of geographically defined prior-ities, but which could encompass both a broader co-ordination of existing services and closer involvement with the local population – began to emerge. But these plans were still at embryo stage when the debate was wrenched back into the immigration control channel by the deepening crisis caused by the expulsion of the Asian population of Kenya in late 1967.

This painful episode has been chronicled more than once elsewhere (Steel, 1970; Rose, 1969). Unseemly panic which affected both major parties ensured the passage of the Commonwealth Immigrants Act of 1968, which substantially deprived the British passport-holding Kenya Asians of their rights of citizenship. The legislation had the immediate consequences of bringing a major politician onto the stage to undertake a systematic campaign for a policy of repatriation. It also had the incidental effect of shattering the coalition that had begun to take on some of the equivalent tasks of lobbying and campaigning that the Civil Rights Movement discharged in the United States. The strength of the public's response to Enoch Powell's appeal to their instinctive desire to turn the clock back generated another of Harold Wilson's celebrated improvisations, the Urban Programme. Sanctioned by legislation in 1969, the Urban Programme was made up of a patchwork of half-completed initiatives and new attempts to square the circle of providing additional resources for programmes for minorities without seeming to withhold them from the majority (Edwards and Batley, 1978; Higgins, 1983). Coupled with the substantially expanded role defined in the 1968 Race Relations Act for the Race Relations Board, and the Community Relations Commission, these new initiatives were designed to provide the basis for progress in the 1970s. The assumption was that the end of the road had been reached on immigration control and that this sector of the front could now be finally closed. Unfortunately, Danegeld, like hire-purchase, is rarely paid in one instalment.

The 1970s: the end of optimism?

The distance travelled over the course of the 1970s is perhaps best measured by looking backwards and comparing the expectation of policy makers and analysts at the beginning of the decade with the reality as it emerged during its course. The analysis at the outset of the period identified a number of intractable problems but its fundamental flavour was optimistic (Rose, 1969). The difficulties that were commonly identified were: a major problem of persistent discrimination, whose existence had been established beyond reasonable doubt by the first PEP study (1967), affecting principally the first generation of immigrants in jobs and housing: the reinforcement of discrimination by continuing hostility on the part of the majority, exacerbated by stereotypes based in ignorance and reinforced by campaigns against immigration, latterly becoming respectable with their espousal by national politicians. Generally, the lack-lustre performance of both major parties was a continuing difficulty: their apprehension about the electoral dangers of over-close association with positive policies in turn inhibited government departments from taking race relations seriously as a policy issue. The existence of separate agencies outside the Whitehall mainstream, to become known to later generations as quangos, reinforced this sense of isolation. Because central government was disinclined to take the issue seriously, the pressure on local government to do so was minimal. Local initiatives tended to be left to voluntary organisations.

These voluntary bodies, together with the quangos with whom they were closely related (initially referred to facetiously by those involved as the race relations industry – a joke that speedily backfired on those who made it when taken up by their opponents – see the journalism of R. Butt, *passim*) had established beach-heads in a number of professional groups – teachers, and for different reasons lawyers, were both examples of such groups called upon early to develop an expertise in the field. Similar, though more tenuous, links which were forged with some 'immigrant' organisations proved vulnerable to the stresses of the political events in the late 1960s.

This gloomy picture was, however, lightened by a number of presumed causes for optimism. The brief (as it proved) economic recovery of the late 1960s had coincided with a period when the issue of race relations was on the policy agenda. This led to the reasonable expectation, fortified by the announcement of the Urban Programme, that resources might be diverted in the direction of expenditure on new measures for positive action. Economic recovery also seemed to underpin the basic optimism about jobs – that there would be, in the foreseeable future, sufficient unskilled and semi-skilled jobs in the manufacturing and service industries to meet the basic needs of the minority communities. Finally, it could then be assumed that the basic 'floor' of Welfare State services would remain available to minorities. This was of particular significance in the key areas of housing and education, both topics to which the Wilson government had devoted special attention. The debate on the future direction of race relations policy could therefore be assumed to be centred on the extent to which additional measures should be funded to meet specific needs in particular service areas. The danger of the creation of a separate and unequal class of underprivileged workers on the European 'guest worker' model had been widely publicised as a danger that British policy makers should seek to avoid (Deakin, 1972).

The other major positive factor in the situation, as it was perceived at the beginning of the 1970s, was the Second Generation. By the late 1970s, it was assumed, black and brown Britons would have reached adulthood in sufficient numbers to talk realistically for the first time about an indigenous black population. This should have three immediate beneficial consequences: first, it would kill off the use of the patronising and inaccurate term 'immigrant', with its negative halo. Familiarity with cultural diversity in education would produce a generation accustomed to ethnic diversity in everyday life. Second, it would help generate securely based community leadership with a clear commitment to action within the context of the British political system. Finally, equality of opportunity in the British educational system would produce a growing number of individuals whose success would carry them into the professional middle class (which apart from the benefit for the individuals concerned would help disperse the patronising stereotype of blacks as unskilled labourers) (Jones, 1977).

In the event these grounds for optimism proved largely if not totally misconceived. The major error of judgment was the miscalculation about the future of the economy and in particular about the continuation of full employment. By the end of the 1970s not merely had the country seen a general growth in unemployment unprecedented since the 1930s; but there was clear evidence that blacks were suffering disproportionately to their numbers (Rees, 1981). In particular, young blacks – the Second Generation – had over the course of the 1970s to face obstacles not foreseen at all clearly at the opening of the decade. The performance of many – though not all – in school had generally fallen well below the level of their ability (Rampton, 1981); on emerging they had to face a job market depleted by the loss of an increasing proportion of the unskilled and semi-skilled jobs that had previously provided the first rung of the employment ladder for the unqualified. Increasing alienation from the society in which they found themselves, from their white peers, and even from their own parents, were commonly reputed to be affecting young West Indians, although the form of such alienation and its implications were hotly disputed.

Other causes for optimism proved to be almost equally fragile. The truce on immigration control was very brief. The incoming Conservative Government's Immigration Act of 1971 tightened the screw a further turn; and although their admission of the Uganda-Asian refugees contrasts favourably with their predecessors' treatment of the Kenya-Asians, in Opposition under Margaret Thatcher the Conservatives reverted to their previous practice of attempting to outflank their opponents by appealing to public anxieties about the level of migration. The undercutting effect of this process for race relations policy should need no underlining. While the scope for positive action did exist it was exploited only to a limited degree. The return of the Labour Party to power in 1974 brought Jenkins back to the Home Office and produced the 1975 White Paper with its emphasis on a fully rounded programme, with action both on racial discrimination (whose persistence was then demonstrated in a second PEP report), and to deal with 'racial disadvantage'. The White Paper argued that

an effective strategy to deal with the problems of deprivation and disadvantage must of necessity attend both to the scale of resources required and to the equitable allocation of the increased resources. Racial disadvantage most often occurs in contexts of generalised disadvantage, and cannot be realistically dealt with unless there are mechanisms for correcting the maldistribution of resources.

Moreover 'legislation is not and never can be a sufficient condition for effective progress towards equality of opportunity' (Home Office, 1975). This White Paper remains the nearest approach to a statement of consistent principles upon which policy can be based; but only its first limb was implemented, in the 1976 Race Relations Act, which introduced the concept of indirect discrimination into law and created a single race relations agency to ensure its implementation. Unfortunately the country's continued poor economic performance undercut action on the second of the White Paper's priorities. After 1976 and the major economic crisis of that year the scope for new initiatives was very greatly reduced, if not entirely eliminated. The concept of selective action in a limited number of geographical areas that would address both poverty and race issues simultaneously had broken down with the failure of the Community Development Project experiment (Specht, 1976; Higgins, 1983); however, the rapid growth in activity of right-wing extremist groups kept the issue on the boil and impelled the Callaghan government to make one further attempt to address these issues. Their new approach involved the transfer of responsibility for inner city policy to the Department of the Environment and the provision of substantial additional resources for a revamped urban programme (Department of the Environment, 1977). But although these initiatives survived the further change of political power in May 1979 their significance has been much diminished by more general developments, in particular the effect of the Conservative Government's policies on public expenditure. So far from providing a floor from which new initiatives can be launched, the statutory services are themselves in the course of being substantially reduced in scope and extent of resources available.

The final ground for optimism, the likely emergence of a distinctive minority leadership, had also failed to materialise in the form anticipated at the beginning of the 1970s. The absence of any significant black presence in the major political parties may be largely a reflection of well justified disillusionment with both parties' record: but it means that the leverage of the kind successfully employed by blacks in the United States cannot be applied here. The absence of blacks on the local government scene is in many ways more disturbing than their lack of participation in national politics: nor has there been any significant progress in the direction of appointments to senior posts in the law, local government, or even the church. This absence of blacks in office, outside token membership of race relations organisations, reflects a continued lack of commitment by ministers and their civil servants to positive race relations policies.

Epilogue: the 1980s, a dream still deferred

If one event gave the final quietus to the lingering remnants of the optimism of the late 1960s it was the 'disorders' (the Home Office term) which broke out in Brixton over the weekend of 10–12 April 1981 and spread to other major cities. The impatience and bitterness of the majority of those who took part in this episode was plain to see: Lord Scarman, who undertook the enquiry into the disturbances, subsequently commented that the rioters' 'fundamental motivation is of course frustration in the sense of injustice and hopelessness engendered by unemployment and social conditions' (Open University interview). In the shower of missiles that descended on the police over those two days perished a number of illusions about the future of race relations in this country: that the fabric of British society was tough enough to withstand unemployment at double-digit level over a period of years; that the essentially law-abiding character of minority groups would inhibit them from extreme responses; that at the end of the day the impartiality of the police was accepted by the vast majority of citizens, even the young; that our 'tradition of tolerance' had developed in areas of long-standing minority settlement; finally, that government could afford to assign the issue a secondary place on the policy agenda to be dealt with by a mixture of benign neglect and selective payment of the never-ending tribute to the recurring demands of the control lobby (most recently reflected in the Conservative Government's Nationality Act). Clearly, the outcome of any attempt to deal positively with the issue of race relations must be ultimately bound up with the outcome of the uphill battle to revive the British economy. Successive defeats inflicted on successive governments in that struggle had by 1981 undermined most of the progress that had been made over the first two decades of the race relations policy. It is a cliché that economic policy has generally come to dominate considerations of social policy over the course of the last few years. It does not follow from that, however, that new initiatives must await the outcome of economic policy initiatives. Those that would argue this case, both on left and right, need to demonstrate that no special problems exist that cannot be catered for on one side of the barricades or another by policies designed to address the main needs of the economy. In practice, the existence of these special problems, in jobs, in housing, and in education, is aptly demonstrated by a range of investigations over the past decade (conveniently summed up in a Home Office publication). Even if the ultimate deterrent of civil disorder did not exist – and Brixton, St Paul's and Toxteth have amply demonstrated that it does – there would be sufficient argument for a programme of positive action in a clear demonstration of persistent special need.

The major virtue of the Scarman Report is that it sets the Brixton debates in the framework of those special needs, arguing that the policing problems specific to the disorders could not be understood except in the context of the social problems of which they are necessarily part (paragraph 1.5). Where Scarman falls short is in the remedies he prescribes, which are essentially devices designed to ensure the more efficient functioning of the existing machinery of government – better interchange of information on good practice, improved co-ordination. These are all very well as far as they go; but the experience of the parallel poverty initiatives suggests that there are sharp limits on the extent to which the existing machinery can deliver the goods. Even the 1977 White Paper policy which ushered in a more effective phase of inner city policy, based on a substantial allocation of new resources, has in practice been largely submerged by broader problems arising from central government's withdrawal of resources from local government.

Young and Connelly's striking analysis (1981) of local government action in the race relations field under the terms of the declaratory anti-discrimination section of the 1976 Act points to a number of possible lines for action. At the local level, these are intended to ensure that the policies of individual departments of the authority take account of the specific needs of minorities and that new initiatives are properly followed through to ensure that they have been effective. At the national level, Young and Connelly call for a change of responsibility from the Home Office to the DOE, and the creation of a task force led by a minister and supported by the regional offices of the DOE. The Government's prompt response has been to designate a junior minister at the Department as the focal point for action on race relations – thereby, a cynic might comment, bringing us back full circle to the policy of 1964. Solutions of this kind represent an elaboration and sophistication of the links sketched out by Lord Scarman and suggest that central government could develop a new role with an emphasis on facilitating action on a local level rather than trying to initiate it either directly or through the race relations quangos. This would constitute one step down the road signposted by David Kirp in his comparative study of British and American race relations policy, in which he argues that 'what is wanted in the racial realm is a public policy that neither becomes officious inter-meddling nor degenerates into mere neglect with the result that race eventually ceases to be a policy problem' (Kirp, 1979).

The overhaul of the administrative machinery implied by Young and Connelly's work at local level and advocated for central government in an incisive report from the House of Commons Home Affairs Committee (1980/1) is a necessary stage on the journey to a coherent policy; but in itself it is insufficient. Two other conditions need to be satisfied: both of them present major difficulties.

The first is the provision of additional resources for programmes addressed to the needs of minorities. Proposals of this kind are liable to be met by a number of objections. The first, and currently the commonest, is that there is no scope for any further expenditure on social programmes of any kind at a time of continuing national economic difficulty. After the 'disturbances' this kind of simple-minded economism was already beginning to look rather tatty: it was given what should be a decisive check by Michael Heseltine, as the Minister responsible for urban policy in his speech to his Conservative party colleagues at Blackpool in October 1981, in which he argued for politics and policies that would deny 'fertile ground' to grievances by satisfying the needs of the inner city populations. This could only be achieved, in such severely deprived areas, by Government.

The second and more sophisticated objection is that there are enough resources available already and the essential problem is how to use them effectively. This line of argument has received some support from Lord Scarman's findings; and is often amplified by reference to the presumed failure of equivalent American programmes and the experience there of 'throwing money' ineffectually at major social problems. This interpretation is in fact open to challenge (Higgins, 1978): even if it were not, it does not answer the essential question, which is whether the proved existence of greater need among ethnic minorities requires a response over and above a more efficient implementation of general programmes.

Here a third difficulty arises, in the shape of the much heralded backlash among the majority and in particular those themselves in need. During the abortive attempt to overhaul the legislation providing for special help to areas affected by minorities, a number of MPs made particular reference to the possibility that resentments generated as a result of allocation of resources to minorities might provoke sufficient hostility to undermine the objectives of policy: 'it is no good thinking', observed one, 'that ordinary white working-class people who exist in all the inner cities and who feel they are deprived are not keenly aware that this is a form of discrimination that is likely to be codified' (Little, 1981).

Faced with this kind of objection, the tendency has been to try to identify policies that discriminate on some more general ground – residence is one obvious example. Yet the evidence suggests that area-based policies are rather inefficient at picking up and satisfying the needs of those parts of the population in greatest need (Townsend, 1976). They postpone, rather than solve, the problem of confronting the issue of positive action.

Race relations legislation and in particular the Act of 1976 provide the legal basis for some policies designed to correct the effects of past discrimination: the initiatives in fields of training and recruitment are sanctioned by the law and offer considerable scope for action, which Lord Scarman's report, like the Home Affairs Committee, identifies as a priority for central government implementation. Yet if the legitimate aspirations of the minorities are to be satisfied, it is necessary to go further. The leadership of the minority communities is still weak and divided: but is likely to grow in strength and confidence as more of the British-born second generation appear in positions of influence. The relatively dispersed pattern of distribution of the minority populations has meant that in the past the weapon of the ethnic vote has not been deployed to secure some response from white populations. That situation, too, is likely to change: although we have a long way to go before we reach anything approaching the American pattern of a well organised Congressional Caucus of black legislators pressing black demands on a whole range of social policy issues.

The pressure from minorities is therefore likely to increase. The question, then, is whether it will prove possible to push ahead with positive policies that command sufficient commitment from politicians of the major parties to survive the now routine objections to public expenditure on social problems. This will involve accepting the diversion of resources from other programmes and client groups. Even granted this acceptance – a large proviso – the minorities will have to prepare themselves to be offered less than the whole loaf over a longer time span than social justice requires. Their growing reluctance to accept short measure is likely to lead to increasingly sharp conflict, given the continuing unwillingness of the majority to surrender scarce resources. These are not exactly the most favourable of circumstances in which to secure race relations its proper place on the Welfare State agenda. But this time the job cannot be deferred any longer.

References

Burney, E. (1967), *Housing on Trial*, Oxford University Press.

Butler, Lord (1971), *The Art of the Possible*, London, Hamish Hamilton.

Deakin, N. (1972), *Immigrants in Europe*, London, Fabian Society (Research Series 306).

Deakin, N. (1978), 'The vitality of a tradition' in C. Holmes (ed.), *Immigrants and Minorities in British Society*, London, Allen & Unwin.

Deakin, N. (1983), 'Peter Shore and inner city policy: the last, best hope?' in J. Higgins (ed.), *The Politics of Urban Deprivation*, Oxford, Blackwell.

Department of the Environment (1977), *Policy for the Inner Cities*, Cmnd. 6845, London, HMSO.

Edwards, J., and Batley, R. (1978), *The Politics of Positive Discrimination*, London, Tavistock.

Higgins, J. (1978), *The Poverty Business*, Oxford, Blackwell.

Higgins, J. (1983), *The Politics of Urban Deprivation*, Oxford, Blackwell.

Hill, M., and Issacheroff, R. (1971), *Community Action and Race Relations*, Oxford University Press.

Holland, Sir Milner (1965), *Report of the Committee on Housing in Greater London*, London, HMSO.

Home Office (1965), *Immigration from the Commonwealth*, Cmnd. 2379, London, HMSO.

Home Office (1975), *Racial Discrimination*, Cmnd. 6234, London, HMSO.

Jones, C. (1977), *Immigration and Social Policy in Britain*, London, Tavistock.

Kirp, D. (1979), *Doing Good by Doing Little*, Berkeley, University of California.

Little, A. (1981), 'Ethnic Inequality in Education', paper for SSRC Conference on the Inner City.

Lunn, K. (1980), *Hosts, Immigrants and Minorities*, Folkestone, Dawson.

Political and Economic Planning (1967), *Racial Discrimination in Britain*, London.

Political and Economic Planning (1976), *The Facts of Racial Disadvantage*, London.

Rampton, A. (1981), *Report of Committee of Inquiry into the Education of Children from Ethnic Minority Groups*, Cmnd. 8273, London, HMSO.

Rees, T., *et al.* (1981), *Ethnic Minorities in Britain: A study of trends in their position since 1961*, Home Office Research Study, no. 68, London, HMSO.

Roche, T. (1969), *The Key in the Lock*, London, John Murray.

Rose, E. J. B., *et al.* (1969), *Colour and Citizenship*, Oxford University Press.

Scarman, Lord (1981), *The Brixton Disorders 10–12 April 1981*, Cmnd. 8427, London, HMSO.

Specht, H. (1976), *The Community Development Project*, London, National Institute for Social Work.

Steel, D. (1970), *No Entry: The Background and Implications of the Commonwealth Immigrants Act, 1968*, London, Humanities.

Townsend, P. (1976), 'Area Deprivation Policies', Barnett Shine Foundation Lecture, reprinted in *New Statesman* (6 August).

Young, K., and Connelly, N. (1981), *Policy and Practice in the Multi-Racial City*, London, Policy Studies Institute.

Chapter 17
Utilitarianism and the welfare state
Philip Bean

To talk of the influence of utilitarianism or indeed of any philosophy on the Welfare State is to be too certain of the boundaries of the subjects and too inclined to treat the Welfare State as if it was a theoretical definition of a particular set of policies. Rather the Welfare State is a convenient shorthand description of an age characterised by a certain stance towards selected areas of social policy by a government whose popularity lessened throughout its term of office. That stance contained many philosophies but was probably not dominated by one; except a form of pragmatism dictated by a belief that certain social policies would give Britain a moral leadership and provide honour and justice to its people (Parliamentary Debates, vol. 386).

It is perhaps for this reason, unwittingly or not, that those interested in social policy have tended to avoid seeing the Welfare State in philosophical terms. Nor does it appear that the architects of the Welfare State encouraged that way of thinking, for philosophical arguments were rarely cited in the Parliamentary debates of that time, or if they were they were presented as oblique references within the main framework – which had developed out of wartime austerity and linked to questions about the appropriate means by which the state could help its citizens.

The general notion of 'assistance' based on a desire to improve the general quality of life remained a dominant theme. 'Assistance' translated often as humanitarianism or Christian socialism was based on a desire to protect and improve where the spectre of the 1930s was held as the type of society to which Britain ought never to return. True, those who opposed the introduction of the Welfare State tended to have a more coherent approach – in the philosophical sense that is. They occasionally railed against state intervention, and sometimes adopted views similar to those of *laissez-faire* theorists of the nineteenth century warning against loss of freedom, loss of initiative and destruction of moral obligations. They also saw economic recovery as taking precedence. The Conservative party's first concern was with the maintenance of social institutions: the condition of the people was second, and sometimes third, in importance.

But to say that the Welfare State, which for these purposes means that period of British domestic history between 1945 and 1951, was a pragmatic, or even an incoherent, exercise in humanitarianism is to ignore some of the philosophical strands that were present. Beveridge was as deeply influenced by nineteenth-century radicalism as many others, whilst key members of the Labour government very occasionally spoke as if they were architects of a theory. Yet it is the Utilitarians, and particularly Bentham, that require greater attention, for the twentieth-century revolution in government, which was the Welfare State, although not attributable to Benthamism as a sole cause cannot be understood without reference to that doctrine. Indeed some commentators see Utilitarianism as a current of thought which began with Bentham and moved directly into Fabianism. (Lewis, 1952, p. 188). And others, notably A. V. Dicey (1962), H. Parris (1960) and J. B. Brebner (1948), have argued that Bentham was, in Brebner's terms, 'not so much the archetype of British individualism, as the archetype of British collectivism'. Here I wish to concentrate on some aspects of the Utilitarian view and ask in a general way not just about the Utilitarian influence but to what extent would traditional (i.e. Benthamite) Utilitarians approve, or would have approved, of that period of British history. The Utilitarian influence is still important in its own right, for it is neither a dead philosophy nor an outdated one, although over the years its limitations have become more apparent. Even so, it is still interesting to speculate on the likely nature and form of the Welfare State had it been shaped according to Utilitarian demands. For had it been so I think it unlikely, for example, that the larger and more impersonal of the bureaucracies would have flourished, nor would there have been such a waste of resources, human and otherwise. But then nor would there have been that sense of compassion so characteristic of the Welfare State at least in its earlier stages. Utilitarianism may be concerned with promoting happiness but Bentham's view of happiness has a somewhat redolent tone.

The nature of Utilitarianism

Utilitarianism, which is primarily a theory of morals, was under Bentham's influence applied to political systems. The origins of Utilitarianism can be found in Hobbes, and Hume, but Bentham gave it an additional credibility and produced a more coherent system. There is no better exposition of Benthamite Utilitarianism than that found in the first five chapters of *An Introduction to the Principles of Morals and Legislation* (1967 ed. used throughout) where Bentham states that nature has placed mankind under the governance of two sovereign masters, pain and pleasure, and it is for them alone to point out what we ought to do and what we shall do.[1]

Critics have often pointed out that Bentham's arguments contain two principles, not one, which are contradictory: that men pursue their own happiness (egoism), and that men ought to promote the general happiness (ethical). For if men pursue their own happiness they may do so at the expense of others and may not then promote happiness in general, or maximise happiness as Bentham wished. But there is no contradiction here. If a man pursues his own happiness it is logically possible, and may indeed sometimes happen, that his happiness is passed on to others, and as within a family his happiness may bring happiness to others. It may not always be so, but sometimes it is, for those that we are close to are happy when we are happy. So too in the wider community, our happiness is affected by, and affects, others, for most would prefer to live in a society which if not a completely happy one is not an unhappy one, and few would wish to live in a society where they were identified as the cause of unhappiness (Quinton, 1973). There was, thought Bentham, a natural harmony of interests when the happiness of one person coincided with the production of the happiness of others.

But Utilitarians have never relied wholly on that natural harmony; sometimes it was necessary to create an artificial harmony. Regrettably, said Bentham, some men's egoism threatens the general happiness, and where this is so the law must impose sanctions and punish, or if not punish then operate as a threat to restrain, those whose egoism could promote misery. These were the political sanctions as Bentham called them, but there existed others; such as the physical sanctions applied by the limitations of the human body, moral sanctions applied by the community, and religious sanctions applied by God (Bentham, 1967, p. 148). To these John Stuart Mill added a fifth, the individual's conscience. So to that natural harmony of interests an artificial harmony had to be applied. There was nothing unexpected about this, said Bentham, although it was regrettable that artificial measures were required. For the business of government must be to promote happiness by punishing and rewarding, and by rewarding Bentham meant introducing legislation which encouraged or pursued the enjoyment of pleasures and security from pains (p. 189). Bentham always insisted that the purpose of government was to promote the greatest happiness for the greatest number.

Bentham did not believe that human beings could be made perfect but he did believe that progress in human society was possible if, and only if, his principle of utility was consistently applied. He also insisted that his principle be applied to all institutions and to all problems. Here was Bentham's radicalism at work and at its best. Small wonder that the principle of utility was regarded as a dangerous doctrine – a point incidentally which Bentham eagerly accepted.

> Dangerous it unquestionably is to every Government which has for its actual end or object the greatest happiness of a certain one with or without the addition of some comparitively small number of other. . . . Dangerous it is to all those functionaries. . . whose interest is to maximize delay, vexation and expense in judicial and other modes of procedure for the sake of profit extractible out of the expense (Bentham, 1967).

Bentham's insistence that all decisions could be made according to the doctrine of utility was the radical feature of his thinking. But where would social justice emerge in such a society dominated by utility? Bentham never considered that question, at least in those terms: what he thought was that the artificial harmony of interests would tend to approximate to what others may call justice. So when two men's interests clash the right course is that which produces the greatest total of happiness regardless of which of the two enjoys it or how it is shared among them. If more is given to the better man than to the worse that is because in the long run the general happiness is increased by rewarding virtue and punishing vice, not because of an ultimate ethical doctrine that the good deserve more than the bad. Link this to a simple psychology (that men desire happiness as being the mainspring of human action), to a lack of interest in natural justice or jurisprudence ('an imaginary personage' Bentham called it) and to the origins of right and wrong ('I do not know the origins, I do not care') and the doctrine itself is radical in its own right, at least by nineteenth-century standards. And when applied to all institutions, to all modes of conduct, and to all questions of politics and morality, it becomes additionally so. The strength of Dicey's position is that he recognised how such a theory could be turned easily into one supporting radical change.

> It is a principle big with revolution. . . [and] as in any State the poor and needy always constitute the majority of the nation. . . the whole aim of legislation should be to promote happiness not of the nobility or the gentry or even the shop-keepers but of artisans and other wage earners (Dicey, 1962, p. 305).

Some similarities between Utilitarianism and the Welfare State

This brief overview of Benthamite Utilitarianism shows that a number of comparisons, albeit superficial, can be made between Utilitarianism and the Welfare State. And in an obvious sense there are many aspects of the Welfare State about which any modern Utilitarian would approve for whilst the aims have not always been to produce happiness, in an explicit sense that is, happiness has often been promoted under the guise of welfare. Or rather the Welfare State was not intended to promote misery.

Consider the Beveridge report and the attempts by Beveridge to remove some of the grosser forms of inequality. Bentham, although not an equalitarian in the manner of someone concerned with promoting a full equality of outcome, none the less saw certain inequalities as likely to foster resentment. These then promoted unhappiness. To Bentham equality was not desirable for its own sake, all that was desirable was the greatest happiness for the greatest number. This is the one fundamental principle: the limits of liberty and equality are determined by it and by the lessons of experience (Plamenatz, 1966, p. 83). Given the war years and spirit of the times when Beveridge produced his report the lessons of that experience were such as to favour forms of equality, even if Beveridge's proposals themselves may not have been egalitarian in any other sense than that which shifted a group of persons off the lowest rung of the economic ladder. A similar Utilitarian view of equality can be seen in Tawney and Crosland, both of whom saw inequality as capable of producing resentment, and gross inequalities as producing gross resentments.[2] This Bentham would have understood without of course accepting the value of equality as an end in itself.

Other examples could be cited 'which may be said to be conformable to or dictated by the principle of utility when in like manner the tendency which it has to augment the happiness of the community is greater than any which it has to diminish it' (Bentham, 1967, p. 127). All measures which promoted happiness would be to the approval of Utilitarians, and even if not measures which *maximised* happiness, if they at least promoted it, that would be better than nothing. And there was and is much in the Welfare State where the aim was to promote something which Benthamites would say resembled happiness, perhaps more than in any other area of legislation. This is the great achievement of it: that it has failed to maximise happiness, that it has not always promoted it in reality (Bentham (p. 276) would call this an unadvised aspect of his principle) and that it has occasionally produced unhappiness ought not to detract from its achievement.

Consider also a slightly different Utilitarian position, that adopted by T. H. Green, and consider Green's Utilitarianism in terms of the Beveridge report which emphasised that liberty came from freedom from want, from disease, from ignorance, from squalor and from idleness, and so in his view did all true liberty which removed obstacles (Green, 1888). For Green saw obstacles as those which impeded and restricted human development. We must of course be wary of citing Green in this context for although a Utilitarian he differed from Bentham in a number of important respects, and from Mill also, for the latter retained too much of a respect for *laissez-faire* capitalism and hence the latent support of privilege to satisfy Green. The minimum area of personal freedom which included the freedom to remain sovereign over one's mind and body may to Mill have been self-evident but to Green that freedom was only appropriate for those whose wants were not basic. Furthermore the negative version of liberty proposed by Mill offered the scope to exploit, in the economic sense that is, those whose wants were likely to increase in terms of hardship or injury. But Green's Utilitarianism was real enough and his vision of a civilised society was based on a Utilitarian premise. When Green spoke of a civilised society, his vision was not that of Mill's who saw civilisation as offering endless debates between educated people who were similar in outlook to himself. Nor, according to Green, was civilisation to be found in Mill's belief that people ought to be left alone to find their own salvation, but in accordance with rights which were commensurate with basic requirements of human welfare. To those not free from want true freedom did not exist or was meaningless.

And there are other areas in which the Utilitarian would give approval, such as found in the methodology of some of the early Welfare State theorists. Consider Beveridge again. Although Beveridge was concerned with social insurance, this was one aspect of his attack on the five major wants. The Beveridge Report was not therefore a piecemeal doctrine but a way of providing a comprehensive means of relief. It is perhaps easy to ignore the importance of Beveridge's method for we are now so attuned to think in terms of comprehensive systems, and large-scale analysis, that we forget most had not been of this nature. Yet Beveridge was simply doing what Bentham had advocated a century and a half ago – methodologically speaking that is.

The similarities however ought not to mislead us. In an obvious sense we must be wary of forcing the Welfare State, and more particularly Beveridge, into a Benthamite mould, for there were differences as well. Beveridge's approach and method was more limited and less radical than Bentham's for, unlike Bentham, Beveridge was not wanting to disturb whole sections of society – only to concentrate on the less well off. The Parliamentary Debates on the Beveridge Report are instructive on this point. Those committed to a radical restructuring of society knew this. 'I say as a convinced socialist that I do not support the Beveridge plan because it is a socialist plan. It is not. It is a common-sense method of meeting our peace-time casualties under the prevailing economic system, the capitalist system. I am quite clear in my own mind that it does not disturb in any way any of the factors from which unemployment and sickness are wont to spring' (Parliamentary Debates, vol. 386, p. 1774). The Beveridge Report was not examined as a piece of political theory or a theory of morals as was Utilitarianism (ibid.) and Beveridge himself would not have wanted it to be so. 'The plan for Britain is based on the contributory principle of giving not free allowances to all from the State but giving benefits as of right in virtue of contribution made by the insured persons themselves' (quoted in Fraser, 1973, pp. 200–1). And later, 'freedom from want does not mean a claim to be relieved by the State on proof of necessity and lack of resources but having as of right one's own income to keep one above the necessity for applying for relief' (p. 201). The needs of the individual, and others' abilities to contribute to those needs, which was and is such a slogan of socialist thinking, had no place in the Beveridge plan. I am not suggesting that Beveridge was or ought to have been a socialist: my point is that Beveridge had no plans, socialist or otherwise, to disturb the structure of society.

Nor were the architects and operators of the Welfare State concerned with maximizing happiness; and of course they never claimed that they were. But to a Utilitarian this would be seen as their greatest weakness. For what the Welfare State did was from the first to promote the happiness of sectional interests based on requirements of 'need' – and then in a pragmatic and occasionally haphazard way. The Welfare State began and ended as a response to a 'need' actual or supposed; it lacked a coherent framework for it was based on the pressure of unpalatable facts. And as such Fraser is right to say that any explanation which does not emphasise the practical, pragmatic, *ad hoc* response of the State is in a major respect deficient (Fraser, 1973, p. 108). Social policies and their administration were geared to meet real and pressing problems, rarely, it appears, to breathe life into some abstract theory or to satisfy some metaphysical aim. Yet in doing so certain areas of 'need' have inevitably become neglected, others ignored and others overemphasised. Imbalances have also occurred which were, and are, difficult to alter once introduced. The shocking lack of current provisions for the elderly is an example. Earlier provisions for the elderly were established by Aneurin Bevan on the basis that the working-class elderly should receive residential accommodation similar to their middle-class financially independent counterparts. In 1947–8 this meant little in terms of service provisions, and by 1980 meant even less. Old peoples' homes are now surrogate psychogeriatric hospitals and the elderly in the community are provided with a third- or fourth-rate service (Ovenstone and Bean, 1981). There seems no immediate prospect that their position will be altered.

Other examples could be found, such as the provisions for the mentally handicapped or the mentally ill. A traditional Utilitarian, committed to the view that one person's happiness was as good as another's, and that each person was to count for one and no one to count for more than one, could point to the position of these groups as examples of the folly and inhumanity created by *ad hoc* reformism. By any standards the position of such groups can be found wanting, whether adjudged on the basis of fairness, natural rights or whatever. The strength of Utilitarianism is that no one can be ignored and no one person's happiness can be discounted. For the aim is to promote happiness in such a way as to maximise it – which means the aim is to produce the greatest happiness possible under the circumstances. In Bentham's principle there is a form of equality rigorously applied.

The lack of rigour in the application of one set or more of principles places the Utilitarian apart from the architects and planners of the Welfare State. When the Utilitarians spoke of a society they saw it as a mass of individuals competing for pleasures; their model may be open to question, but the individual was the unit and a society was built up of units. Institutions and organisations were the sum of the individuals who staffed or manned them. Democracy was to the Utilitarians the only acceptable form of government for only in democracies would governments be concerned with promoting happiness, and only then if those in power had to submit their position regularly to the electorate. Frequent elections, said Bentham, would be required to remind governments of their obligations to abide by the principle of utility. It may be that Bentham failed to understand the complexities of the task, be it in governments or in people, for if we were the sort of people he thought we were we would be successful only in the pursuit of pleasure and the avoidance of pain. Yet that defect is also a strength. If we suppose that men will want to succeed as much as possible, and try to satisfy their desires, satisfactions or whatever, they may care about the type of society in which they live. They may see themselves as moral beings, having rights and duties with some conception of the world in which they pursue their, and others' pleasures. The Welfare State provided the rights but it was rarely concerned to emphasise the duties and so the opportunity to produce a society which was less segmented, less full of the clamour of pressure groups, and less full of sectional interests was lost.

The *ad hoc* response to unpalatable social facts, as Fraser called the Welfare State, may have contributed to its ultimate demise, but there was more to it than that. The Utilitarians would have known what was wrong from the outset. For the Utilitarians had a clearer conception of 'need' than most politicians or social welfare theorists, since need was to them linked to the pursuit of pleasure for all members of the community. It was not the tortuous pursuit of party politics where the party in power aimed to represent the interests of one class to the exclusion of others, or worse still, to do as the Marxists wish, that is to claim the *superiority* of one class. For that, like all doctrines claiming superiority of one group over another, whether it be race, class or otherwise, leads to conflict and violence. The Utilitarians would know that 'need' was in part contained in their view that each person pursued his own pleasure, in part in their maxim that each was to count for one and no one to count for more than one, and in part in their principle that one person's pleasure was no more or less important than another's. Based on standards such as these the needs of all would be considered, not those of a few.

The limitations of Utilitarianism applied

For all its strength and its virtues Utilitarianism is not a philosophical theory which is currently in fashion. The post-Welfare State period is dominated by other concerns, where the rights of the individual are set against the powers and demands of the bureaucratic state. The individual protesting against the planners' decision to build a trunk road, the demand for the rights of mental patients, even the demand for children's rights have become commonplace. The latter stages of the Welfare State with its trend towards collectivism, its professionals, its experts etc., have been seen to swamp the individual who must, by some method, legal or otherwise, stand out against these recognisable forces. The theme is no longer that of the greatest happiness for the greatest number – not that it ever was in that form – but that of the strength of the individual whose resources, moral and otherwise, allow him to stand against, and possibly defeat, decisions made in his and others' interests.

This view, that the individual is now posited against the bureaucracy and insensitivity of the state, is a direct descendant of that Welfare State which was amongst other things paternalistic and slightly suffocating. It is also a direct descendant of a positivist view of social science which created the so-called experts whose knowledge and expertise of human affairs could somehow be expected to be gained from a short course in social science. The very assumption that experts could be created able to offer their expertise on various aspects of human existence – ranging from child care to old age and even to dying – was a product of a Welfare State which emphasised the value of social science research as a way of changing human society. And the paradox is evident: that the major beneficiaries of the Welfare State have been those very professionals of welfare who have found such a lucrative trade in the solution of social problems. These experts are not practical people indifferent to social theory whose aim has been to meet the challenges or the complexities of modern living but resemble more a state-financed oligarchy whose power is difficult to resist. Bentham would not have approved; of their status or of their views.

Nor indeed would John Stuart Mill. And yet it is Mill who now commands more support than Bentham, and I think is likely to in the future. (Not the early Mill but the later Mill after he had stopped being a traditional Utilitarian.) Perhaps we recognise now that he understood more of the dangers of Utilitarianism and of State Welfare. For Utilitarianism, in its traditional form with all its emphasis on happiness, has within it a capacity to be authoritarian and inflexible. Herbert Spencer recognised this: the pursuit of the greatest happiness for the greatest number, said Spencer, often sacrificed the freedom of the individual to the real or supposed benefits of the state, or to the majority of the citizens (Spencer, 1969). Bentham's own rigid application of Utilitarianism, particularly in the field of penal policy showed the authoritarian side of that doctrine. Mill was by contrast more gentle, more understanding, and less committed to the application of one point of view. Bentham cared little for freedom, he only cared about happiness.

Many of the more gross errors of the Welfare State were foreseen and forewarned by Mill, although he did not speak of the Welfare State in that form. Mill, who was neither Socialist nor Conservative, saw the importance of promoting that area of personal freedom which could not and ought not be violated. He also saw clearly some of the modern problems of the relationships between man and the state, and whilst we may not always accept the solutions he offered they are becoming more widespread in the theories of F. Hayek and M. Friedman – the former often unfairly maligned by his left-wing critics for so-called Conservative views. Hayek and other latter-day liberals warn against the uncritical provision of welfare and the unreal expectations so many welfare provisions create.

But Mill was more than an old-fashioned supporter of *laissez-faire*. It is true that he said *laissez-faire* should be the general practice: every departure from it unless required by some good is a certain evil (Mill, 1920, p. 950), and it is also true that his view of welfare provisions was similar to that of Bentham's principle of less eligibility, thereby giving unqualified support to the Poor Law (Mill, 1920, p. 968).[3] We do not need to accept uncritically all that Mill said to see there is more to Mill's position on social policy than his support for *laissez-faire*. His concern for the then position of women is, or ought to be, recognised as being in advance of his time, as I hope will his discussion about industrial democracy (Mill, 1920, bk 4, ch. 7). For Mill saw more clearly than most that low status groups will not always be content with their conditions – and nor should they. Unlike some other theorists, contemporary or otherwise, he also offered possible solutions.[4]

It is however his call for that minimum area of personal freedom which is being given a more modern appraisal and becoming acknowledged as an acceptable stance against the intrusion of the Welfare State – or the therapeutic state as some critics call it, for the notion of welfare has long since given way to that of therapy. The modern approach shows itself in the increasing demand for rights – and sometimes for natural rights. (Bentham may have called natural rights 'nonsense on stilts' but that shows how far away we are from traditional Utilitarianism.) More often the demand is for a form of a Bill of Rights, or in its more extreme form for a Therapeutic Bill of Rights aimed at protecting the individual from the therapeutic influence.

The demand for rights is not likely to be transitory for it is based on an intense reaction against some of the assumptions built into the Welfare State itself: that rights are coterminous with welfare, and that welfare itself has no limits placed upon it. In the first there are no better examples than in the 1959 Mental Health Act (or the 1969 Children and Young Persons Act) where, as the Royal Commission said in relation to mental patients, the need is to provide swift and certain treatment. The patients' rights were to receive that treatment (Bean, 1980). No consideration was given to likely objections from the patient or that the patient may be wrongly detained or even that the decision to detain is wrong in principle – there is for example no right of appeal in the 1959 Mental Health Act relating to non-criminal compulsory admissions or to the type of treatment given. In the second it is not so much that the Welfare State has changed into the therapeutic state, for that by any standards is a dangerous position to be in, but that welfare is too often selective (i.e. relating to the position of women as in the Beveridge report) and arbitrary (resembling what Mill referred to as the dangers of charity: charity said Mill, almost always does too much or too little). Faced with these suppressive requirements rights are seen as a way of protecting the individual, and perhaps the only one given the way society is structured.

We do not need to invoke traditional Utilitarianism to see how the demand for rights is being created, although Bentham was instructive on this point. 'As to the rules of beneficence, these, as far as concerns matters in detail must necessarily be abandoned in great measures to the jurisdiction of private ethics.' Or again: 'It is a standing topic of complaint that a man knows too little of himself. Be it so: but is it certain that the legislator knows more.' 'It is plain that of individuals the legislator can know nothing . . . [and] . . . it is plain that [the legislator] can know nothing of advantage' (Bentham, 1967, pp. 419–22). This theme that the individual knows best how to promote his own happiness and is responsible for it himself runs throughout much of the Utilitarian literature (but not in the writings of T. H. Green). Bentham tended to regard state intervention as not so much wrong in principle as in practice: governments according to Bentham rarely know how best to intervene and so when they tried to do so they rarely acted in ways beneficial to the people. Perhaps we shall continue to see the wisdom in Bentham's view without accepting too much of the remainder of his position.

For my argument is that 'rights' are beginning to replace 'needs' as the dominating area of concern – or if not replace then operate alongside so that 'needs' will also be required to be linked to rights. We may continue to see the merits of Bentham's arguments but it is Mill to whom we may refer in the next decade.

Notes

1 The first five chapters of Bentham's *An Introduction to the Principles of Morals and Legislation* (1967 edn) provide the essence of the Benthamite Utilitarian doctrine and the first five sentences of chapter 1 summarise the argument.

> Nature has placed mankind under the governance of two sovereign masters, *pain* and *pleasure* [italic in original]. It is for them alone to point out what we ought to do as well as what we shall do. On the one hand the standards of right and wrong, on the other the chain of causes and effects as fastened to their throne. They govern us in all we do, in all we say, in all we think: every effort we can make to throw off our subjection will serve but to demonstrate and confirm it. In words a man may pretend to abjure their empire: but in reality he will remain subject to it all the while (p. 125).

2 R. H. Tawney (1931) for example argued that a community requires a common culture because without it, it is not a community at all. But a common culture rests upon economic foundations. It involves in short a large measure of economic equality; and Crosland (1956) held that the first argument for greater equality is that it would increase social contentment and diminish social resentment.

3 In this respect Mill was still a traditional Utilitarian assessing the value of state subsistence in the same way as Bentham assessed punishment, i.e. that the position of the punished be marginally worse than that of the free man otherwise punishment would be valueless. And Beveridge too seemed to follow that tradition. It is true that he spoke of 'social insurance' (para. 26) where 'social' implied an element of compulsion where men stand together with their fellows, and it is also true that one of Beveridge's guiding principles was that of social security, which could only be achieved by compulsory cooperation between the state and the individual. But he added, in a manner reminiscent of Mill, that the state in organising security should not stifle

incentive, opportunity or responsibility. In establishing a national minimum it should leave room and encouragement for voluntary action by each individual to provide more than the minimum for himself and his family (para. 9). Did Beveridge perhaps share Mill's view that the greatest error of socialist thinking is 'to charge upon competition all the economical evils which at present exist and forget that wherever competition is not monopoly is: and that monopoly in all its forms is the taxation of the industrious for the support of indolence if not plunder'? (Mill, 1920, p. 792). Perhaps so.

4 The two chapters in Mill's *Principles of Political Economy* entitled 'On the probable futurity of the labouring classes' (bk 4, ch. 7) and 'Of the grounds and limits of the laissez-faire or non-interference principle' (bk 5, ch. 11) show Mill at his best.

References

Bean, P. T. (1980), *Compulsory admissions to Mental Hospitals*, Chichester, John Wiley.

Bentham, J. (1967), *An Introduction to the Principles of Morals and Legislation*, Oxford, Basil Blackwell.

Brebner, J. B. (1948), 'Laissez-faire and state intervention in nineteenth-century Britain', *Journal of Economic History* (Supplement 8), pp. 59–73.

Crosland, C. A. R. (1956), *The Future of Socialism*, London, Jonathan Cape.

Dicey, A. V. (1962), *Law and Public Opinion in England during the Nineteenth Century*, London, Macmillan.

Fraser, D. (1973), *The Evolution of the British Welfare State*, London, Macmillan.

Green, T. H. (1888), *Lectures on the Principles of Political Obligation*, London, Longman.

HMSO (1942), *Social Insurance and Allied Services*, Cmd. 6404 (The Beveridge Report), London.

Lewis, R. A. (1952), *Edwin Chadwick and the Public Health Movement*, Longman.

Mill, J. S. (1920), *Principles of Political Economy*, London, Longman.

Ovenstone, I. M., and Bean, P. T. (1981), 'A medical social assessment of admissions to old peoples' homes in Nottingham', *British Journal of Psychiatry*, vol. 139, pp. 226–9.

Parris, H. (1960), 'The nineteenth-century revolution in government: a reappraisal reappraised', *Historical Journal*, vol. 3, no. 1, pp. 17–37.

Plamenatz, J. (1966), *The English Utilitarians*, Oxford, Basil Blackwell.

Quinton, A. (1973), *Utilitarian Ethics*, London, Macmillan.

Spencer, H. (1969 edn), *The Man Versus the State*, Harmondsworth, Penguin.

Tawney, R. H. (1931), *Equality*, London, Allen & Unwin.

Chapter 18
Reflections on the welfare state
Barbara Wootton

While I am delighted and honoured to be a contributor to this volume, I must admit to an uneasy feeling that the title suggested for this essay originated in a presumption that my personal life span might more or less coincide with that of the Welfare State. I hope, however, to convince the reader that the Welfare State will far exceed the five years which is roughly the expectation that the Life Tables now predict for me. But there is one marked difference between our two life stories. I was born on 14 April 1897, whereas the Welfare State has no precise birthday. Like Topsy it has just growed, and presumably, if it is not to enjoy the immortality that I could wish for it (though not in its present shape), it will presumably fade away, rather than disappear on any fixed date of death.

Certainly at the turn of the century no 'welfare state' was so much as a gleam in anybody's eye. At that time the only public provision available for the needy was the Poor Law administered by local Boards of Guardians, and absolute destitution was a necessary qualification for any help from that quarter. Some consciences were, however, already stirring, particularly in relation to the poverty of old people. In 1895 a Royal Commission on the Aged Poor made many horrific disclosures about the conditions of the aged, without, however, suggesting any remedies. Thereafter a succession of Committees was appointed to consider a variety of schemes for Old Age Pensions, but gave their blessing to none. Not until after the publication in 1903 of Charles Booth's momentous survey of the *Life and Labour of the People of London* was Parliament goaded into action. In 1908 an Old Age Pensions Act conceded pensions of 5 shillings a week at age 70 to everybody with an income of less than £21 per annum. The figures of course mean nothing today, but some idea of relative values may be gained by comparison with the average earnings of a farm worker. In 1914 these had reached 18 shillings weekly and then (as now at £94 a week) the recipient stood at the bottom of the male wages hierarchy.

If, after all, the Welfare State did have a birthday, the 1908 Act was it. At least that Act was widely regarded as an alarming omen for the future. Well do I remember my mother (herself recently widowed) walking from room to room in dismay at what she saw as the total demoralisation of the working classes. Why save for one's own old age, if that would merely put one beyond the level at which the state would provide?

The next seventy-odd years saw a succession of measures designed to provide protection, sometimes for those presumed to lack the resources necessary to protect themselves, occasionally for everybody, rich or poor, against the various costly contingencies to which the modern world exposes us. It would be tedious to list all the step-by-step extensions that followed the modest beginning of 1908, but a few major landmarks, aimed at consistency or comprehensiveness, or at the inclusion of needs previously overlooked, do deserve mention. Most significant of these was the introduction of compulsory insurance by the National Insurance Act of 1911 which provoked the doggerel 'Now we're all employed, everybody but tramps has got to lick the stamps, and put them on the cards on Saturday morning'. Not that this poem was an accurate assessment. The Act only gave a limited section of lower-paid workers (but not their wives) access to medical care and unemployment benefit on a very modest scale in exchange for tripartite contributions by employers, workers and government. However, from 1920 onwards, the scope of the scheme was steadily extended in relation to both the range of population compulsorily insured and the benefits provided, until by 1946 virtually the whole working population was brought under compulsory insurance against the costs of sickness, industrial accident, unemployment, maternity, widowhood, old age and death. Meanwhile two years later the old Poor Law was replaced by a 'National Assistance Board' which provided support from government funds for persons who were not actually destitute, but whose incomes fell below a prescribed level.

These last two developments were preceded by, and largely due to, the most significant landmark of all – the Beveridge Report of 1942 on Social Insurance and Allied Services. Beveridge himself, as far as I know, never used the term 'welfare state', but that title might fairly have been applied to his comprehensive plan for defeating the five giants who are paraded on his opening pages, to wit: Want, Disease, Ignorance, Squalor and Idleness. The report was indeed founded upon the principle that it was the duty of the state to provide protection against these monsters, and the author's purpose was to show how that could be done, particularly in relation to Want, which he judged to be 'the easiest to attack'.

At this distance of time it is difficult to recall the immense enthusiasm with which the report was received: indeed only those now of fairly mature age can have experienced it. On the day that the morning papers published their summaries, strangers greeted one another in the streets and on commuter trains, sharing their emotion in a way that is more often associated with great catastrophes than with great rejoicing. The war was not yet over, but this document of less than 300 pages, bearing the signature of one man alone, promised that in the post-war world, in defiance of the Bible, we need no longer have the poor with us.

The twin pillars of the Beveridge scheme were the universalisation of social insurance, and the provision from government funds of a means-tested minimum income for those (whom Beveridge expected to be only a small minority) whose resources for whatever reason still fell below a 'subsistence standard'. In addition the report made two further proposals. First of these was the payment of family allowances financed from government funds (later rechristened child benefit) for all children other than the first-born (who have however since been included), without means test, or any specific contribution from the beneficiaries. The second additional recommendation was a blue-print for a free National Health Service (NHS). All these proposals were put into effect within less than a decade of the publication of the report. But how shocked the enthusiasts of 1942 would have been, had they known that thirty-seven years later Professor Peter Townsend could publish a massive volume of 1,211 pages entitled *Poverty in the United Kingdom*! Beveridge must surely have turned in his grave.

What then went wrong? Of course all the figures of benefit soon proved much too low, but that could easily have been adjusted. Sad to say, in view of subsequent history, the beautiful simplicity of the Beveridge scheme proved its undoing. The principle of flat rates of contribution, and of benefit at a level which was supposed to cover the bare essentials of living, though regarded by its author as fundamental, was inappropriate to a grossly unequal society in which the working community set great store by wage differentials, and in which, as Guy Routh put it many years later, a person's attachment to his standard of living has an 'elemental quality' 'not unlike the attachment of an animal to its young' (Routh, 1980). It was all very well for Beveridge to suggest relying on voluntary insurance for any necessary supplementation. Few could, or in my opinion can even now, hope to afford that, unless in a very distant future. Yet, as illustrated below, the idea of relying on voluntary contributions to replace the social security system is once again fashionable today in certain quarters. Moreover the picture that Beveridge envisaged, in which payment of supplementary benefit to persons already receiving social insurance benefits (for age, unemployment, or sickness) would be quite exceptional, has never been realised. By February 1980 42 per cent of all registered unemployed persons were also in receipt of Supplementary Benefit (SB) (1980, p. 65) as also were substantial numbers of pensioners and of the sick or disabled.

In the forty years since the Beveridge Report two forces, generally driving in opposite directions, have nevertheless continued to defeat that document's attack upon the Giant Want. The first was the ever-increasing complexity of the social security system, consequent upon discovery of the endless variety of individual needs which no single benefit rate could meet. Sick or disabled persons, for example, not only cannot earn their daily bread, but must have someone to wait upon them. Attendance allowances have therefore been introduced for what are judged to be suitable cases. Similarly, mobility allowances are now payable to disabled persons who cannot get around under their own steam, while people dependent on expensive heating systems are (though very inadequately) given help with their fuel bills. And so on.

The second disturbing influence on the structure of the Welfare State, notably in the past two or three years, has been the desperate attempt of government to save money. Recent examples of typical pettifogging economies are the increased charges for school meals, the proposed taxation of insurance benefits not previously taxable, and the obligation laid on employers to pay for the first few weeks of an employee's sickness. Meanwhile old-style social security is now surrounded by a network of other specialised benefits, mainly means-tested, in which every such test is constructed independently of every other, whether it applies to rent or rate rebates, SB, Family Income Supplement (FIS), legal aid, or parents' contributions to the university education of their offspring.

The result is one appalling tangle, which only the experts can hope to unravel; and not all even of them invariably succeed. The Department of Health and Social Security (DHSS) thoughtfully issues through HM

Stationery Office leaflets keeping the law relating to social security up to date. A single issue of these documents may run to more than thirty pages. Meanwhile the Supplementary Benefits Commission (now superseded, see below) has regularly published an annual handbook, hopefully sub-titled 'A Guide to Claimants' Rights'. The final edition of this volume runs to 125 pages of text plus 4 appendices, costing (in 1980) £2.40. The first 87 pages explain the 'normal' rules governing assessment and payment of allowances, after which three further pages give eight separate instructions about how to claim 'an urgent need payment for day-to-day living expenses', outside the normal rules.

Obviously few claimants, whether in normal or in 'urgent' need, will be able to tackle the matter on their own. Inevitably they will have to seek the help of a social worker, or of one of the Voluntary Welfare Rights Groups which are dotted about the country, but not thickly enough to be universally accessible.

It looks therefore as if to Beveridge's original five giants, two others must be added – the Giant 'Complexity' and the Giant 'Government Parsimony'. According to one view, capitulation to Complexity is inevitable because the state is required to make, on behalf of individuals, an endless variety of decisions which they ought to be free to make for themselves. As Arthur Seldon puts it, 'the welfare state has been a grievous *cul-de-sac*', and is bound to fail in the face of market forces which conflict with it. Hence 'the question is not whether it *should* [italics original] continue into the twenty-first century but whether it *can*'. Seldon anticipates that the centralised Welfare State will be increasingly replaced by 'local voluntary services which develop organically in response to changing circumstances of preference or technique in the coming 10–20 years'. He also doubts whether the NHS will survive 'as a comprehensive structure to the end of the century', and foresees that by 1995 25 per cent of children will be in private schools, and that the number of persons covered by occupational pension schemes will have risen from 1½ million to 15 million or more. In short 'if the state had not been misused to provide education, medicine, housing and pensions', these would have evolved 'in response to. . . demand and supply' (Seldon, 1981).

But would they? The fact is that state welfare provision was developed only because people had signally failed to provide these services for themselves – for the simple reason that they could not afford to do so. Demand did not evoke supply because it was not, and could not be, backed by the necessary financial bait.

To be fair to Seldon, he shows some awareness of this, and directs his criticisms primarily against state provision of services in kind, arguing that cash should have been redistributed sooner, and on a larger scale, than it was. But he also expresses regret that social benefits have so often been distributed universally, instead of by what he calls the 'sensitive, humane refinement of means tests'. Nevertheless it is as good as certain that, should his prediction that the NHS will not outlive the century be fulfilled, the result will not be that everybody will get the medical care that he needs from the doctor or hospital of his choice from his private insurance or his own pocket. Indeed Seldon himself only claims that 40 per cent of the population will thus be able to protect themselves, and he shows no concern whatever about what will happen to the other 60 per cent. Without an effective public service, their needs will undoubtedly go unmet, and they will again lapse into the position so vividly described in Margery Spring Rice's survey of working-class wives in the 1930s – published just a decade before the birth of the NHS, though it reads more like an account of the Dark Ages of the nineteenth century (Spring Rice, 1981).

In the immediate future therefore it is unthinkable that the welfare state should be allowed to wither away, or that we should be frightened by the Giant Parsimony into continuation of the present policy of soaking the poor.

With Giant Complexity we must also keep up the struggle as best we may, always being careful that nothing is done now in the name of simplification, which either lowers present standards of provision, or is liable to prejudice desirable future developments. In the present government's view, the 1980 Social Security Act amounted to a significant victory over Complexity. Indeed on the face of it that Act's decision to establish a single advisory committee with oversight over the Social security system as a whole certainly seems a sensible alternative to the previous dual arrangement, under which one committee kept a watchful eye on the insurance sector, while an independent commission had a wider policy-making function in relation to the SB 'safety net'. But it is early days yet to assess the effects of the Act's radical reconstruction of the whole insurance-cum-supplementary-income maintenance system.

Particularly questionable is the decision that the rules governing entitlement to SB should become statutory orders formally enacted by Parliament. This virtually abolishes (apart from cases of urgent need) the 'discretionary payments' which are now assessed under the commission's general rules by its officers who pass the actual money to the claimant. These payments have increased of recent years so much that they are now awarded under one head or another to the majority of beneficiaries and can therefore no longer be strictly called 'exceptional'. But what will happen to them under the new system? If they just disappear, the result will obviously be disastrous. But can they, or will they, somehow be codified into the new rules? Even if they are, the claimant's right under the Act to appeal to an independent tribunal against his assessment will not admit a claim that a rule is itself unfair (that is a matter for Parliament), but only that it has been wrongly interpreted, or is not applicable to his case. Nevertheless the changed status of the rules relating to SB, like the establishment of the new overall advisory committee, is claimed by government as a useful simplification. Parliamentary draftsmen are not, however, notorious for the lucidity of their language, and the loss of 'discretionary payments' may well mean hardship to individuals whose circumstances really do call for special treatment.

In the longer term, more radical changes should be initiated. First of these should be the abolition of that nineteenth-century Bismarckian invention, the so-called social insurance system. Although to Beveridge the insurance principle was fundamental, it is now quite out of keeping with modern ideas. The best that can be said for it is that the title 'insurance' enables beneficiaries to enjoy the dignity of asserting that they have paid for what they get. That title itself is however a complete misnomer as applied to the present system, under which governments decide first what they propose to spend on 'social objectives', ranging from retirement pensions to support of the unemployed or the sick, and from redundancy grants to the NHS, and then apportion the cost between employers, employed persons, and the taxpayer as they think fit (House of Lords, 1982). The result is a most inequitable distribution of the cost between these contributors. The charge on the employer takes no account of his ability to pay, while the employee's contribution, which was at first virtually a poll tax, now makes only a rough and ready discrimination between wage earners at different rates of pay.

Meanwhile Beveridge's pioneering invention of a family allowance (since rechristened 'child benefit') is financed from the general tax revenues and therefore does take some account of ability to pay. Benefit is payable on behalf of *all* children from birth to age 16 (or 19 if in full-time education). This is therefore the first case in which the state contributes to certain citizens' expenses without exacting any specific contribution from the beneficiaries, and without any limitation by means test.

Incidentally it is perhaps a little surprising that this should be the first such benefit. Sickness and unemployment are in general misfortunes for which the sufferer cannot be held responsible, nor can any of us avoid growing older. But in these days the birth of a child may fairly be regarded as a voluntary, or at least not an unavoidable, occurrence. It might therefore have been expected that as between the birth of a child and the cost of unavoidable disasters or of the loss of income owing to retirement, it would have been in the latter classes of case that no specific contribution would be required. Almost certainly the explanation is that child benefit is the descendant of income tax allowances for dependent children, which previously assisted the relatively well-to-do with the expense of parenthood. Anyhow its most remarkable feature is that it has established the first group of people who *are in fact paid merely for being alive.* That of course is also nearly true of men over 65 and of women over 60 in receipt of retirement pensions, but with the important difference that they have been previously compelled to make a specific contribution for this benefit, and are also subject to the one condition that in the first five of their pensionable years their weekly earnings do not exceed a prescribed amount.

Together these two groups of the young and the old add up to 24½ million individuals or almost 44 per cent of the total UK population. That leaves over 31 million between these ages, a substantial proportion of whom will at some time in their lives be drawing sickness or unemployment benefit, FIS or SB – this last being, as already noted, often in addition to their 'insurance' benefits.

The above are all hard cash payments to be spent as the recipient chooses. If they were all wholly financed from the general tax revenues, not only would the cost be much more equitably distributed, but an initial blow would have been struck against Giant Complexity, since it would no longer be necessary as in the 'insurance' cases to make detailed investigations into contribution records. Even stronger is the case for retaining the obligation on the taxpayer to carry the cost of certain services in kind, such as doctoring or education, since it can reasonably be held that the whole community has an interest in, and should therefore take responsibility for, the health of its members and the educational opportunities available to them.

After abolishing the 'insurance' fiasco, the next step forward would be to improve the position of the 31 million persons not entitled to unconditional benefits such as retirement pensions or child benefit. This would mean launching an attack on Giant Parsimony, who has recently been very active in this field. Thus the present government, although generally thought to hold Arthur Seldon in high esteem, has consistently ignored the implication of his regret that past policy failed to redistribute cash from the richer to the poorer classes so as to enable most such people to satisfy all but their most exceptional needs by the exercise of free choice in the open market.

Redistribution of a kind there has been, but in deference to the Giant Parsimony it has been predominantly geared in the opposite direction to that suggested by Seldon. In their first budget of June 1979 Mrs Thatcher's government remitted £1,560 million of the annual income tax payable by persons in receipt of incomes of over £10,000 (House of Commons, 1979). Since then it has been mostly the poorer end of the income hierarchy which has been affected by tax changes, and these have generally increased, not lightened, their burdens. The lowest band of tax rates has been abolished, and short-term social security benefits are also presently due to become taxable for the first time, pending which *all* the unemployed in receipt of benefit have suffered a 5 per cent cut, although some of them will still not have incomes above the tax threshold, even after benefit becomes taxable. Nor have sickness and unemployment pay kept in step with inflation, and the same was true also of the income tax threshold in 1981–2 though there have been promises made about the future. Last but not least, from the beginning of 1982 no new claims for earnings-related-benefit (ERS) have been admissible.

Inevitably, as the result of all this, more of the sick and unemployed have been driven to fall back on SB, for which the consequential increase in claimants has been estimated at 100,000. Altogether, sundry changes in the SB scheme since 1980 along with the abolition of ERS are expected to worsen the position of about 1¾ million claimants while 500,000 will be better off (Child Poverty Action Group, 1980, p. 43).

Looking still further ahead (I am thinking of generations rather than decades), I suggest that we should plan a long-term attack upon Complexity in his great stronghold where he employs a vast, and vastly expensive, array of bureaucrats, administering detailed regulations, not just about contribution records, but about the conditions of entitlement to benefits. This bureaucracy's job is to find out, for example, how soon after you fell ill, did you claim sick pay? Was it a recurrence of a previous illness from which you had recovered and signed off? What exactly is the definition of voluntary unemployment? Could it have been your own misconduct which caused you to be dismissed? If you are a lone female housing a lodger, may not the two of you be living as man and wife and may he not be contributing to your maintenance as a 'common law husband'? And so on.

This bureaucratic army will never be finally disbanded, nor can Complexity suffer a fatal blow, unless and until the principle underlying child benefit is universalised in a *social wage payable from the public purse to every citizen merely for being alive* and without regard to his or her income, marital status or other sexual relationships. In the present state of our economy, any such proposal to subsidise everyone up to millionaire level is of course unthinkable. But if such a social wage was initially payable only to persons below a certain level of income, the proposition would descend from Cloud-cuckoo-land to the real world. Even a small social wage would at least eliminate some applications for short-term benefits, and so make some reduction in the bureaucratic procedures which these necessarily involve. Nor should it be overlooked that, the higher the social wage or income which would be payable as of right, the greater would be the saving both in present benefits and in administrative costs.

It may of course be argued that a 'social wage' subject to means test would be merely a dressed-up version of what we already have in the SB safety net. Moreover means tests (as ordinarily so called) are not generally associated by those who have experienced them with the 'humane and sensitive refinement' referred to by Arthur Seldon. Objection on this score would however be minimised if questions of entitlement were handled by the Inland Revenue Department, where the atmosphere is rather different from that of some DHSS offices – also if payments were made, as with child benefit and retirement pensions, at post offices.

Nevertheless, crazy though it would be in present circumstances, I should still cherish universalisation as the ultimate blue-print for the Welfare State. First and foremost the restriction of any allowance by even the most courteous means test inevitably creates a 'poverty trap', where any increase of independent income means loss of the allowance. Universality puts a final stop to the possibility that anyone can be financially better off not working than at work.

I would hope therefore that we should creep up to the remote goal of universality, as now represented by child benefit. We could begin by gradually raising the age of eligibility for a (re-named) child benefit and increasing its value, while, at the other end of life, pensionable ages could be correspondingly lowered.

How far and how fast we could travel is generally thought to depend upon where we could get the money from: but that is not quite the right form for the question. Money is only a token that issues by some mysterious process from 'the City'. The volume in circulation can be manoeuvred as, after 2½ years of 'monetarist' policy, we in this country should know. The real issue is whether we shall ever have the *material resources* to guarantee to everybody a standard of life at which he can expect to cope with all the normal hazards of the contemporary world, as the top half of income recipients already do, for the most part without emergency recourse to public funds.

Here the immediate situation is crucial. The experts tell us that today we stand on the brink of a second industrial revolution in which new technology will multiply our productive capacity beyond all precedent. That means that the possibility of the Welfare State providing a universal social wage depends on two factors: first, on whether the magnitude of the coming revolution is or is not exaggerated by its prophets; and second, on what is the public and political reaction to the full force of that revolution if and when it comes.

As regards the first point, if the speed and violence of the revolution have been grossly exaggerated, then the remaining pages of this essay should be put into cold store. But it is worth remembering that we have heard similar, though less dramatic, prophecies before, and that, never-theless, the work force of Great Britain has absorbed about 9½ million additional workers since the turn of the century, and has achieved an unprecedented rise in general living standards, with no persistent upward trend in what has always been a fluctuating volume of unem-ployment. Today, however, it has become fashionable for journalists, academics and politicians to elaborate over their gin and tonics the thesis that we must prepare ourselves (and others) for the 'leisure society' in which regular employment will be the exception rather than the rule. This thesis is also echoed with alarm over the beer tankards in the public bars of London or Liverpool. Extremists (notably Dr Mishan of the London School of Economics) even draw the conclusion that any increased output of material wealth would be actually pernicious, at least for a country as rich as ours (Mishan, 1967).

That doctrine I find criminally short-sighted. If it prevails, it will be one of the greatest acts of defeatism in the history of this country. Let Dr Mishan speak for himself if he has got all the material wealth that he wants, but not for his fellow citizens who are still living in hovels, not houses, and risking death from hypothermia. To satisfy all legitimate needs for domestic comfort, better food and clothing and recreation, would require an unimaginable outpouring of goods and chattels from factories now silent or non-existent. Mishan is right that we don't need to be flooded with such fripperies as electric tooth brushes, but completely at fault in his generalised attack on productivity.

If the human brain is clever enough to invent silicon chips, thus making it possible in certain industries for one man to produce as much as five men did before, that brain must also be capable of devising the economic and financial organisation necessary to re-employ the displaced four, and to market the consequential five-fold increase in production. Instead of dreaming of a workless world, every economist and politician should be wrestling night and day with those problems – difficult tasks indeed, but surely not so difficult as getting safely to the moon and back; and the rewards of success in human terms would be immensely greater than those of that adventure. If the new technology is directed, as it should be, towards the abolition, not of work, but of poverty, it might indeed herald the apotheosis of the Welfare State.

References

Child Poverty Action Group (1980), *Poverty*, (December), London.

House of Commons Official Report, 3 July 1979, col 553.

House of Lords Official Report, 18 January 1982, cols 417–25.

Mishan, E. J., (1967), *The Costs of Economic Growth*, London, Staples Press, *passim*, especially p. 14.

Routh, Guy (1980), *Occupation and Pay in Great Britain 1906–79*, London, Macmillan, p. 179.

Seldon, Arthur (1981), *Wither [sic] the Welfare State*, Occasional Paper 60, London, Institute of Economic Affairs, pp. 7, 8, 14, 25.

Spring Rice, Margery (1981), *Working-Class Wives* (2nd edn with foreword by Cecil Robertson), London, Virago.

Supplementary Benefits Commission (1980), Annual Report for 1979, London, Department of Health and Social Security, HMSO, p. 65.

Townsend, P. (1979), *Poverty in the United Kingdom*, Harmondsworth, Penguin.

Index of names

Subject index